36582

THE JOURNAL
OF A DEPORTEE

MAURICE CORDONNIER

36582, The Journal of a Deportee ©

Published by CH Publications
2011

ISBN 978-0-9568697-0-8

Printed by Graphic Impressions
Springfield Lyons House · Springfield Lyons Approach · Chelmsford · Essex CM2 5LB
Telephone: 01245 260349 · www.graphic-impressions.co.uk

FOREWORD

I wrote this journal in the autumn of 1945, shortly after my repatriation and whilst I was in convalescence, and while the harrowing events and the vivid memories of my friends were still fresh in my mind.

I dedicate this testimony to my comrades from l'Aisne and from Saone-et-Loire who didn't come back. I shall NEVER forget them.

Many thanks to Jill Constable and Janet Osman, for translating my work from French into English so that it may be read by all my English friends.

Note that the German in this book is how I heard it and may not be entirely correct – but we came to understand what it meant!

One will forget,
Those from the prisons,
Those from the dungeons,
Those from the cells,
Victims of the traitors,
Of the spies, of the
5th column and of the Gestapo,
Victims of barbarity and of
Sadism.

Never before did this happen to any other nation.
We already forget about our dead, famous or unknown,
Heroic or weak, those of the torture chambers and
Those of the gas chambers, those made martyrs as
They tried to escape, those dying of thirst and of misery,
Those who were
in the camps and in the convoys.
Alas there are so very few
S U R V I V O R S!!!

Their role has ended. They have to take their leave now. Others, who
Didn't lose anything, who are rich, powerful and respected already have
Their say. They have forgotten about the widows, the orphans, the sick
And embarrassing deportee. Be quiet; only those who never said anything,
Or never did anything under the German occupation have the right to speak.

Quick, let us turn the page.
Certain memories   are really
Far too painful to bear!!! But,
Whilst they are still around,
These old camp serial numbers,
With the memory of thousands
And thousands of dead people,
With the memory of a brother
Who left one night to meet with
An unknown death. THEY will not
Forget them, THOSE who have been
Their comrades....

CORDONNIER Maurice
Serial Number 36582
BREMEN FARGE Commando

Chapter 1: THE ARREST

21st April, 1944. Goodnight Georges!

My story begins here. I went down the steps which run alongside my friend's house. Marcel, a colleague of mine and a railwayman like myself, and I have just returned from Georges' having drunk a glass of Marc and feel its warmth spreading through our whole bodies. It is midnight. Tomorrow, we will have 'brioches' to eat! We have been invited to Georges' home to celebrate his birthday. We are savouring the delicacies already, since we know how good our eldest friend is in making the real pastries of pre-war days, despite the lack of eggs, butter and milk. All this in spite of the Jerries! Without a sound, Marcel and I return to our hotel bedroom. We get into bed quickly; my friend is always reproaching me for being talkative! We switch out the light; tomorrow morning at 5.00a.m we shall be at work again.......

Knock; knock; knock! Half asleep, I think I must be dreaming and do not answer. Knock; knock; knock! There is no doubt about it – somebody is knocking and it is louder this time. Marcel is awake too. As he is closest to the door, he switches on the light; he has hardly turned the key in the lock, when the knocking begins again. What has happened at the station? Doubtless some derailment or other and, as usual, they have come for some extra help. But I am not dreaming; it is the Boches at the door, armed and helmeted. On their arms are the black shield and the letters SD of the Gestapo. In a split second, everything is clear to me, for they are already searching my suitcases. There is a civilian with them, sub machine–gun on his shoulder.

"Cordonnier!' shouts the interrogator.

"Here!" I respond. Am I really as dangerous as all that? I wouldn't have believed it! He speaks to me in good French.

"Do you know why you are being arrested?

"No, I don't. What is going on?"

"Come on now, hurry up; get dressed quickly, you're coming with us."

It is quarter to four. I have the presence of mind to put aside my summer clothes and to dress warmly. I tell them I'm on duty at the station at 5.00 but they pretend not to hear me. Marcel is petrified. While I am putting on my shoes, watched by the two men in green, the civilian disappears, then returns and tells Marcel to get dressed and that he will soon be free again.

I am ready; let's get going! I run into the manageress of the hotel at the end of the corridor. I can tell from her manner that she is upset. I offer to settle my account for the month but she refuses saying there is no hurry.

The cool morning air wakes me up. Once in the street, the Boches search me again. Where are they going to take me? I arrive at the 'Mairie' – there are men in uniforms everywhere. They force me up the stone steps. The uncertainty depresses me and I feel terribly tired.

I am taken into the room on the left. I'm hardly through the door and bewildered by the bright light, I recognise friends who have been arrested before me. Everything becomes clear. Shopped; Denounced! We're in a pretty bad state – what a mess!.

On an order from a German wearing hand grenades fixed to his belt, I sit down on the ground in a corner, facing the wall. I try, however, to see which ones are here. The leader, deputy leader and a patriot from my group, two others who I don't know and lastly a friend who has been arrested too. For what reason? The three from my group are hardly recognisable, so great is their apparent exhaustion. They have certainly been beaten up – my turn is not far off. On my left, Louis Bellot and Maxime Chevrier are lying on their stomach and are covered in dust. Louis is hardly moving but from his breathing I gather he must be in considerable pain. Maxime looks at me and edges towards me. He is all in. "Done for", he whispers to me. I shall find out nothing from him....

Pierre Lhoste is behind me but how can I turn around? I can feel the eyes of the Jerry boring into me, his revolver too. Nevertheless, I turn around for a couple of seconds. The sight of Pierre terrifies me. He is leaning in the corner of the wall, legs apart as if out of joint. His face is ashen and with his very thick dark beard and haggard eyes, reminds me of a corpse. He sees me and makes a negative gesture with his finger. He has said nothing...... I must not be afraid. I shall deny everything. But why this arrest? He is thirsty and asks for something to drink; the guard does not answer him.

I ask myself unsolvable questions. I reflect. I'm frightened. Then the door opens several times and a new prisoner enters. I listen with fear as the hobnailed boots strike the mosaic floor of the corridor. How long can this comedy, now becoming tragic, continue? I have noticed that the Boches are collecting up the radios - there are about ten of them on my right.

My uncomfortable position on the ground is tiring me: I can hear a lot of noise but can see nothing. Have the Germans guessed that we listened to London? Yet I, who have no radio, have a defence. Could I have been denounced for having listened to the British every day at Georges' house? But he would have been arrested too! I make up my mind to deny everything. A German enters and calls several of us. I remain motionless where I am. The manager of my hotel has been arrested too. He is made to sit down beside me. He asks:

"Have you been questioned?"

"No not yet."

That earns him two kicks in the stomach and a heavy punch for me. I am disturbed in my thoughts by the dull noises coming from the next room. I understand: the dance goes on. My friends! Their cries are muffled. I hear questions: "Where are the weapons?" Blows and more blows. Then I hear just one word: "Never".

When is it going to end? How long have I been here? I am hot. I risk an "Abort bitte" to the guard watching me. He then consults one of the leaders and comes back to get me. He holds me by the arm, takes me behind the mairie to the WC. It is a fine day and quite still. The German remains on guard outside the door which he has forbidden me to close. I take advantage of this freedom to destroy the letters which I have on me. I go back to the mairie, already regretting that wonderful moment when I glimpsed escape into the gardens and then the fields. My mind goes out to the Resistance. My friends are still there. They are being called, Louis Bellot, Maxime Chevrier and the garage owner, to whom the Boche throws a wallet; obviously his identity papers which his wife would have brought him. I pity Louis Bellot, he is red faced, his eyes are haggard and his hair is plastered down over his face. I shall not see him again.

I hear cars coming and going. Each one seems to stop. What is happening at home, at Chateauneuf, in the Nièvre. How will they hear the news and when? The church clock has just struck half past ten. It was 8 o'clock when Olivier Melin was the last one to join us in our present situation. He looks at me, impassive.

A tall civilian, whose stature makes him stand out, comes over and asks me:

"How long have you been in the Resistance?"

"I don't know that organisation; besides I am not from Etang and all that doesn't interest me." "Do you belong to the 1942 call-up?"

"Yes, my papers are in order. I can show them to you."

"How long have you been at Etang?"

"Eighteen months."

He goes away. He is not French, as he has a slight accent. I'll find out later. Very dark haired, eyes black and piercing, arms too long and with the demeanour of a thug. I will recognise the famous Stouklik anywhere. Eleven o'clock. A tall Gestapo NCO enters suddenly and gives brief orders in a jargon which I don't understand. He goes out and then comes back again. This time he has an enormous baton in his hands.

This is obviously the instrument he used to beat my friends. This brute in a green uniform must be over 6 feet tall. "Auf stehen. Alles, alles." I stand up.

We must be leaving for the prison. We can hear a lorry again. I am at last on my feet and walking. My stiff legs give me pain. We all go out of this cursed room. We breathe fresh air. At the top of the mairie steps my glance sweeps over the small square. People are coming out from Mass. I see a lot of people but recognise no one. M.Lapray's lorry is waiting for us. A lot of women! They are all looking at us. It is a sad moment for Etang-sur-Arroux. Fortunately my parents don't know yet! My mother cannot see me!

So many guards!!!

The Germans have parked their cars in a line from the bridge to opposite the bakery, owned by my friend Maxime Chevrier, who has been arrested with us. I can feel his parents' eyes peering through the shutters opposite. A Boche, with a phlegmatic air, indicates the lorry. He still has his grenades fixed to his belt. If the ones in the Resistance suddenly turned up, we would surely come to blows. There were about 20 green clad men, all together.

I get into the lorry without even turning around to try and see a friend or acquaintance. There was no sign of Georges. So much the better, as long as he can get away. We sit down on the two benches intended for us. Jean Rousseau and Maxime risk waving goodbye to somebody outside. A Boche comes forward menacingly and lifts up the tailboard of the lorry. A dry click shuts us all inside. We are already in a mobile prison.

M. Mitoux will have the chore of driving the lorry. A civilian opens the small left-hand door and begins to pile in the radio sets which I saw just now at the mairie. Then comes a counter-order and he takes the sets away again, helped by the Germans.

I look at all those who have just been shut in with me. Their expressions are sad. Mine can't be much better. Maxime and his friends are in handcuffs. Louis Belot and Pierre Lhoste are not here. Who is the chap on my right? I have never seen him before - a spy, friend, suspect? Mme. Lapray has enough courage to approach the lorry. She is bringing her husband something to eat: "Something for the lorry" she says. M. Mitoux slips a wristwatch to M. Godillot.

Noon. We're off. The lorry's engine revs louder. We question Maxime Chevrier. "What has happened? Who has talked? Did they beat up many?" M. Lapray presses him with questions. He wants to know everything and quickly. I listen. I mistrust my neighbour on my right, who seems odd. Max is annoyed and admits that he couldn't hold out against the blows. He has told everything. He gave names; "Everyone must look after himself" he said.

But how? What has he told them? Talk suddenly stops, for two Gestapo civilians come and sit beside us, one on each bench. They tell us to be silent.

One of the Germans, tall and fat, hair plastered down over a receding forehead, hooked nose, our first guard, wearing a leather jacket, and has in his hand a long revolver which I recognise as English make. The second, French, much younger, hardly twenty, looking like a yob, has a small revolver in his belt.

Chapter 2: ON OUR WAY

At first, I cannot make out which way we are going. As we pass in front of the station, all becomes clear. The suddenness of the departure does not stop me thinking of that station where I enjoyed working, because of the camaraderie between colleagues and the beautiful countryside too. Le Beuvray, La Grotte, Uchon, L'Arroux, Le Meuvrin and so many walks! So many memories! Now I have to leave all the friends, nice people, young men and women I often saw at the station, the hotel, in the street….We are going towards Autun. Through the slats of the lorry, I can see several grey cars. What a fancy escort!

Max's friend asks permission to smoke. It was granted. In spite of the handcuffs, he takes out a packet of cigarettes from his pocket and offers them around. I do not smoke. He even offers the packet to the warders who do not deign to accept! As soon as they begin to inhale, my friends' faces relax. For them, tobacco is a real comfort. "That's better!" says one, in a tone of conviction which was touching. I have not said a word since we left. We arrive at Autun. To my great astonishment, the lorry does not slow down. We are going on to Chalon. Mr. Badet, sitting in front of me, sighs. Etang is already a long way behind!

We pass through deep woods, the country is hilly. The maquis is not far away but our guards do not take their eyes off us. The German has his finger constantly on the trigger of his weapon. At the cross-roads of Saint-Leger-sur-d'Henne, we hear what sounds like gunfire. Our guard gets up, tells us to stay seated and looks out through the small windows of the lorry. They are ready to fire. A ray of hope! Alas, it is only an engine backfiring.

Where is Louis Belot? Where is Pierre L'Hoste? They must be in one of the cars. In front? Behind? Several of them stayed in Autun. We stop. We are in the middle of the country, fields, hedges, woods. We are at a cross-roads. The driver looks pale. We start off again. We would like to stop for a minute. We are told that is impossible and are obliged to use a corner of the lorry, one after the other, without blinking an eyelid. It is also forbidden to show ourselves at the windows. I am reduced to looking furtively through the slats. I see people walking along the road. I had forgotten already that it is Sunday. Some people are having fun, young people like me, going with a small bag towards a sports field. Our lorry going by seems to intrigue them. They turn around.

The weather is fine outside. The sunshine makes us even more sorry for our confined and insecure position on our two benches which are likely to tip over at each sharp bend. Our driver is not driving according to the road conditions but adjusts his speed on the order of the German sitting on his right.

Chalon: I have never been there. I could make a wish but it seems such a ridiculous idea that I just think about the place that is waiting for us.

Half past two. We are slowing down. The Prison: I can see high walls. I feel moved; my heart is beating louder, for we have stopped. We get out. With my eyes I say goodbye to the driver who is observing us, powerless. This evening he will be home again and will tell everyone in Etang what happened.

Chapter 3: The PRISON

One door, two doors, three doors, a clinking of keys and grill bars which open and close after us. It is dim. Everything smells shut up here. The nails in my boots seem to make too much noise on the cement. After crossing the long vaulted corridor, we are made to stand, facing a wall. To my left, a glass fronted office, on my right, every two or three yards lots of small black doors. I gather they are the cells. Above each one, a number in cast iron. On the doors, in the top left-hand corner, a number is written in chalk; I don't know yet what it signifies. At head height, on the same level, there is a spy-hole. We remain motionless. Behind us a sentry walks up and down, bayonet fixed. Hands behind my back, I don't dare to blow my nose. The neighbour I mistrusted in the lorry speaks to me:

"We are bound to die of hunger around here"

"Who are you? I don't know you. I never saw you at Etang."

"Me neither."

I receive a heavy kick in the pants; the wall stops me from falling.

A civilian makes us write our names on a card.

Above me are two large floors. Everything is symmetrical in this place. An open door at the end of the large hall gives a little light. All is quiet. Our lorry has obviously left again. My friends are called up in turn. I am going to be last. It must be interrogation time. No — it's nothing like that at all.

Surname, forenames, age and address and these are the only formalities. Also, the interpreter asks me if I am Jewish or Catholic. A German typist is taking it down. I am taken back to the wall. This time I am alone and my friends must already be in the cells. A guard makes me raise my arms. Am I then more dangerous than I was five minutes ago?

Soup is being given out. I lose all sense of time. In spite of myself, I am interested in the passing bowls. It is a thin "bouillon". It steams a little but smells of nothing! Are they intending to put me away? When shall I see the men again who were lined up with me a few minutes ago? I can hear a lot of noise coming from outside — laughing and women's voices. About fifteen women come in through the door which has been left open since my arrival. Are they prisoners too? Then the sentry takes me away from my thoughts: Komm! Los!

I follow him, lower my hands, and then put them up again on feeling the rifle butt.

I go up the stone steps.

On the first floor I notice cells everywhere. The bareness of the walls chills me. I quickly cross the first floor and go up to the second by a wooden staircase this time. I turn to the right and a few more steps, this is it No.86. The prison is absolutely immense and yet here I am in a chicken coop! The locks are enormous and all identical. With the aid of a large key, the door is opened.

I stoop to enter, at the same time negotiating a step. The adjutant searches me and I am relieved of my two watches, my identity papers, wallet, photos, belt and knife. I am left with my comb and a handkerchief. All my things are put down on the floor. "Shut the door", the Boche jailer cries to me with an accent.

It's the first time I have had the chance to study him. Tall, thin, a shifty expression, a small Hitler-type moustache. He shouts again – "Shut the door of the cell."

He knows his job, for hardly have I pushed shut the heavy barred door, than a latch is fastened, the second door closes, a key turns twice and I am alone....

What with the prison, the cell, the isolation, I am on the same level as a thief or criminal waiting for interrogation, judgement, sentence, but with something extra – the blows with the stick and without doubt, the torture chamber.

I remain immobile in front of the door which has closed on me. What are they going to think at Chateauneuf? When will they find out? And yet they will have to know, for in two days time, I had been due to go there. What sorrow I'm going to cause them. They will no doubt cry, especially my mother. Fortunately, she knows nothing about what I have been doing. Robert though knows everything, or almost, and my father does too. My father was quite ill when I last saw him. He had warned me that if anything happened to me, it would kill him.

Us! Denounced! Why this sudden arrest? It's Maxime, one of my best friends who must have talked. What did he tell them about me? We mustn't appear anxious but rather indifferent. What questions will they ask me? I would appear to be alone here but a spy might be watching me through the keyhole.

My cell – Number 86! Two metres by about 4. Whitewashed walls, vaulted ceiling. On the right as you come in, a partition is fixed to the wall and on the floor a sort of bronze barrel – that's the W.C. When I first came in I had not noticed the repugnant dirtiness. Plaster, dust, crumbs of mouldy bread all impregnated with the smell of urine. At least there is a window. It's not very big and at least two metres from the ground. It is divided in two; one half is fixed and the other can only be opened from the outside by using a rope running the whole length of the ceiling of the cell and going outside above the door. All the panes have disappeared! There is just one piece of glass left in one of the squares. In the wall, which is about 70 to

80cm thick, huge criss-crossed iron bars deter any attempt to escape.

It is not very dark and in my present surroundings, I have only heaven as my witness. I am kneeling in front of the barred window. Prayer! My only succour. Even though I might deny everything, if they brought me tangible proof, if my main accuser was my best friend – as I conclude at present, I would certainly not be much of a match for Monte-Cristo.

Torture chamber, hanging by the feet, blows, threats, I can see these things in my mind's eye – but don't dare to think about them. I can hear cells being opened and closed. The sound of keys disturbs me. I always think they're for me. This prison seemed so big to me and yet I am not alone here! Small consolation!

Sunday, 23rd April, 1944 I am looking for my knife. All my pockets are empty. I remember the searching. I look at my handkerchief and my comb – the only two objects they left me. Not even a pencil, out of the 7 or 8 that I had! It's certainly not worth the trouble being a bureaucrat! I look again. At last, here's something valuable – a pin has remained hidden in a lining!

Here it is! I put it back where it was. This accursed little hole in the door still frightens me. I keep thinking I can see an eye there.

What silence. Night is falling. I listen, ear to the huge ice-cold bars of this accursed door. Nothing....

Yet there are guards about – I can sense them. They have, with good reason, confidence in the solidity of the bolts and the doors. I don't dare to move. Just one gesture but I don't make it. Am I afraid of myself? "Imbecile", there have been others before you!

I am emboldened by the silence. With my pin, I write on the wall, in the left-hand corner: Sunday 23rd April, 1944. Then in the right-hand corner, I make a small vertical mark: the first day in No.86. Now I shall know where I am. Luckily, I have my big pullover and my shirt. It can't be very warm at night.

How long have I been sitting on this plank? It's dark and I can't see any more....Tomorrow....I no longer dare to think....I lie down. I am not comfortable. I have placed my hat and handkerchief under my head but I'm still too low. I manage to doze but not for long. I am obsessed by unanswerable questions: "What are they going to accuse me of? Derailments, sabotaging wagons, intercepting documents destined for the Germans at Montchanin, defacing wagons, sending German wagons to destinations other than the right ones?"

Unfortunately, I was not at Saint Didier or Millay. I was not involved in the action at Tronsanges either. But what about the rest?

They don't know about it because I haven't talked to anybody. What about my small red case? Did they open it after I left Etang? Marcel knew nothing but he may have thought of sending my things home. If they discover my correspondence with England, I've had it! And so will the others from the free zone along with me(?)...

Also, what about that letter I gave to Louis Belot a week ago? Where is it? Supposing by ill-luck there is a search made at his house? Supposing they find it? I'll deny it, as I know their tortures. They are capable of anything.....If I can't hold out and confess, they will finish me off. If I keep quiet, I've a chance of coming through and then perhaps they will just send me to Germany to work....The uncertainty really upsets me. I would like to face a tangible danger, one I could foresee! That is not the case here. I try to reason with myself. I am afraid because I don't know. I'm cold. My teeth are chattering.......

Tired out, I had fallen asleep but I am woken with a start by various noises – buckets falling over, being filled at a pump, shouts in German, cells being opened and closed. I wait. I listen. Will it soon be my turn? The cell next door. They seem to be opening everything. This time, it's for me. I recognise the step of the gaoler from yesterday. No. I'm wrong, he's going by.

It was opposite, or below. Aren't they going to come then? I hope they do, yet fear that they will, both at the same time. The comedy of the locks goes on for half an hour, then stops.

It's day break.

How narrow this door is! It's solid. I take a firm hold of the bars with both my hands and with one foot against the wall, pull with all my force. It doesn't give an inch! Silently, I try with sharp jerks to make it move. I think I am going to go mad. I should like to be able to break everything up and yet, I'm here, like an idiot – less than nothing, good for nothing. Like a rat in a trap! What's not so funny is that I have nothing to eat. Yesterday, I did not think about it but, today my stomach gives me no peace.

I mark up Monday on the wall and a second notch, next to the first one. I inspect the walls of my room down to the last detail. A few inscriptions. "X..... condemned to death for having resisted on the ...."

Father of 7 children, Jean 18, Andre 15, etc. ....

Inscriptions half worn away by time and the last layer of whitewash.

Here there is a swastika. Further on, the cross of Lorraine can just be made out.

Above the door, some words attract my attention and give me courage: "God alone commands."

On the board which serves as a bed, prisoners have used a knife to engrave initials, a date, a proverb, and marks close together evidently signifying their days spent here.

I try to draw on the wall but with my pin I can only write my name in capital letters, very even, in spite of the plaster which flakes off, made fragile by the dampness. I had not noticed that cross over the bed and the words "God will judge". Although my mind has been occupied by this minute inspection of my four walls, my anxiety has not decreased.

The day is going by.

A sound of boots in the yard below makes me think they must be changing the guard, although they opened some of the cells this afternoon. I don't understand. Have I been condemned? Why no water and no bread?

I'm thirsty and have a temperature. Tonight I have scratched myself a lot and I notice bites on my hands. Is this from bugs or fleas? The sun has set; It barely shone into this cursed room at all, apart from hardly ten minutes through the bars!...

It's a bad night and I am shivering.

25th April I hurt all over. With my clothes and shoes on I cannot rest. I hear the hours striking. Time is going by, monotonously and every note of the nearby clock sounds like a death knell. I remain lying down in spite of the daylight. I pray fervently and ask for the bread and water which those who are free can obtain so easily. They don't know their luck!! The water, so plentiful at all the fountains in the town is flowing. Of course, this is not the only trial awaiting me!

The noise of locks, keys, the boots of the guards, calls, blows, shouts, orders, German curses, numbers, buckets being filled with water and other noises which I can't make out make the time go by. I feel less alone. I try to sleep, to forget. I cannot. Children are playing in the street. A woman calls to them. How happy they are!

I rise, and look at the window which is too high, the bars too wide and the wall too thick. I curse all prisons and all cells. I curse the masons who built and worked here; I curse too the men I can hear laughing outside. Men are mad, for you have to be mad to fight a war.......

I lose myself in pacifist reasoning. Why am I here? How silly a prisoner is. What use is this discussion with myself?

26th April. I forget my uselessness and think only of the lack of water and of the impossibility of escape. I cannot keep still any longer. I walk up and down but after five paces am obliged to turn around like and animal in its cage. I would like to make a noise, to call out – but don't dare. I try to recite decades of the rosary but can finish none of them, or, counting on my fingers. I make a mistake and say fifteen instead of ten

Last night was terrible for me. Only the same clock outside tells me the time. The half light of a slow dawn plunges me into a dream. What a cruel awakening after such a sad night. The décor does not change, the bars, the door, the walls, my board for a bed, everything is still there! I am in a tomb and no longer dare to think of my room of three days ago – the contrast hurts. I no longer have the strength to listen to anything. I jump…..A violent rattling strikes against my door, then another, then a third. A German is there and kicks open the door. A civilian is with him, repulsively dirty. He shouts at me with a strong accent – "The jug". I am astonished. "The jug" he says again. Faced with my silence, he comes in furious, stepping over all of my personal effects which I had been made to put down between the two doors. Observing the absence of a jug, he calms down, goes out, turns, throws a broom in my face and a piece of cardboard as big as my two hands and has the doors closed again. I understand I have to sweep up. My broom has no bristles left, however, with the wood I gather up most of the plaster and other dirt. I wait. I am brought an iron pot full of cold water. Having got rid of the broom and box of rubbish, I drink long and without stopping from the water which smells a little of rust, for the pot is completely covered in it. At last I am saved! I have some water. I was just a victim of an oversight. I feel rich now I have a jug!

11 o'clock. Inside, the prison is coming to life again. My door opens just as violently as before. A German takes all the personal effects which were behind the door. A young chap puts down in its place, a small bowl of soup. It's very hot and I burn my fingers. I put it down on the floor, sit down, pick it up again with my handkerchief and drink from it as though it was a basin. It's boiling but I'm so hungry. It's a thin, dark green soup with some leek in the bottom and there are two small pieces of Jerusalem Artichokes, which I eat with my fingers. That's better! I could eat it again but let's not think about that! The gaoler comes back, takes away the empty tin and throws me a piece of bread. He has a large basket of it to give out and shuts the door again, without a word. I once again have to push the huge door, so that the hook on the outside fixes it to the wall. I look at the bread – it is sacred!!

I think back to the orgies at the college in Cosne, when we used to fight each other with bread rolls, or when we threw them into the Nohain or into the W.C.s. Those who are free complain of the rationing but if they only knew…… The meal is over and I drink some rust-smelling water. I begin my walk again – three paces, about turn, five paces, about turn. I close my eyes and walk like an automaton! If only I could write…If it was only a letter, ten lines long, in order to ask their pardon for all the trouble I have caused. My father will not be able to get over this. My Mother who stopped me going to England, I want her to know I do not hold it against her but I should never have listened to her. My eyes ache. The worm-eaten floor and the whitened walls tire me. Something is missing. Outside, black clouds pass across the bars. I try to see something more so I climb onto my bed board. Roofs, skylights, chimneys, tops of windows….. Standing on tiptoe, with my back against the wall, I can see the top of a tree. It's green but it's a long way away! I stay there contemplating this greenness I am privileged to see, as opposed to those in cells below me. I can see some birds. A sparrow comes right up to my window. It seems to be complaining and crying.

I am brought a straw mattress. Surprised, I don't dare take it. A bowl of soup, a slice of bread – I devour all.

My water is replenished. I am well off but I am bored. My mind is working too much and in the evening I am tired. I am at ease on the mattress. I'm very hungry. I try to sleep but it is impossible. I always jump each time I hear steps or a cell being opened. When will the interrogation be?

We should have received the weapons yesterday by parachute. Will they have found the depot at Nevers, which Max confessed about, in spite of not wanting to do so, to these German wretches? I shall deny everything to the end. If they talk to me about Georges Richaud, I shall deny that too. Names, they want names – that's all they know. After all, I am not from Etang. I know nobody there. Let them ask the locals.

28th April. I am still at the tribunal but my cell is the court-room and I alone am the accused and the accuser. "You know him; you are still in contact with the public at the station". I will answer, Yes, I know them, by sight that's all. I am not into politics. I have always been correct with respect to the Germans. I have always done my work conscientiously. Fortunately, they don't know anything – at least they have no proof.

"Why do you come home so late at night?"

"My work; the delays to trains; I am allowed to move around at night."

"Why do you listen to London so often at G. Richaud's?"

"That's not true."

"And this, do you recognise it?"

"This newspaper, this letter you have intercepted."

"I don't know. I don't understand. I have always learnt English as a pastime – furthermore, you will have noticed that I also have a German book in my case."

Already I see myself under the blows, suspended by my feet. I grit my teeth and I think of those who London spoke of one evening – "They all held out – they said nothing."

30th April. Six p.m. It's a long time with no food. I drink a lot and often lie down.

Sometimes I feel suffocated. It really is too small here. What can the others be doing? I can hold on as I am young but what about Joseph Godillot and Gerard Pillot?

When I'm in the mood, I crush fleas!

1st May. "Clean the cell" the gaoler with the Bavarian accent repeats each morning. I have a bucket of water and a rag. It's quickly done and I go back to sleep again.

I have made a rosary with a string from the mattress!

I am brought a companion – a small man, badly shaven and clothes all torn.

"Why did they arrest you?"

"I stole a bicycle. And you?"

"I don't know. They think I'm in the Resistance."

"That's bad. I had a lot of pictures – all those of the group. It was a French policeman who arrested me. It's the chief's fault. I didn't want to steal the bike. To get to 41 and start stealing...."

"What's your name?"

"Joseph Romanin. What's yours?"

"Maurice Cordonnier."

He writes his name next to mine and puts underneath "two friends". He is in fact a friend for me but I don't trust him. I let him talk.

"How small it is in here. Have you been here long?"

"A week"

We walk side by side.

"I'm from Chalon. This is the road to Autun."

I help him to look outside, him standing on my shoulders. He makes signs and calls to a woman at the window opposite. She can't hear him. He calls her again. She looks then disappears after closing the window.

Joseph gets down again. The nails in his shoes have hurt my shoulders. It is my turn to look out. I have taken my shoes off. I am quite steady and hold on to the huge bars, whose thickness does not surprise me. Houses, windows – a street with people coming and going. Some are strolling, some are in a hurry. Will they please look this way?

Down there on the left is the front of a butchers shop. Far away, in the opposite direction, I recognise my green tree with the birds twittering in the branches. Children's voices. It is impossible to call out with two big walls a long way apart, which separate us from the outside world. Germans, policemen in navy blue. I climb down. I won't have any Lily of the Valley this year. Joseph tells me he is a Mason and has always been unhappy. He doesn't believe at all in the possibility of a landing. I want to convince him of it. He does not pray. I cannot go to sleep without it. He has been brought a mattress and blanket.

It is dark. Another lodger is brought in. Pierre Orlic, dark, tall, strong, one finger missing on the right hand. He is a Serbian and does not know why he is there. He has four children and owns a large farm. I cannot complain for I have the good fortune to be single!

Chapter 4: THE TRIAL

"Kordonniere!"

"Here"

"Los, los, schneller!"

I go out, a little surprised but without hurrying. Below, all is a hive of activity – soldiers, officers; civilians are coming and going, calling in German. My name rings out several times along with Max's. We go down the two flights of stairs. The noise and fresh air down here hit me. Los, Los. A gaoler puts a pile of handcuffs on a small table. I am bound up and led with Max into the street. A car takes us away. There are five of us tied together; I don't know who the other three are; they all sport beards. Two Germans travel in the front. We go through streets, the town and passers-by turn around to watch.. Still we travel on. Right, left, then a barred gate opens, sentries and warnings in German.

A large courtyard, fir trees, a civilian sweeping up. A few steps, first door on the right, a large room with a desk, telephone, typewriters, three Jerries are there smoking large cigars and a young woman is typing, smiling ironically. At the back is a pile of wireless sets. In one corner, some guns.

Now, all the prisoners are attached to the wall by a ring, ready prepared like animals at a market. Others are already waiting in this position. A German takes off my chain and signals to me to sit down on the floor, head against the wall. I want to see them, so as to recognise them again. You never know, later on...... A French woman is larking around with them, under our noses. Another joins her, worried about what she will be able to cook today. She speaks of cauliflowers and beef steak loud enough so as to be heard. Other women are there too but they don't belong to the establishment. They are bringing parcels to their sons; they wait. A tall officer is puffing out huge mouthfuls of cigar smoke, sitting on the desk itself and answers the telephone. I can hear blows, cries, blows, more blows then nothing. Then the blows begin again. It sounds like a stick being hit against a table. Here, of course, we know what it means. Max is very white. The old man in front of me is too and all of us bow our heads as if we could see the instrument of force being raised in front of us. The typist lights a cigarette, looks at me and shouts-

"Turn around Mister – you're at Gestapo HQ now. You understand? Gestapo!"

I obey in silence. A civilian comes in, well dressed and portly – I recognise him. He's a Boche. He taps his gaiters with a small cane baton. The two women come with some parcels which were sent with them to the prison. Other women are talking in the corridor. We cannot see them. My neighbour, bound like me, gets up. To the French typist, he says:

"They're my wife and sister. Could I ..."

"Silence".

"Ladies you cannot come in here. This is the Gestapo HQ".

The man sits down again. The women have gone out. The disturbing noises begin once more in the next room. The steel handcuff is cutting into my wrist and I can no longer feel my hand. I've had enough. If only it were over. They go on beating. Behind me, an old gentleman is seated on a chair but attached like me to a ring. The clock shows midday. The German telephonist comes out of his daydream and kicks me in the back. I understand my fault and turn to face the red and yellow flowered paper. He sees the man behind me who looks tired and is trying to lean against something to sleep. He slaps him. The man must be all of 70, lined, almost bald, his straw hat, which he had put on his knees has fallen to the floor. The German questions him:

"Did you shelter terrorists in your mill?"

"Yes"

"What's this?" he adds, shaking him by the lapel.

"The rosette of the Legion of Honour!"

"I don't know that, what does it mean?" He tries to tear it off, when an officer stops him and explains to him in German

"Papers please." He gives the man his wallet

"Naval Officer during the Great War" laughs an interpreter.

The telephone rings. I am tired. It's 12.30. A civilian comes in, a piece of paper in his hand. He calls Maxime and myself. I walk with difficulty because of the handcuffs. A corridor, then a large room with swastika flags – at the back, a life size Hitler. It's not the first time I've seen him with his moustache and arrogant air but I have never felt his presence as much as here! A Hun points the way and a civilian follows. Now we are in a huge dining room. The table is laid with numerous place settings and the piles of bread cut into chunks remind me of my hunger and above all, that there are people who still eat at table, with a tablecloth and plate. What a waste, for these men!

Where are they taking me? I climb a spiral staircase and cross a corridor, passing a large box of sawdust and a spade stained with blood.

More steps. A door opens and I am in a room which is small, wood panels

24

everywhere and it seems to be sound-proofed. Also, there is a table, typewriter, blotting paper and two revolvers. On the wall under a large photo of Goering is a large map of Europe, on which is written the pretentious word "Deutschland".

I am made to sit down.

A German sits down at the typewriter. Another, in civilian clothes I recognise as he was in the lorry and his name was Goldberg. He looks at me but I don't move. Nobody speaks. He goes to open a cupboard and takes out a truncheon. It looks brand new. He places it before him on the desk after waving it around in the air several times. He sits down, calmly lights a cigarette and opens a pink folder. My file, no doubt!

Newspapers, letters. What is there against me in all those papers? How helpless I am with these handcuffs which paralyse both of my wrists. He searches in his pocket and takes out a small 6.35 revolver, which he places in front of me – about a metre away.

It is the school of fear. I am tempted to jump on the weapon but I hesitate. Is it loaded? Is it a trap? I know that he has another one, three times as big. He had it in the lorry.

"How long have you been in the Resistance?"

"I am not involved in politics, I don't know this organisation."

"It was Chevrier who recruited you, do you admit it?"

"I don't know. He never said anything to me. Moreover, I am not from Etang and I don't know half of those you arrested at the same time as me."

"You know Joseph Godillet, Oliver Melin, Louis Belot, Pierre l'Hoste.?"

"Yes, they are colleagues at the station but….".

"They were with you.?"

"No."

"Have you any weapons?"

"No."

"Have you heard talk of a parachute drop?"

"I don't understand."

He gets up to strike me.

"Ask the others, I don't know anything, they didn't say anything to me."

He puts down the truncheon and shows me an enormous pistol; its black butt frightens me. The man really looks like a pirate, with cruel eyes.

"Where are the copies of "La Liberation" which Max gave you?"

"I don't know. I don't understand."

"Liar, you are going to tell me." He shouts abruptly, training his pistol even closer to me – "I know your political feelings"

"Reading a newspaper won't change them"

"You are in the Resistance. Your great friend Maxime Chevrier says so and you used to pass the papers on to Pierre l'Hoste."

"That's not true."

"I'll call in Maxime Chevrier, he'll soon make you talk"

"It's not worth it. I know he bears me a grudge. He has told you a lot of stories. He did in fact show me two newspapers but I didn't read them. I didn't know what they were."

"You were to give them to Olivier Melin or Pierre l'Hoste?"

"I rarely spoke to them and Melin always frightened me."

"You are a terrorist. Who was with you at the Saint Didier derailment?"

"I swear to you I never......"

"I'm not asking you to swear but to confess."

While I am speaking, the typist is taking everything down. I am in a sweat! Are they going to leave it at that? Their weapons are again lying on the table.

"If you don't confess, we will arrest your parents, your two brothers, father, mother, everyone.

"What do you want them to tell you? It's almost two years since I was with them and anyway I have never done anything against the Germans."

"I am not saying you have done anything."

"So, you......"

"Sign here on the three copies. Sign, you have been sentenced."

"Translate it, I don't understand German."

He points a revolver at me.

"I can't sign what I don't understand."

"You understand. In any case, it's your declaration. You will either be released or sent to Germany."

"Why?"

"You should have been there a year ago."

Tired out, I sign, trembling. The writing is bad, illegible, anyway under duress it means nothing. I am almost relieved. If the matter goes no further, I have come through lightly.

"To what am I condemned?"

. . . . .

"Will I remain in prison long?"

. . . .

"How long will I have to work in Germany?"

"People always work there, you will be taught to work."

He goes out.

Two guards take me away. Stairs, the yard, the car. There are five of us again and I am once more tied up with Max, who tries to talk.

"Did it go OK? Did they beat you?"

"No."

"So much the better!"

At top speed we pass through Chalon, a town I don't know. This is the road to Autun, the high wall, the barriers. There are lots of people here. I recognise Messrs. Lapray and Godillot. I look at them. The lorry is there too. The women draw back and we go in. The gates shut again. Once more I am back in the dreariness. I am given a bowl of cabbage soup, which is cold. I drink it quickly and my gaoler takes me back upstairs. I have received a parcel of linen. Questioned by my friends, I tell them all went well but give no details.

Chapter 5: I AM WAITING

5th May. Life goes on at the prison. We are dying of hunger. We have plenty of water and the cell is washed twice a week. The Red Cross came once and brought us sugar and biscuits. Some are better off for they have Red Cross bean soup. We could have some too but the Boche prefer to breed pigs.

8th May. We have a new boarder. He too, does not know the reason for his arrest. He has some dripping and cheese in his bag. He gives some to us and we devour it. He is very bored. Every day we look out of the window – behind our bars. It must be so good to be outside! No luck today, there are Boches at the window opposite. They must have seen me. Quickly we lie down on our mattresses. Not a sound, not a word. Suddenly, the lock turns, the door opens, boots and movement everywhere. We get up and, standing to attention one behind the other, as is the rule, we wait. It is the little moustached man who comes in.

"You looked outside – you climbed up here?"

"No."

He is addressing himself mainly to me. He comes nearer and I move back. He looks threatening and takes out his revolver then does an about turn and writes a number in his note book.

"Close the door." He has gone and he goes downstairs again.

I am told off by my friends. You won't be getting up there anymore. They'll be looking for us now. Since we can no longer communicate with the outside world, let us try with our neighbours here. I tap against the wall. I listen. No answer. I'm frightened of being caught. Earlier, I saw an eye through the spy hole. I listen – my three friends are asleep, or pretending. I ask them to help me and listen, ear against the wall. They refuse, under the pretext of being deaf. A knock, two dull knocks. It begins again, there's no doubt – someone is answering, someone has knocked. Enemy or friend? I bang once, twice, three times with my wrist against the wall. Three knocks answer.

I go to the door to listen to see if there is anything suspect, either in the corridor or on the stairs. Nothing. I call to Joseph softly: "Come and listen" There is someone next door. There is some knocking, it may be Morse code.

"Joseph, give me a leg up. I am going to call out of the window."

"Are you mad?"

The tapping has stopped

10th May. Hello room 86. Quick, to the window.

Answer by speaking loudly against the wall. Let's try.

"Who's there? Maxime Chevrier from Etang.

I cannot hear well

"Who gave us away?"

"It was a …. From Autun called Gressard I don't know him. Do you?"

No answer. Cells are being opened again. Shush — someone is coming up. No, wrong.

12th May. Jean Meullens has gone. Freed, or just moved to another cell? The Romanian has come back from being interrogated. His back is completely blue and bruised from his beating but he did not tell them he belonged to the 'maquis'. He has a fever but will not give in and we walk side by side in our cage, for a long time. He still has an old bit of cigarette stub which he can't smoke through lack of matches. He always has it in his mouth!

The door opens.

We are all at attention at the first noise of the lock. It's the madman. "The bawler" as we call him — young and well turned out, with the red ribbon of the Russian front. He surprised us, for he is wearing slippers!

"You're smoking here? You're utterly mad."

I am astonished and notice that Joseph is still looking at him, ironically at attention with a cigarette between his lips. A blow throws him off balance and the German takes his tobacco from him. All my friends are suffering greatly from this privation, as much as from the lack of bread. As for me, I'm hungry but don't care about the rest of it.

15th May. Another new man, tall, fat, kind, called Gabriel Durand. He is a butcher. He too was arrested at night for no apparent reason. He gives us a little sausage that the Germans were kind enough to leave him.

There are just 3 of us again now, Gabriel Durand, Pierre Orlic and myself.

We chat sometimes with the chaps next door, either through the wall or the window, in the evening from 6 to 7 when all is quiet or on Sunday afternoons. We are wary, because the woman opposite is on the side of the Boches and has told them that we make signs.

Sometimes the madman in slippers stands guard outside the door of our cell. He has already caught me twice at the window, standing on the shoulders of the strong Gaby, who is sometimes very sad too, for his wife is at home ill. She has sewn a small medal on the nightshirt he received. In fact, every fortnight we are allowed a laundry bundle but not food or letters. We still have no spoons

23rd May. Gabriel Durand has gone to be interrogated. I tell the chaps next door and pray while he is away. He returns. He has not been beaten, so all went well. I am pleased. We talk a great deal in order to think as little as possible and above all to fight against depression. As soon as one of us is silent, he begins to think, becomes sad and is shaken by the others. In turns we walk up and down, sometimes all together but one behind the other, after having piled up our mattresses on the boards. We make a tour of our square! It is so dry, that the nails have come out of our shoes.

Pierre Orlic amuses himself by trying to stick them back by spitting on them!

Each man tells his story, his life, gives his opinion on the war and the landing, which is so slow in coming. They don't give a damn about us, says Pierre.

I am still confident. Only the uncertainty frightens me. Will I not be called again? Will I be asked other questions? In prison, I could be serving as a hostage if there are other derailments. What will they do with us if the English land or if the Resistance tries to free us?

Far off, in the street, we can sometimes hear a wireless. The news. Listening at the window is dangerous but I risk it as soon as I hear the radio. I cannot understand much.

It is Radio Paris and sometimes Switzerland. The war goes on. If there are Germans at the window opposite, I have to put my ear to the ventilation grille at floor level, in spite of the cold draught. I catch a few words, bombing raids, terrorist attacks, Hamburg, Kassel, Wilhenschafen. In the Pacific, things are going well but progress is slow. No mention of the Russian front.

25th May. For some time, we have been getting more water. A large bucket and a jug in the morning, mid-day and evening. We are able to wash but have nothing with which to cut our toenails. I do not hesitate – after washing; I cut mine with my teeth, under the amused glances of my friends, especially Gaby who asks which circus I worked in?!

In cell 87 nobody answers anymore and I am alone with the cells below. Only No.85 is interesting. I can talk to them for hours thanks to the alphabetic code I have written on the wall for speed. On the other side, the guy has done the same and, without seeing or speaking to each other, we have real old conversations, some serious, some banal or ironic.

"Hello, who's there? This is the Resistance."

"This is the Gestapo"

"Hello, your name?" …….

"Where are you from?"

"Montchanin."

"This is Etang; pass the message to the next cell."

"Etang is below. Call 87"

"Why?"

"They were at the window...

"Be careful."

I transmit, Pierre receives, Gaby keeps watch.

As soon as there is an alert, the noise of a key, a lock, boots in the corridor, on the stairs or along the passage, we quickly lie down on our mattresses and pretend to be asleep.

28th May. It is Whitsun.

Thanks to our primitive calendar on the wall, we can count the days. Today, my young brother is due to make his first communion. I am sad, don't speak but I pray. At noon, I found a piece of beef fat in my leek soup. Every Sunday, we actually have 2 mouthfuls of meat in the soup. I should like to bend these bars and get out – get out quickly. Any attempt to escape would be suicide, what with the guards on patrol, the stairs which creak, the iron gates, the keys which I don't have. What a nightmare. When we see the sun, it is for 15 minutes in the evening at dusk.

30th May. It's Tuesday, the day for the laundry parcel. Those from Etang will come by lorry. They will be down there, at the door and I won't see them. Gaby is nervous this morning. He would dearly like news of his wife. Pierre Orlic is definitely counting on some linen too, for he's not changed for a month. He still has his shoes covered in dry mud – the Germans arrested him at work, in the fields.

6 o'clock. We are cleaning the cell. It makes a change for us. We would like to work a little.

8 o'clock. Already I am looking out of the window. I can hear people passing in the street which I don't know. I propose to my friends that we write something in the cell. I have already sent something secretly in the two preceding bundles but without mentioning it to them.

"What about a pencil or paper?"

"I have found about 10 pieces of thin paper and a stub of pencil between the wall and the plank of my bed."

Astonished, they look at me. Not bad – let's write!

I write my letter hunched up in the corner to the right of the door, so as not to be caught. It's a long one. Above all, I want to reassure my parents, tell them all is well and ask them for forgiveness. I send them my love and don't even ask for a bundle.

I do Berrot's letter for he can't write. Gaby writes in his turn. Also, I cut my finger on the piece of glass at the window. Bleeding, I write with my blood on a dirty handkerchief: "Everything OK, how about you?

I take another piece of paper and trace out a few sentences in scratches made with my pin. One letter is now in the lining of my shirt which I have unstitched a little, the other under the elastic of a sock!

My two friends do the same. Gaby hesitates a little and moves his paper. He tears his shirt in several places and he can't find anywhere to hide his letter. His paper gets torn and he has to write it again.

10 o'clock: What a long morning! The exasperating noise of the locks has started again. The gaoler passes by us several times, knocking with his keys. Every rattle is a source of anxiety and questions for us. At each lull, one of us climbs up to the window, taking good care not to be seen by those at the windows on our right on the other side of the road. Those people are collaborators and they allow the Boches to come into their homes.

Gaby would like to see his wife again, or his friend who is a butcher who lives at the end of the road. It is with the greatest trouble in the world that we hoist him up to the bars. He doesn't see anyone and gets down again. It's my turn to look. Opposite, the neighbours have laid the table with cloth, plates, glasses and a bottle. What a meal!

11.30: Here's the soup! It is as usual, very clear. Each man comes up with his bowl. Nobody speaks. Gaby and Pierre have a spoon. I wait for a while but I am so hungry that when one of them offers one to me, I have already finished, as I have already eaten the piece of bread.

12.00: Collection of empty bowls and distribution now of a handful of biscuits marked 'SN'. I guess it must mean 'Secours National'.

13.00: The linen still has not come. Next door in 87, the chap from Chalon has had his, together with some food. He tells me through the wall he has some gingerbread, cheese and saucisson. In cell 85, Max and the man from Toulon have also had a parcel and a card from home.

If Max has had something, those from Etang have come back and I have no news. There will therefore be nothing for No.86.

Well, here are the parcels, one each! There is some clean linen from home. At last I have a spoon! I change my clothes quickly and make a parcel of my dirties in the box that the clean ones were in. Someone has written my name on it. I don't recognise the writing. With my pin, I scratch a small letter – "I am well, are you? Thanks for the spoon and the bread.

With my clean clothes, I am alright. In doing up my shirt collar, I am extremely surprised to see that the letter I slipped there a fortnight ago, has come back again. They did not see it in Etang. Perhaps they will see today's?

15.00: The man with the pipe comes to collect the dirty washing.

"No notes in it?"

"No sir!"

He's gone. We climb to the window again. There are some people in the corridor below, opposite. I make some signs and a young woman answers me. I don't know her. She blows me some kisses. I smile and answer. A young girl is eating cherries at the window opposite. At every moment one of us is watching. I try to ask for some parcels. They can't hear me, so I shout. They are frightened and move away. The evening goes by. I have seen nobody local. The sun goes down. As usual, we have our evening visit on the right hand wall. How sad this yellowy red light is which lengthens the shadow of the iron bars! This evening, my washing and my letter will be in Etang, if the guard has not noticed anything. On the other hand, if he has looked at my collar, socks, handkerchief, I shall be for it!! With Gaby, we have composed a song to the tune of "As long as there are stars".

We sing: -   We are jailbirds, we're under cover,
                 We sleep in a cell at night.
                 We've got bugs and a nice little bed
                 All is well, everything smiles on us
                 And yet we are proud in spite of everything
                 The end is nigh, we will see it through
                 Luckily for us.

It is dark. The sirens are blasting. Fortunately, our gaolers are going to have a fright. What joy there is here! 2 or 3 bombs well placed on the barracks and we'll be able to choose our moment. Planes, dull bangs, flak, silence, then the all clear. It is not light yet. We have already thought about how to defend ourselves in case of mass execution in the cells. The bed frame is solid but with the three of us, we could prize it away and push it against the door so as to remain out of range of gun shots and stop any incursion into our prison which would become a refuge in case of serious attack.

3rd June. Pierre Orlic has been questioned. Perhaps he will be released soon. I prepare him a letter which he puts in his cap. It is fine outside but in here the atmosphere remains dreary. I am used to the lack of space, of air, of greenery, of light. Each morning is a nightmare for me, the dawn of a useless day going by and above all, my freedom is lost. Life, already so short, is further diminished for us by reclusion. Pierre Orlic and Gaby talk about business matters, money, the buying and selling of animals. Their discussion irritates me and I cannot understand these prisoners who talk as though they were at a market, whilst one question only should be raised – How to get out of here.

I am hungry. I drink a lot of water straight from the jug. Gaby grumbles at me.

"Why do you drink so much? You're mad."

I don't answer.

4th June. Last night we heard firing. The day is monotonous, humid, sad and still full of anxiety, of worry at the slightest noise of a key, of boots, or of the front door bell, when it only rings once. Just one ring means the Germans have come, two rings, is for the French prison. This morning I heard the small bell of the priest who comes to say mass for the common-law prisoners. We are not allowed out, but pray just the same. A sad Sunday. Slowly the sun disappears. I don't sleep at night. Startled from my doze by the noise of the lock, I jump –

The Corpulent Kraut calls to me –

"Los, Los!"

I go out, without even taking my jacket. It is cool, cold even. Not a sound. Below, an electric lamp is alight. What do they want from me at this hour? It must be 11.00. I am led by the guard towards the exit but we turn to the left, into a large lit room. I am a little afraid and suddenly terrified by the spectacle before me. Two men are hanging by their feet, their hair brushing the dust on the tiles. Another man, laid out on a table seems to have fainted. Goldbarck is there, the tough guy with the large baton. He approaches but speaks to the guard saying "It's not him".

Has there been a mistake? They make me turn about, inspecting the plan of the cells. We go up again. At the first floor, we stop. They open a cell, call a name similar to my own but I can't catch it. I rejoin my friends and tell them briefly what happened.

5th June. We are visited by four officers. They have come to see us and have looked at the interior of our room.

Gaby has had a parcel via the head of the French prison, chocolate, sugar and saucisson. We eat. Gaby has cut off a small piece of saucisson for each of us with the nail which serves him as a knife. That was a long job – the slices are not very round but taste fine!

6th June. 9.00. In the street, the usual morning hum is beginning, shutters are banging, children are playing. I come down from the window, walk about, listen, ponder. I think about everything and nothing! "Courage men, they've landed". Have I understood correctly? Gaby makes me climb quickly up to the bars. I am bewildered and can see nothing. I come down again and call the neighbours, in 85 and 87. "Have you heard? Yes or No? A landing"?

Impatient, we wait for the wireless opposite. Will it be on shortly? Yes! I can hear Calvados mentioned- 11,000 planes. Quiet chaps! It's certain, it's just happened. I call Max. He can't understand the wireless and is afraid of being seen. I explain to him and he is pleased.

87 are rejoicing too. All is well. I climb up to the window again, thanks to Gaby who lifts me up each time like a feather! Ears pricked, breath held, I listen and then come down again into the shade.

I draw a map on the wall with my pin. England, Northern France, Normandy, the Cotentin peninsula are working out a strategy. Already we feel we are no longer prisoners.

10th June. The gaolers are worried and we are celebrating.

On the 11th, we have a new prisoner, Georges Gardon, pleasant but with no spirit. I smother him with questions about the latest news. He has nothing with which to reproach himself but on his return from being questioned, we suddenly understand. He too, is in the Resistance and accused of being one of the leaders. He has been roughly treated. His buttocks are no longer white but black and inflamed. I moisten my handkerchief and make him some compress. He is weeping. I comfort him. That's fairly easy for he is a Catholic. He admits to me that he wants to end his life. I try to buck him up, for the sake of his wife and children. He is afraid and jumps at each new noise, wanting to confess everything. I dissuade him. He is in pain. I am worried about him but don't let him see it. "They've landed, there's no doubt – you found that out yourself, outside the prison. We must hold on"

15th June.

I am the information bureau, the ear of the cell. If I am not listening at the window, it is at the ventilation hole. For my trouble, I catch a cough, thanks to the treacherous draught. I have a fever, one must not be ill. Shivers, sweating and involuntary trembling takes hold of me. Here's the soup. It's boiling. I swallow it and stretch out on the mattress with the blanket tucked around me. I am hot and fall asleep

17th June.

I feel better and come out of it with a good cold. Georges Cardon has been interrogated again. Everything seems to be working out for him so the news feels good. There is fighting in Normandy. We have been given soap and papers for the WC. These newspapers give us some news, gleams of hope, for we know how to read between the lines. Each paper is passed around, so that each day we read and re-read.

Today there is a convoy leaving the French prison. The Mobile Guard – militia, are patrolling this cursed road to Autun. I can see some Boches too. I have made a pack of cards with the papers and my pencil. We play Manille and Belote but have to be careful. Next door were caught and deprived of soup for this reason.

19th June.

Pierre Orlic is unhappy and dares not play with us. Doors open and shut again, there are shouts. Men are going up and down the stairs. I wait and wait. It's for us. They want me again. I can see the ones from Etang on the stairs. They are still recognisable with their beards. I guess it must be them, rather than actually recognise them. Maxime, Olivier, Gerard Pillot, Jean Rousseau. Where are the others? We tell Gerard Pillot about the landing. I walk in front of Pierre L'hoste without recognising him. He has a shaggy beard and is talking to Maxime Olivier who confirms to me that Louis Bellot is dead.

It's medical inspection – just a formality, carried out in front of a woman interpreter and a Russian soldier in German uniform.

"Have you got TB or syphilis? Asks this woman. She makes us undress. The soldier looks at us. We get dressed again. It's over. No doubt – departure is near. Our case has been settled. Germany is awaiting us!

All four of us have received a linen bundle but no letter.

22nd June.

"Pierre Orlic, Maurice Cordonnier!" Bring zor zings. We are moved to another cell. I didn't even have time to say goodbye to Gaby and Georges.

We go down and to my great amazement; we are put in cell No. 1. It is damp and has no window – also, where is the mattress? We do not know what to think. Other men join us - all those from Etang, or almost. There are about 15 of us! Morale is good. The landing is the major subject of conversation but also the reasons for our banal arrest. It is obvious that some people talked. Olivier is furious. Pierre L'Hoste remains calm.

We are called in turn to be shaved and to have our hair cut by the prison barber. Every time one of us returns, he looks young again and a smile is back on his face! Pierre L'Hoste shows us the Christian religious thoughts he has engraved on the wall of this hideout, where he has lived for forty days.

We give a letter to the barber with a little money, because we have just been given back most of our personal effects. The news is good! If we go, it won't be for long. It's getting late. We are going to bed but with no mattresses.

I have been moved to yet another cell and am with a friend from Frouard, Bernard Besancon (he died in the death convoy to Dachau). We are in No. 17, three times as big as the other ones and brighter! We are welcomed by about 20 bearded men who question us. They are all from Autun. They were stealing petrol from the Germans. They are nice and offer to write to our homes as they can get letters through! At last my parents will get some news. Here, things are better! Through the grille in the doors, we can look into the interior of the prison and see the flags where, with arms crossed, one of the Resistance chiefs died after throwing himself from the 2nd floor. There is also the place where a priest was half strangled by the Boches and died three days later.

23rd June. The night was short. We have been called and it's now time for departure. I see my friends again. Doors open and liberate others. There are about 100 of us, all facing the wall. I stand next to Pierre L'Hoste but a German moves me again. Here come the handcuffs. I have a small bag with clothes in one hand. We are tied up in pairs. Preparations are slow. We are given a piece of bread and some cheese. At last we are going out, to leave this cursed prison!

I am in front, with an ex Legionnaire. His set face is furrowed with lines and scars. He has lived in South Morocco for the last five years and he doesn't speak much. An escort arrives with revolvers, bren guns and machine guns! It seems they have plenty! Forward! The doors are opening. The street at last! I take deep breaths. I've got air good and cool! The cursed floor of No.86, the jug, the bars, the friends who stayed behind – all that is already a long way away. The street, with its closed shop fronts and half-open doors is waiting for us! The few passers-by look at us from afar, fearful, powerless. Are we going to the station? Some roads are closed. The cross-roads are blocked off with a zigzag of sandbags and barriers.

Chalon: The town looks pleasant but in my situation, I cannot judge. It is 8.00a.m. Having arrived at the station, we stop. About 15 women appear to be waiting for us. I do not know them. They are laden with parcels and come close. Surely they must have relatives amongst us? The Germans sign to them to stay to one side. They regretfully move away. Our convoy moves into the marshalling yard and a number of wagons are waiting for us. To my great surprise, we get into the passenger coaches. It was a difficult exercise as we were encumbered by handcuffs and tied to somebody else! The guards are ever present on the ballast. In the distance there are some railway men, friends, I'm sure. I am confident and my thoughts are solely of escape! The journey passes without incident. At Beaune, I wanted to warn somebody I knew but saw no-one. Dijon! Lorries are waiting for us at the station and take us to the prison. The décor is no different here from Chalon. Walls, sand, bars and the sky – when you can see it!

200 of us wait in a large room with grilles which look out onto the courtyard. We

can see the prisoners in the cells upstairs. One of us makes signs. We communicate with a mirror and the reflection from the sun. They haven't heard the news either. We tell them as best we can. They are hungry and thirsty. One of them has been there for 2 years. We are fairly calm and can talk at leisure, even talk loudly with men we don't know but who are already companions. A bell sounds. Some detainees cross the yard, accompanied by guards who shout insults at them and hit them. We are going to be served soup. It's late. Each of us receives a bowl of very clear soup, in which the cauliflower is sparse. It's very thin.

24th June. We go back to the station. Without any doubt, we are going to Compiegne. Goodbye Dijon! The 'comedy' goes on. Bound in pairs, we travel towards the capital. My companion in chains is Max and we talk a great deal. Olive is with us but Pierre is in the next compartment. Our guards have the same black shield but I have never seen this uniform before. To my great surprise, I can hear them speaking in very correct French – at least with no foreign accent – They are French! They look like thugs. They've got the gift of the gab and are very cocksure. They have started a conversation with the man opposite me. They believe themselves very clever in conducting a roaring black market trade and making a lot of money. This evening they hope to get into the nightclubs of the capital. They are proud of their job and on the ring of their big German belts, I can see written in French "For my honour and my country". They are ex gaolbirds, for they know Clairvaux and Fresnes rather well, where certain eminent collaborators liberated them at the price of dishonour.

There is a 1 hour stop at Laroche-Migennes. What memories this large station brings back to me, whose every corner and detour is familiar to me since I've been going to Auxerre. Escape, which should be so simple, is impossible with our handicaps and the sentries.

We set off again. The sirens are going as we arrive in Paris, the Capital. It's an air raid with a plane, flak and observation balloons. Each man sees something that he knows – a certain area, a church, the Concorde, the boulevards, even just the Eiffel Tower! It's sad to pass so close to home or to a friend and to continue this journey in handcuffs. My right hand and my heart feel equally constricted.

Gare de Lyon. We see some colleagues. Pierre finds his brother and is able to speak to him and give him his watch and wallet. Some railwaymen bring a box of peaches and distribute them in the compartment. The gesture does as much good as the fruit. We slip them a note scribbled in haste in the WC!

Manoeuvres are carried out and it takes us 12 hours to reach the Gare du Nord, where the Red Cross give us some hot coffee. The night is a strain with our encumbrances. Max, my companion in chains, is ill and I have to follow him, for my right wrist is constantly obliged to follow the movements of his left wrist. He stretches out under the seat and I have to stay in a squatting position, off balance and unable to sleep. He moves a great deal and if I forget the damned chain even for a moment, I injure myself or receive a stream of reproaches from Max. My right hand no longer belongs to me, for in spite of myself, if indulgent; I impose this tiring position upon myself.

25th June. It's cool this morning. We have pulled up again. We hear that the line is blocked. That's possible after what we saw in Juvisy. They should do the same everywhere! The Germans refuse to prolong the delay. Are we going to leave the train and get into waiting lorries? I am in a trailer with my friends, and of course, still attached to Max.

Forward!.....

Chapter 6: COMPIEGNE

The pace is extremely fast. There are at least 50 of us, standing in the trailer with nothing to lean on, encumbered by our one parcel and obliged to stay in the position dictated by the handcuffs and our companions. At each jolt, each bend, the least steady among us stagger, stumble, fall and bring down others as they go. On top of each other, wrists grazed, cries, insults, complaints, we travel inexorably along this bedevilled route, thrown forward at full speed. Countryside, sparse villages, etc. When the two flaps of the lorry allow it, and according to the number of jolts, we can see the daylight filtered by the silhouettes of the sentries.

As in a storm, we are thrown to and fro, to right and left at the mercy of the bends. At each moment it feels as though we are turning over and the driver, if he is aware of it, certainly does not realise what is happening.

He is German!

24th June 1944. Compiegne. This is the life!! On our arrival, a real feeling of physical and mental relief comes over us. At least we are on solid ground and the calm atmosphere is reassuring. We have the impression of being free. Of course there is barbed wire all around us, surmounted by watch towers but here the Germans cannot, as they did in the prison, stop us from being in the fresh air, and above all, from seeing the trees, the grass and the countryside. We have some space and this space is a renewal for us, recalling us to life!

In the cells, we had begun to forget what bird song was and the sky with its sun and the countryside. Here, we can really appreciate the grandeur of these things which we had lost and which man becomes indifferent to when he experiences them every day.

The first day is spent in completing all the formalities for entry into this Stalag 122 camp. We are given a speech lasting several hours. There are not many Germans about. We chat while awaiting orders, either sitting or lying on the ground. We only half listen to the reading of the regulations, for they are talking about a canteen, a sports field, Red Cross soup, a library, etc…..We were not expecting any of this.

We are forbidden to keep more than 600 francs. How ironical for the man who no longer even has a wallet! We are given a serial number typed on a small piece of yellow card. Mine is 42.535. We have to put on a table all our identity papers, under pain of sanctions, but since we are not searched, I do as many others are doing, and give them nothing.

We remain for half an hour, 200 of us in a large room where there is some straw to lie on and two iron buckets acting as toilets. Of course space is limited and the air cannot circulate, for it is forbidden to open the windows. Some lie down; others in groups exchange a few words. Some, pensive, say nothing. The waiting is soon over and we are divided into several groups and led to buildings numbered A1, A2, A3, etc. after having crossed a large recreation area bordered with trees. Maybe I'm dreaming but in passing I see some prisoners engrossed in a game of bowls, while others are playing basketball!

However, as soon as we appear, whistles start blowing everywhere and as if by magic, all the players or walkers disappear behind the red brick wall. We wind up in building A1. A few steps, a corridor, several numbered doors, a blackboard announcing the day's menu, a newspaper pinned to the wall together with some typed notices. Room 5 is ours, long and wide, lit at the back by two large windows looking out onto gardens, a watch tower is visible on the right and hidden behind a barbed wire fence, the sentries are patrolling up and down. The beds are bunks of 2 or 3, one row on each side and fairly tidy. Two tables, a few benches, sufficient for 50, especially when you eat on your mattress. We all have two blankets, between which I quickly forget my fatigue! We have chosen our beds and staked our claim. Our group takes up a whole corner, of course, and we sleep side by side. At last, we have a bed. We were received by about 20 men from the Auvergne who have been here a fortnight. They seem rather dirty. They want for nothing, not even onions with which they seem to be having a feast, for they each have a string of them tied to their beds!

They are extremely outgoing men, taking no moderation in their gestures or language, which is often incomprehensible and sometimes vulgar. Ordinarily, I would keep away from them but in here they are not obnoxious to me, for they have the advantage of being able to make everyone laugh!

We eat well, we have got air, and we can walk outside. We are almost at liberty yet we wait and wonder about the days to come.

I still have a spoon from the prison. I have been given a small mug for drinking and a small blue dish to serve as a bowl. We have a hut leader who cuts the grey bread into fours, supervises the soup and the sharing of the extras, i.e. butter or jam.

The soup (carrots, slightly rotten potatoes, and beans often scored and indigestible) is better than at Chalon but still insufficient in spite of the improvement brought by the Red Cross.

Since we are not working, the chores are frequent: cleaning, fetching the soup, emptying the buckets, installing or transporting beds, chores at the station, in the town, or just between the rows of barbed wire, where we are digging ditches. There is no shortage of water here. About 100 taps give us as much as we need and each morning sees us in a file, chest and legs bare, going into the big tent. Later in the day, one man might wash a handkerchief there, another a towel, even a shirt which will dry on the barbed wire, under the eyes of the watch tower guard who hardly bothers to hide his machine gun.

The camp is on a hill overlooking Compiegne. The wind, often blowing, makes the gardens which we are cultivating, very dry. The leaders are mostly Frenchmen who speak German. Some are Block Leaders or Deputy Block Leaders, with an armband bearing one or two stripes. The policemen have red stripes. The Camp Leader, short moustached, a former Rifleman Captain wears the large Basque berry, an armband with dark green stripes and smokes a pipe. We are obliged to salute him, together with all the other German soldiers, when we meet them in the yard. At attention, head bare, eyes towards your superior – that's the order of the day, otherwise you risk, like the Marquis of Moustiers, doing a spell in the "cooler", camp prison where you languish without food, water or air!

Twice a day, the camp inmates, except the sick, have to assemble for roll call. There are about 5000 of us and for 10 to 15 minutes, we remain standing at attention, motionless, in ranks of 5 and in columns of 7 or 8. The Head of each hut counts his men and gives the number to the Germans. They then check. It's quickly done, for the young Boche who reviews us, is used to it and often goes around on a bicycle. A whistle blows and the crowd breaks up like a flock of sheep, suddenly set free.

In each hut, there are books or packs of cards available, or the remains of the half parcel, given by the Red Cross. I don't play much. I walk up and down in the corridor, re-reading several times, the Compiegne newspaper. Fighting is continuing in Normandy – in a fortnight we might see what's happening and I examine the map, work out the miles and time needed to break through…

We talk a great deal about these crucial matters and work out strategies behind these cursed barbed wire fences. Is escape possible? Yes! In spite of the search lights which constantly sweep over us at night, in spite of the Alsatian dogs, a tunnel could get us out of here at night but it needs time to build it and that we haven't got. The one which ran from the Chapel is, in fact, no more use than the one from the Canteen through which 17 escaped.

We have only one chance: the train – we will try it little by little. We know the price of failure – 10 men were shot for each one who escaped. There is one man who is feared in the camp – the man with the dog. Short, fat, booted, wearing a cap with a long peak like a jockey. In one hand he carries a riding whip, in the other the dog on a leash. He is frightening with his huge head and bull neck. Woe to the chap who doesn't see and salute him – the dog quickly recalls him to duty!

We often walk around the large open area. We rub shoulders with men from all over France and from every kind of background. There are many priests amongst us, even bishops. It is therefore easy for Catholics to say their confession while walking with one of them! Communion takes place every day during mass at the Chapel. At each service, the Chapel is full. This is the place for spiritual relief and thanks to the comforting words of Monseigneur Theas from Montauban; we come out each time fortified and confident, in spite of the uncertainty of the days ahead. A German is always present at these services but in the role of a spy, for what we feared has come to pass, mass has been stopped and our priests and bishops sent to Camp C, next to ours, yet inaccessible because of the strict instructions and the barbed wire. Already I regret the presence of these men, who despite being just as dignified as when they were free, stood side by side with us to peel carrots and potatoes, dressed in their cassocks and violet scarves.

Air raids are rare and yet a few planes sometimes come to fire on our warders. On the other hand, a new man who arrived in the last convoy was killed by one of them whilst he was out in the latrine buckets. In fact, we are strictly forbidden to leave the huts between 7 in the evening and 7 in the morning.

30th June. I was ill throughout the night. The rotten beans are the cause. Indigestion, violent colic, vomiting! Unfortunately, I am not alone and there is congestion in the WCs and in the corridor, already soiled by the ill. The blue lamps hardly light the way and people often mistake their room on the way back. I don't like this corridor; it's dark and too long. It is cold, full of draughts and seems to me even more lugubrious when lit by the beacon opposite.

1st July. People are talking of an imminent departure. The old hands believe it and explain to us in advance what the call will be like. Preparations matter little – all that interests us is the freight wagons and escape, for we must succeed. At 13.00 as planned, it's roll call in the yard. There is a large table with a green cover, chairs and benches for the German scribes. Some officers are present with their briefcases, from which they take out large papers, lists, no doubt. The man with the dog is there – even more arrogant than usual. The whole camp is present, down to the cook with his white apron. A small table is brought out and the Camp Leader and police chiefs sit down. We form a large circle, as though around a circus ring.

Roll call begins. In alphabetical order, names are called out, spoken by the man in the green armband who is never without his pipe- the eternal pipe, always full and alight. It's as though we were at a market, with the auctioneer pointing out the animals.

Each man impatiently awaits his name! In other words, the certainty of departure. It's a pathetic moment and goes on and on. The letters A take a quarter of an hour. The B's are even more numerous and our friend with the moustache, satisfied, blows puffs of blue smoke about him, unceasingly. In order to appear more eloquent and above all to be heard better, he gets up onto the table. Men pass by in single file, bareheaded, before the German officers who stamp their card as they pass. Any man not saluting is slapped or bitten by one of the dogs as they too form part of the guard. Names are often mispronounced but it's too bad for the man who doesn't reply 'present', or who makes one of the guards walk a step. We are now at the C's. Max is called. It's my turn. NO it must be wrong! I'm staying. I wait and keep listening. Max is already over there with the others. He turns, looks at me as if to say "So you're not coming. Why not?" I don't know Jean, with whom I often recited my rosary has gone and so has Gerard. They've come to the end of the list but another begins, then a third, fourth, a fifth. It's 5 p.m. Many are already sitting on the ground, not knowing what to think. Olivier and Pierre are there. We notice that many railway men are staying behind. It's not an oversight. What do they want to do with us? Roll call is over. We are proud of the grace which has been given us. We are privileged and selfish. 4 thousand are going away, so what about us? A respite? Liberation? I hardly dare to think of it. I go to rejoin my friends who are going away. They are preparing their bundles. Max is really the worst off for clothes. I haven't much but share the little that belongs to me between him and his bed neighbour. In an hour they will have gone to Camp C. I walk up and down with Jean. For the last time, we talk of Etang and of our dear ones. He shows me some photos. I recognise some of the young girls. All that is a long way away and yet the war is coming to an end, for they've landed, although Jean does not believe the end is near. Now they are all leaving us from hut A1, in rows of five, each one carrying a case, a bag and a rolled-up blanket. Gerard has put on three pairs of trousers, one on top of the other! In spite of the search which was promised, he is taking the letters from his wife which he received in prison. "Goodbye Jean, Goodbye Gerard, Goodbye Bernard...." The last handshakes are the most sincere. They are going to the next camp to be searched – tomorrow, they will go.

2nd July. There are only four of us left in our room, whereas before we were 50! Everything is rather solemn. We caught sight of the men as they left the camp this morning and now we feel homesick, abandoned, forgotten. Because our numbers are reduced, the chores are more frequent. When working in the kitchens, everything is OK but cleaning now disgusts me. Pierre is Block Leader and therefore exempt from work. That doesn't worry him. If we could work in the garden, we would have some vegetables but we haven't been there long enough. A police chief comes to ask for gardeners, or florists. Well, we'll take the chance. He takes our name, just Olivier's and mine and exempts us from the digging. Work is easy if you're you own boss. One thing above all made me decide to apply for this job. I leave camp A to go and fill my watering cans with water from a well outside the gate to camp B, where there are British, Canadian and South African prisoners. Moreover, I have to go and fetch, pick and rake from beside the gate. A few yards away is the road leading to the station, to Paris and to freedom! Every morning and evening I am only a few steps away from it. It opens in front of me to let in cars, Red Cross or reinforcement carts but there are sentries and watch towers. My main task then, with Olivier is to weed the beds and grow Marigolds I don't like that flower and yet I give it more water than a gardener gives his lettuce! The German in command of us is satisfied but doesn't guess that when I go so often for water, it is to talk to the Mulattos in English.

Cigarettes? They don't want to give me any but let me taste some good cheese…. It is forbidden to talk to them but I go up close to them and they wait for me between each journey for water. Our little job stops us getting bored but is tiring. Fortunately, our chief procures some bread for us and a policeman in the kitchens gives us some crusts.

One group of railwaymen has just been set free! An array of hope! In the offices we can hear typewriters working; perhaps our names are down for a future liberation. I begin to believe it when I learn that those who have just gone had been arrested in reprisals and not for anti-German activities.

10th July. A convoy has just arrived. The blast of whistles has told us to go back to our rooms. They are Bretons, full of lice. Their clothes are sent to be disinfected and they are left naked with just a blanket around their shoulders. Some have been 13 days travelling from Brittany. They have a lot of provisions and we vie with each other to share in them. They have all been in prison and many have been maimed by the Gestapo. One is being led by his father; a truncheon has made him blind. Another young man is walking like someone with no sense of balance – what is the matter with him? Apparently the militia have torn at his chest with red-hot pincers. He is covered with red scars. In my room, the new men are almost all from Flesselles, a small village in the North of France where every man has been arrested, from the local policeman down to the old doctor. All were denounced by the same man, who is here too but is now marked down by the others.

For a week, I have been eaten by fleas. I never used to fear these dirty insects and laughed when they were mentioned. Now it's different for my whole body is covered in bites, as though I had measles. I can no longer sleep at night and spend whole hours during the day, chasing after them.

In the Canteen, they are selling onions, honey from Guinea and brushes Unfortunately, we have no money here and everything is at black market prices some men receive parcels of bread, wine and jam. They are not given the box and the Germans put jam, cheese, meat, pate, etc. into the recipient's bowls. We look at the list of those people receiving gifts. How could our names be on it when maybe our parents don't even know of our departure from Chalon? I have lost my knife! Or rather, I think it has been stolen. A departure is imminent. Our numbers are even higher than a fortnight ago. Compiegne is just like a huge slave market, for every day one sees the columns line up and the square darkens during roll-call.

14th July. At least we are going to celebrate the victory which is near – but the departure too. Maurice Boudet has made a little speech and we have eaten better than usual as Pierre has received his parcel from the Block Leader. It's a large Red Cross parcel and Oliverre and I have a three kilo parcel to share between us. Of course, we have guests, amongst whom is the large mechanic from Dole, very amusing with his witticisms. Yesterday, the whole camp, under the surveillance of the Germans, organised big sporting competitions – running, walking, football, basketball. Everything had an attraction but I don't understand these men who spend so much energy before the painful trials, which we will soon have to endure. One thing really nauseated me and that was the boxing matches. A few champions were presented by Maurice Bourdet who was in the ring announcing. The Germans were greatly amused and the crowd looked on, engrossed, some had even climbed up the trees and had basketball nets, just like in the countryside when the Tour de France is passing through. The celebration, interrupted by an air raid, fizzled out but the competitors, very happy, were rewarded by Red Cross parcels.

15th July. It is 2 p.m. Roll call has been announced. This time, it's the 'off'. Like the others, I await my turn to be checked off and the Camp Leader, with his eternal pipe, is smoking the tobacco so coveted by my friends. Perhaps my friends will be lucky enough to stay behind? No, they are all coming. As the food will be confiscated, we get rid of it to our friends and bed neighbours – tins of salmon, cheese and the kilo of jam from the Red Cross. We keep some sugar and a little chocolate in our pockets. Fortunately, I still have a little cloth bag which I got in prison. My only luggage! A shirt, two towels a few handkerchiefs, my spoon and my cup. We give back blankets, bowls and mugs. I go to be searched. The German makes me take off my shoes and socks, then satisfied, or weary of his job, lets me pass. I have my railwayman's armband and papers in my little used inside pocket. All this will come in useful, after the escape.

It's 7 o'clock. We are in C Camp, locked into a hut – 200 in a room. We are suffocating. All the windows are bolted and Alsatian dogs are masters of the corridor. Our group has been split up. At the risk of being bitten, we try to see each other again. The task is impossible, for no crowd is more impact than the one passing. I start to look for an iron instrument, for escape is more than ever imperative. Everything has been removed from here, down to the catches on the windows. The gauges and engines in the shower room have been taken down and I see I am too late. Certain colleagues are tearing away the last bits which can be moved. Fortunately some of the group still have their knives and pliers can serve as a lever. All is carefully hidden under clothes or in golfing trousers. Before we go, we are given a ration of hot water called tea. There is as much as you like, but I am content to just taste it and don't trouble for more. We leave C Camp and cross for the last time the wide square of A Camp in the middle of which we receive a piece of bread and slice of saucisson to last 3 days. Those with cases load them onto a trolley which will take them to the station.

It is 8 o'clock and still in ranks of 5 along the beds of marigolds near the exit, we wait for other groups to form up. Some, impatient and ravenous, are already biting heartily into the bread and saucisson, others have cut the loaf through the middle with a string hanging from their shoulder!

It is 8 o'clock but I am hot with my double layer of clothes and 2 pullovers. The able men move off the sick too. A large cart is there, pulled by horses. The sick, the elderly and the infirm will go by car then. The first column begins to move. "Can you walk Mr. Sarraut?" asks a German. The former minister goes off in front, on foot like the rest of us.

Before the exit, we pass before the German photographers who take several snaps of the group of policemen who precede us. At last we are in the road. The guards are 3 metres apart, gun or machine gun in hand. Some even have grenades. We walk quickly and with a long stride on the paving stones, to which we would like to say "Au revoir" Goodbye. I cannot evaluate how many of us there are but in front and behind, I can only see backs, shoulders, caps, bare heads and foreheads and each man is carried along, over each bump in the ground, like a surging sea and yet powerless. The noise of our shoes mingles with that of the German boots.

Olivier says nothing, nor Pierre but some are chatting. One group in front of us is whistling the tune of La Madelon, then the Marseillaise. I join in but the Germans reprimand us several times. We go through Compiene, the Compiegne that we don't know and that we are already missing, even before we have left it. The roads are deserted. All the shops have their blinds pulled down; all the stores have closed their doors. There are few windows open. The private houses have even glazed over their shutters and nobody therefore will have the courage to make us a small sign, to say goodbye to us. We understand though – The Germans have issued threats and Compiegne has already seen many departures like ours.

A few civilians and above all women, watch us go by however, from in a little street. One woman anxiously remains behind her shutters but a German sees her and she closes the shutters making them bang loudly. In spite of all the precautions taken to isolate us, letters will get away, families will be warned. Here is an open window. One, two balls of paper could be passed under the blind and fall – I don't know where, but maybe with French people, who will read them and let those involved know.

We go forward to the station and notice another group of young girls and women. They wave goodbye with handkerchiefs. Some are crying, they must have recognised a brother or a husband. A little girl in her mother's arms bursts into tears. Our pace doesn't slow down. This evening, Compiegne station will again see a little of France going away.

On the platform for the slow train, the German troop is waiting for us, complementary to the scene. We cross two lines. Our goods train is there. I recognise all the wagons, so familiar to railwaymen! Those of the SNCF, like those of DR, have all been repaired or chosen as being suitable for the occasion. The small windows have had grilles added to them, surrounded by barbed wire.

A German divides us into groups of 60. The door of our 21 square metre German carriage is open. Our new quarters are certainly restricted, but we don't complain, for I had not expected too much as warnings on Radio London have been heard about the convoys to Germany with 120 in a wagon. The roof of ours looks especially solid. We settle in and spread out a little straw.

An interpreter comes for the last time to recommend that we behave and we do not attempt an impossible escape. He will be on our side and make sure we have water and bread during the journey, provided we don't cause him any trouble. He is a young soldier. I don't trust him for he is probably as much a cheat as all the others. "No getting cold feet" is the order of the day but already there are recalcitrants. Two currents of opinion form in the wagon, so we keep quiet. Some think that the war will soon be finished and think such an enterprise too dangerous, in view of the short time we will have in Germany. "We have children and we will not let kids do anything here. We are leaving but maybe we'll be back in a month!"

The door is closed and fastened from the outside. So, there are sixty of us in here. It is hot. The air, already heavy outside, in spite of the evening breeze, is stifling in here, for we only have two little windows. Night is falling, Pierre has made a small parcel of our letters, and is looking outside through the slats. The Boches are there. Almost all of us are lying or sitting so that the air can circulate. Pierre is looking at the barbed wire. It seems firmly nailed to the outside. Our companions are grumbling, because Pierre remains standing at the window.

A locomotive is shunting and passes not far from us. At last a bump tells us that it has been coupled at the front of the train. It is 11 o'clock and only the light from the signals illuminates our lugubrious immobility. Where are we going? Several times we have heard Austria mentioned and Czechoslovakia but nobody knows anything. Testing the brakes – all is well. A final blast on the whistle and off we go! Pierre is still standing at his post and takes a last look for us at the station and its yard. The letters have been thrown – "Hey, stats. Pick up my letters by the points" a last hope. Perhaps they will have news of us. Many of us are already in shirtsleeves. On my left in the corner, a priest is reciting his rosary. Our jackets, vests, bags, which for the moment are a nuisance, are hanging on the nails and rings sticking out of the wall.

Chapter 7: THE 103

We travel on. The dry but regular clicking of the wheels on the rails; the sudden jolts due to slowing down or accelerating; the irritating swaying of the whole body of the wagon hide, with the help of the night, the work which awaits us. I can hear whispering and can gather what is going on. Pierre has moved and must have been at the door which rattles so loudly at times, for several minutes. I ask Olivier quietly, "What's going on? Should we go? "No, there are plenty of them and they have all they need. I listen, I wait. Somewhat moved, Olivier too is worried. I don't dare move and think about the damned sentry in the front observation van.

Pierre does not return – the night is black.

Several times people step on me. Others disturbed in their sleep and obviously unaware of what is going on, let out cries and curses – then everything becomes quiet again. The obscurity adds an eerie quality to the business attempted by a few to save 60. The risk is great, which is why we will all leave from the open door. In the next wagon, they are getting out via the skylight, from which they have been able to remove the wire. But only the young ones will be able to go. Here, the old ones will jump first. "The 7th plank from the bottom" Pierre had said and so the knives are at work at this blasted wood which is too thick. One must reckon on a thickness of several centimetres and a hole 10 by 10 in order to get a hand through. The sky is very overcast outside and there is no moon. We are not going fast and the train seems to be going up a steep incline in the middle of the country. Several of them take turns in pulling at the wood, piece by piece. Nobody says a word. "Are you ready? Olivier whispers in my ear. "Yes it's done" we'll be able to open up in a couple of minutes.

I quickly put my pullover back on and my jacket and firmly tie on the little bag of clothes and food. I feel for my wallet containing my papers, my armband and my Deutsche Reichsbahn insignia. Everything is in place. I check my clothes a last time; put a double knot in my shoelaces, hooks and jacket buttons secure, beret pulled down over my ears. I notice Olivier is already crouched as if about to rise.

Pierre comes back. "Well?"

"Nothing doing. The openings made, the fastening undone, the wires taken off, but nothing doing. They should have attacked the other door, like I told them to begin with, but it's too late now and tomorrow night we shall be in Germany and won't be able to open it then. The wheels of the door must evidently be stuck and it would need two more holes to bring the thing off. It doesn't budge an inch as though it was held by a hook, but it must be blocks which are stopping the wheels. We have tried five times, pulling with all our might. If they notice, all hell will break loose. Is it a big hole? Big enough for a hand and what is more serious, the other chap has dropped the fastening. Was it big? Ordinary. Possible to cover up? Benezon is putting some straw in the hole.

Pierre lies down again on the floor. We don't move any more. And the other door? Is that blocked too? Failure! And yet for so little. The train is so slow, so favourable but unfortunately this wagon is solid and well fastened. How fine it must be outside. A headlamp sometimes sends some light through the skylight. Suddenly, there is a gun shot and then another. We stop. What is going on? It must be an escape! The ones next door? And what about us, the wagon, the door and the hole? Anxiety roots me to the spot and I hold my breath to listen – to find out beforehand, if they have seen anything – what will they do?

What time can it be? Midnight? One o'clock. Men are marching. Boots pass to the left and right of the wagon. Germans are calling to each other. A luminous beam suddenly filters through the skylights and the hole in the door. "Sabotage! Sabotage! Hurried steps come closer. The light disappears, and then comes back more strongly. We are caught! Everyone stays still. Violent thumps bang against the damned door but in spite of the noise, nobody moves. All at once it opens. "Where is the saw? We want the saw, or we'll shoot! It's the interpreter. He is no longer the passive man he was earlier; he is fuming with rage and threats. Blinded by their lamps, we remain lying down, but ill at ease, as if disturbed from sleep. They are not taken in. "Everyone stand up. Give us the saw. Who has the saw? I warned you. You have 2 minutes, the officer is giving you 2 minutes." Then, losing patience, some soldiers who have just come in, rush at us brandishing revolvers and sub machine guns. There is general panic. Some, completely petrified, knock others over, step on them and fall in their turn. "Give them your knife", one frightened man says to his neighbour. "Give them your knife – you don't want them to shoot us". Several knives are therefore thrown down from all corners of the wagon and I see with apprehension that one has fallen at my feet.

Furious, the Germans strike us everywhere, with their boots or rifle butts. They pick up the knives and pack us all into one corner of the wagon. "Thirty seconds men, then we won't answer for the consequences". Everyone is in some way guilty. Each man must therefore take the same share of responsibility, right to the end. About ten Jerries are there, guns still pointed! The young officer, foaming, really frightens me.

"It's too late. Everyone get undressed!" No order was carried out with more speed than that one. Jackets, shirts, trousers, shoes, pants, socks are thrown off pell-mell in a moment. With fear, modesty no longer exists. Our nudity increases even further our fear and increases our feeling of helplessness. The officer goes away, and then comes back with another. We are in a sweat, despite it being night time and the door being wide open. The dancing starts again. This time, the blows fall on bare skin. "Who made the hole? Point him out" Blows rain down. I get two in the back and three on the head. I fear, especially for my glasses which I have managed to keep, and which, for a short-sighted person, are the most precious thing. Bunched up against each other, we wait. Some, eyes haggard, have lost all control over themselves, which earns them extra kicks.

The Germans climb down and close the door.

"If you don't denounce the guilty man, we will fire into the closed wagon."

"It's you, give yourself up"

"I haven't got a knife"

I find these accusations between friends painful and yet it's a critical moment. The Germans come and go, talking loudly to each other in their jargon.

"It was you, I saw you, you moved several times."

"I didn't move, liar – only the railwayman could have done it, I don't know anything about opening a door like that!"

Several voices repeat together –

"Yes, it was the railman."

The door opens again and the electric lamps blind us. The interpreter is still there and dominates all the others by his build. The helmets and guns which surround him make us think of an execution squad. This time, nobody comes towards us and we remain, terrified, huddled on either side of the door.

"The railman, the railman. Step forward," cries the interpreter. Olivier, Pierre and I have to push the others aside in order to escape from the human mass. Olivier, the tallest and also the eldest, goes forward first.

"No, too old, it's not you."

"I was asleep. I have no knife."

He motions him to move towards those at the back. Pierre and I appear together. Hardly have I shown myself, when all eyes are against me and suspicious too.

"It's him, it's him, I recognise him."

Fists are menacing, fingers point at me and say

"It's him."

The men, in their calumny, give me away. To escape death, man is capable of the lowest things, but here, fear of death is the master. If the Boches kill me, all the others will be safe. Standing in the middle of the flour platform, I am interrogated

"It was you. Where is the saw?"

Two revolvers pointing at me disturb me. If I was not confident, I would be afraid. However, I defend myself with vigour.

"It wasn't me, I swear it. I do not have a knife. I left mine in the bundle at Compiegne. I was asleep when you came and I've seen nothing."

(German) - "It was you. Admit it, or I fire."

(Voices) – "It was him."

The soldiers, impassive, look on. Outside is the night, inside the electric lamps, the two revolvers, the accusation and the condemnation

"I am innocent. I swear it."

(German) – "Point out the guilty man."

"I don't know. I was asleep."

From the back of the wagon, a voice calls out – "It was Lhoste."

The German has heard. "Lhoste? Who is Lhoste? Where is Lhoste?"

Pierre, who had stayed in the group on the right when I was pointed out came forward now and comes towards me.

"It wasn't me, I swear it. It wasn't me. Nobody moved in our corner and I was under the window. There were others at the door."

"Liar. It's not true, it's him, it was Lhoste who stayed by the window at Compiegne." The Germans become impatient and several take aim at us.

"It wasn't us and you know well enough that it wasn't us. Why don't you say anything? You are scum."

"It was you. It was Lhoste, it was the little man who walked about all the time. He stamped on me each time. It's the Iron Thread, Lhoste. Yes, that's right, I recognise him. Iron thread, it's him. Give yourself up, coward, give yourself up."

"It's untrue. I swear it wasn't me."

"I swear it," I say, stretching my arm towards the ruffled heads, haggard eyes and accusing hands of those on the left.

"Move away," says the interpreter.

Pierre and I remain motionless in the centre. The young officer approaches. The interpreter counts, one,

"No, I swear to you."

"Two"

"No"

Two shots ring out between our legs. At the moment when instinctively, we had moved aside, so the shots hit the wall behind us.

"Who was near the door?" Asks the interpreter. "Go back as you were at the beginning."

Each man has to try to attain his former place, while stepping over our clothes.

With Pierre, I regain our place under the window, separated by 3 or 4 men who are friends from the Nord. Nearest to the hole is Benezon, the tall curly haired man. The accusations begin again.

"It was the Jew, it was the Jew Benezon."

The officer climbs up and places the butt of his revolver against the chest of the newly accused man.

"I am innocent, you can kill me, I'm innocent."

"It was him, it was the Jew Benezon."

Hands in the air, I am trembling, hair standing on end, face stricken. As far as I am concerned, he is done for.

"I am not a Jew," he cries,"I swear it, I am not a Jew."

Furious, the German turns and repeats several times, fuming with rage: "Alles, alles" The interpreter translates. Everyone on this side.

At the same moment, the blows begin again. One of the soldiers strikes out with his huge bayonet. This time there is no doubt they are going to shoot us. Already, from the machine guns turned on us, we can hear the clicking of the loaders. Hunched up together, naked, jostled, stifled, panting, despairing, we can feel our hearts beating at unknown rhythms.

"We have children; we want to see them again. Let the guilty one give himself up," says a voice.

Pierre has two little girls and others are married too but the real guilty man is single and it was he who cried the loudest in accusing us. We make ourselves as small as possible, waiting for the bullet which will go through us. Half crushed; I cannot get free, in spite of frantic efforts. The Germans get out. The interpreter makes us get down, naked, two by two. I await my turn. They are going to shoot us in a quarry nearby. Seventeen escaped from the next wagon. Two men go, and then others follow in turn.

In front of me is an elderly man. It's his turn. He hesitates, turns around, looks at me trembling. I take pity on him and go in his place. I jump on to the ballast, slip and fetch up against stones, but my mind is elsewhere. I get up and walk. Where? I don't know. A German catches me by the shoulder and gives me two good punches behind the arms, under the elbows. I understand and raise my hands up high. Then I get another blow in the back. I turn around. A tall Boche pushes me with the barrel of his machine gun. I walk quickly, heart beating violently at the unpleasant feel of the round iron pressing constantly against my spine. I am hot; I can feel beads of sweat all over my body. And yet the ground is damp and a few drops of rain are falling from a very cloudy sky. Behind the soldiers lining my path, I can make out a forest but I can only see the tops of trees. On my left, the motionless train, the closed wagons, the rails, the wheels, the sleepers, the ballast and the gleam of the electric lamps, shadows; on my right, boots, surmounted by capes, shining bayonets, guns at waist height. I cannot see any faces and no longer look for them; they are in the dark.

A blinding lamp lights up the ground and the stones. Tired, I lower an arm, and then on an order from a Jerry, raise it again. I still walk just as fast. Final steps, at night, somewhere near Soissons on 16th July and my mother will not know anything ever. Farewell everybody. The German makes me run. I can see others in the distance. "Los, Los…" We are only changing coaches. This time we will be at the back of the train.

There are a lot of us here. I climb into a coach already full of naked men. The 43 remaining from the next wagon are here too. Even more are arriving, the last ones from our coach. We are made to sit cross-legged but since instinctively, each man leaves a space between himself and the next, there is already no more room. The Jerries make us close up and thereby hit us with batons, as one would cattle. Those at the back cry out and those just arriving stagger under the blows. We squash up, backs against chests, shoulder to shoulder, we make contact with the other men's skin. Olivier and Pierre are there. I am a little ashamed to see all these naked men, old and young, right down to the priest who still has his rosary in his hand. The last two must have arrived, for all the Jerries seem to be regrouping near our coach. The interpreter orders us to count our number. How many are there of us? Have others escaped? A young man counts but goes wrong. We must be quicker; otherwise they'll hit us again. "103" he cries at last. The door, with an awful roll, closes again. The fastening goes down outside, bars are attached with rifle butts. We sigh into the night. There is no window here, no straw, no clothing. It's dark. We are alone — that's to say the Boches have shut us in and are no longer threatening us but there are 103 of us!

A whistle blows and a heavy jolt off balances those who are standing. We are off again. I get up, in order to try and recognise myself in spite of the obscurity.

Not a ray of light. The shutters, despite being closed and latched, start to judder. I manage to hold onto a wall, for nothing is more unstable than a goods wagon and ours is small. It is hot. I feel that with the sweat from our bodies, the air will soon be unbreathable.

Some, not many, have remained seated but the most comfortable position is standing up when this is possible. How long will we stay like this? Our loaves of bread are still in the other wagon. Olivier and Pierre have disappeared but I dare not call out to them. What's the use, in this noise, where everyone has something to say?

The going is fast and my situation makes me think of the cattle trains going to Dresden, which I saw go by when I was at Etang. The night is long but we must be patient. Tomorrow, it will be a new day – we will see….

"You're here then?"

It's Olivier, I recognised his voice. Pierre is with him.

"Yes, but not OK. What a journey, one can hardly stay standing."

Actually, that's the best way to keep going, for there is a little air filtering through the joints in the planks. I dare not sit on the floor, there are spikes everywhere and a sort of powder, the colour of which I can't make out but which is already burning our feet.

I cannot even stoop without jostling my neighbours and being grumbled at. I won't be able to stand up the whole time though. I need to sit, as soon as somebody stands up. My whole body is sweating and a smell of sweat and urine fills the atmosphere. Space! We need space! Arguments are breaking out and intolerance is everywhere. What selfishness! Those standing near holes or joins in the shutters, stay put and don't move. Those in the middle are jealous of those on the outside!

It is only when two trains pass that we can feel a small draught. The darkness is less intense. I am obviously getting used to it and perhaps day is breaking. Of course, they'll bring us something to drink. I hadn't noticed that there was an iron barrel in the middle of us; it obviously serves as a toilet. I am beginning to be thirsty but try not to think about it and above all not to speak. I move as little as possible and keep my mouth shut! I feel strong and able to hold out a long time. I therefore feel proud and cannot understand those who are already exasperated.

It is day – we are travelling much faster. I spotted a small place from where two men have just risen. I sit down at last between two spikes, after having swept away the chalk with my hand (for it is definitely chalk) that is covering the floor. I can either lie down or rest my head. My legs are folded up and I rest my head on my knees. I try to make myself as small as possible but am still too big to avoid touching a bare foot under my left buttock and the ribs of a large damp back, touching my shins.

Each time the wagon sways, we hit each other involuntarily. I try to sleep in spite of the heat and nauseating air which abounds in this lower part of the wagon, the kingdom of feet, legs, and the buttocks of those standing. At the next stop, we have decided to ask for some water. If only the shutters were open! Our means of ventilation are certainly sparse – just a few holes which the breaking day has highlighted, and a few slits between the boards of the walls and floor. It would be better, if these meagre gaps were not blocked with dust or chalk!

A splinter of wood begins to hurt my backside but I can't move and feel as though I'm rooted to this stifling room. I sit on my hands. Sweat is running everywhere and my eyes are stinging. I wipe my forehead on my knees, but these are just as wet. I can feel a head and hair leaning against the small of my back. I am tired and would dearly like to be able to put just one elbow on the ground. I notice some men stretched out completely and asleep, piled on top of each other!

It must be around 10 o'clock. The train stops. Brutality is law here. Each man is jealous of his neighbour.

"I haven't slept all night and you, you are lying down all the time. Change places!"

It's always the same ones who remain leaning against the walls or near the air holes. Of course, it is the strongest ones who are alright. The rest are condemned to lack of air and sleep. The oldest of us is 65. About ten of us agree to ask him to organise our positions. It needs a bit of discipline, tolerance and understanding, so that we all arrive alive! "Quiet, quiet" It's impossible. Some men are enraged. They fight amongst themselves and argue. In the midst of all the tumult, I say nothing and keep still, for fortunately there are about 20 bodies between me and the argument. "Shush, blast you, shush or I'll bash you". Punches and kicks sound in the darkness. Those lying down are trampled on and it's quite a job to get to the tub, which is already full.

"Shut up, in here. Shut up chaps". Cries and complaints from the disgruntled are the only reply. Everyone is equal here but alas no! Even here, each man's fate is different!

Why does that one stay constantly by the hole in the plank and why is this one stretched out full length and still others leaning against the wall – they can rest and have air! We in the middle, seated or standing, have neither rest, nor support nor air. My right hand is burning from this damned splinter of wood which I try in vain for several moments to pull out – then I succeed! Quite a piece of wood! My neighbour, who has seen me, starts to cry out like an idiot "Sabotage, sabotage". I try to calm him. It's impossible. I am frightened of attracting to myself, all the arguments which just now were foreign to me. Fortunately, nobody can see clearly. I manage to stand up, carrying my small piece of wood. Suspicion falls on another person who defends himself vigorously. "Look out, look out, the Germans". There is silence. Not a sound outside. We have stopped at a siding, for between 2 planks I can make out several tracks and some wagons. Our senior takes the initiative and recommends that above all we begin no more sabotage and proposes that we organise a rota so that each man can, from time to time rest and get some air, priority being given to the sick. He tells us that moreover, we have an interpreter who will ask for water shortly plus permission to empty the tub.

Unfortunately, we can see nobody outside. The atmosphere in here is becoming unbearable. The planks are hot. I hold on to an iron ring, quite damp. In spite of the request from our old man, nobody changes places. At least, the privileged ones don't want to give anything up. A violent jolt and we are off again. I take advantage from the fall of a tall man by the window and take his place but he gets up again and tries to punch me on the jaw. Fortunately for me, he has received a thump from the man he has just trampled on. I have decided too that I shall keep this place, standing up. I can look out through a slit of about 3 mm but the view is limited to the stones in the ballast which pass by like a continuous road. I thought I would have a bit of air but it is just as scarce. Outside in the sun, it must be quite warm but in our wagon we're in a suffocating chamber. I'm lucky however to be fairly well removed from the tub, which is already full and likely to tip over at any moment.

At the slightest movement, the urine spills over, spreads and runs up to my feet, after having wetted those nearest, or passed under those who remain seated, lying down, and unrecognisable but resigned. My feet are burning horribly but I say nothing to anyone because many have complained of the same thing. On my left, I recognise the old priest. He is sitting down and saying his rosary. Feeling some remorse for a fault not committed, I call to him softly

"Father, remember this. I was next to you. It wasn't me who made a hole in the wagon"

"I don't know. I was asleep."

I don't press the point and leave him to his prayers. I try to do the same but don't have the will. Perhaps he is praying for us all? Outside, it must be light but in here, everything remains ghostly and strange. I have the sudden impression that we are all dressed. Then, no longer thinking, I am convinced of it!

I am thirsty. In the noise of our moving cell, the light and obscurity seem to clothe our bodies with a phantasmagorical quality. Feeling the nudity of those next to me, I realise again my own lack of clothes. I cannot quite believe it when I look at us all! Pierre and Olivier remains stoic.

Above all, we must not talk to or fight with the intolerant ones. In spite of the regular noise of the train, the arguments continue.

I can't go on. Insults are pouring out from everywhere and one feels that all the shouts are coming from throats already dry and irritated. A stop ....at last....a station. I can't see the name of it and we don't know where we are. "Achtung, achtung. Wasser, wasser bitte. Achtung, bitte wasser, ein wenig" (Attention, attention, Water, water please. Attention, please water, a little). Will they come? Will they stop, open up? We shall die in here if this goes on.

"Water, water, give us something to drink. There are 103 of us."

Everyone is standing. I am crushed against the planks by those who have just risen but don't move. Steps outside. Obviously Jerries. They pass by.

"Wasser, wasser bitte. Water, we are dying of thirst, open a window, and give us some water."

Various shouts try to attract the man walking down there on the ballast. More steps, then nothing. If only we could see but there are only stones. If we could get some silence so that we could listen but with the few mad men here present, it's impossible. If only we could breathe but these planks are so tightly fixed. With my splinter from earlier on, I manage to remove some of the dust and see out. What? Opposite, the door of another goods truck. Steps, more steps! The uproar does not die down. Nerves are stretched to the limit and I notice that the face of the interpreter is bleeding. He was fighting earlier on. The noise of boots comes nearer again and .... I see a green outfit, well known and a pail of water. Yes, a pail of water. Others have seen it too. "Wasser, wasser". The imploring cries, the prayers, the complaints begin again and such impatience exasperates me to the highest point. I could hit them. They are like kids. No will at all, it's deplorable. The Germans must really be laughing. I am ashamed of them and from the expression of my friends; I see I am not the only one to think like that. The bucket is on the ground; the water is sparkling and swaying limpid in the sun. The German, a sadist, shakes the handle and lets it fall several times. A bucket.... At last, let's be patient. What a scramble in here! The weak ones are stepped on, crushed in front of the door. The stronger ones walk all over them without thinking, only thinking of the bucket of water which is there, on the ground but which a strong hand seizes and takes away. That's it – no more water, not even the vision of water or the noise of the bucket. A general despair falls on our thirsty and burning lips. We start off again with no drink.

Leaning against the wall, I try to forget. I pray a little but think even more of the water. A glass of water! Whereas here everything is dry, my lips, my mouth, my teeth and even my tongue, which seems as though it's covered in horn. Olivier's lips are completely black. Perhaps I am mistaken but I can't see the exact colour of my skin. I must be terribly dirty. I can feel the thickness of the grime when I wipe my forehead and my hair is as though stuck into one lock.

16th July. We have been shut up since 2 in the morning and it must be noon now. Already the tub is overflowing and a filthy smell catches in our throats. I still have my glasses, which astonishes me as our crushed conditions don't allow for fragile items!

Our wagon is a veritable crate, opening on both sides. The iron doors seem badly hinged and the movement makes them move with a noise now familiar……. On one wall, I recognise and read an inscription which makes me smile – wagon with non-airtight roof. To be used only for non-perishable goods!

I believe that if I was not constantly on the lookout against my neighbours, I would soon have no space left to put my feet! If I raise my right foot, inflamed by the chalk and urine on the spike scratches, the place is at once taken by an elbow or a knee, or another foot. If I let go of the little ring, thanks to which I can keep my balance, it will be fought over by several different hands. If I move slightly away from this blasted partition full of splinters, I could not return to lean against it. Every man is watching the movements of the others in order to use them to his own gain and profit from 10 cm so as to be a bit more comfortable and a little less tired. We cannot drink, we can hardly breathe. Try and sleep. I sleep a little standing up. I sit down. The change of position does me good but legs quickly stiffen when they are bent. The wood is hard to the buttocks but what does all that matter? I am tired and let myself fall too, head thrown back onto the leg of someone who must be asleep too, for he has not moved.

Is it a nightmare? I wake up to panic. We have stopped. The door moves. Yes, the door is opening! Day, light, air! The Germans draw back on seeing us, or perhaps from the bad smell which must emanate from us. Our interpreter speaks to them but they don't want to understand. They still want to know who the 2 guilty ones are – the 2 railway men.

I come forward with Pierre. They ask for our serial numbers and write them in a notebook, then bring in another young man.

"Who made the hole?"

"I don't know, they've gone. He's from the other wagon."

The officer has the door shut again.

"Water, water please. Wasser, bitte!"

All we have had is some air. The tub, still full, is becoming an obsession. We must empty it. The Germans are called again but no-one answers.

When we are not moving, we can feel our breathing slow down, our energy decreases. We must hold on. We scratch between the planks with splinters. The dust, compressed and evidently already very old, comes away with difficulty.

Kneeling, crouched, sitting or lying, poked on all sides at the slightest movement and still unstable, we scratch and scratch. We then risk placing an eye to the slits and see stones, sleepers and a shadow of a wheel which is a comfort!

Despite the foul smell from the filthy floor, I place my nose to the groove. A sudden start makes me falter and I receive grumbles from my neighbours. I have a little air from this slit. That's better. I shall stay here, quite still. We go on and on…. I no longer want to listen to those who are arguing because I am revolted by such an attitude. My left leg is numb and the whole of my side feels paralysed, as if weighed down by something heavy and crushing. My head is wedged between my leg and a back and I can breathe better since my cleaning operation!

Night is falling. What's the time? No matter, I try and sleep. What about the others? Some are standing against the door and evidently finding air. Some are sitting on the floor, others half lounging and half lying, are in a heap. I no longer think about anything. I no longer want to think. I have commended my soul to God and let myself go, crushed with fatigue.

Every jolt wakens me. Is it really true? Is it a dream? I can hear someone wheezing, then blows and cries. Another fight! The night is long. When we are moving, things are alright and I hope our goal is approaching but where are we? My saliva is drying up in spite of the fact I never open my lips, which seem soldered together by a layer of putty. I fall asleep.

I am awoken by a loud noise. The Germans are here. We get up, pushed by kicks to one side of the wagon. We are counted. Two tall Boches make us file past between them. Their batons fall flat on our bare backs. Nobody speaks. Soon it is my turn. I pass and am struck too. 103 – All correct!

The door closes again. The frontier. Pagny no doubt. I don't know. Outside, I could only see the night. This is Germany says the Algerian who understands the officers words. Still, we travel on.

17th July. Our thirst is unbearable. The train stops in a large station. Snoring, gasping, whistles, the noise of machines, buffers, in the distance the screech of scraped iron. I stand up. The situation is unchanged. I feel heavy. My head aches. Far off I can see something though. A peak half hidden in bluish clouds, then I see nothing more except water. A spring and grass, a tree trunk with roots going down into the water. I am cold. The water makes me cold – so cold that I cannot drink it and it runs on the stones, between the rocks with such a noise, like a train which can't stop, carried along by speed. Suddenly, everything is quiet. A grotto, taps, one tap, just one tap and water flowing from it and I'm going to drink water from Lourdes. What a mirage. I was dreaming! I am suffocating and can feel the sweat running over my shoulders and down my arms. As I am touching another arm it stops, makes a detour and runs again, mixing with the other man's sweat. Where are we? Abruptly, the doors are opened. Below are the Germans. The comedy begins again! All of us are pushed onto one side. Distribution of water! A bucket is there, in fact there are cardboard beakers too. There is the general scramble, quickly scotched by threats. Opposite is a large Red Cross wagon and the word "Koblenz". All becomes clear to us now.

Soon, it's my turn to drink! The containers are different sizes. There are 5. Each man calculates the best place by the largest! I go up but am so confused, I don't even see which container the German gives me. I drink. It's freezing. I swallow more, then drink. That's it, somebody else's turn. That's better. I am sweating as though I'm in a steam bath!

18th July. It's a terrible night. The tub had been emptied at Koblenz but it is overflowing again and we are more and more thirsty. If only we knew where we were going to. If we could glimpse the name of a station but nothing. Nothing shows behind these damned planks except a procession, hardly perceptible, intangible of buildings, trees and unknown countryside which is all the same The stinking atmosphere of heaped up bodies and the wind of madness which can be felt blowing over us, makes me think of another world. The Algerian calls out in German at every stop to obtain water and have the tub emptied. He even talks of the mad ones and others hearing him shout at him too and at the Germans. Insults, blows, the strongest will kill the weakest. "Dirty Boches – I would kill them. Come here then you fools. We fear the stops now, for if the Boches hear, they'll shoot us. Bad luck to be the man who lies down. He is unable to rise again and is at once buried under other bodies. I stay crouched for a long time. We stop again. A station – but which one? I can see civilians and soldiers, all clean, well dressed, and indifferent. They are doubtless awaiting a train on the other platform……. Other people in France are also waiting for trains at stations. "Achtung, achtung!" (Attention, attention)

The Algerian starts calling again but they don't seem to hear for some even move further away! We start off again. Olivier and Pierre are still there, like me – stoical. Some don't even take the trouble to go to the tub and make a mess everywhere. I am just indifferent.

Indifferent too, to these fools who hit each other and expend their remaining energy by trying to get space which doesn't exist. These fools who dip their lips in the indescribable liquid from the iron vat. Tomorrow night will be a disaster. Some are amorphous, others are rasping. I too seem to lose my reason for a moment. I start to look for Benezon. I call him, search for him, stumble, fall, crash among bodies.

My glasses have come off. I lose them, then I find them again! I have not found Benezon. Why was I looking for him? I no longer know........

A stop! Then we start going the opposite way. Then some shunting. A large bridge with a slope which allows me to see over to an immense river, with further on, other bridges and a large town with many ruins. It must be from the bombing. One of us cries "Hamburg". I don't believe it. Then another man says the same. We had been told Austria or Czechoslovakia. I don't understand any more. Diverted maybe? That's impossible. The shunting goes on, then we stop. Heat envelopes us as though we were in an oven. I can hardly part my lips. My eyes are stuck together and remain closed as soon as I try to go to sleep. My hair, in indescribable disorder, is stuck together with something sticky which I dare not even touch. My inflamed feet are burning worse than ever. Even if I wanted to, I would not have sufficient saliva to utter one word, make one complaint.

Raus, raus, alles. (Out, out, everyone)

The door is opened. The sun, blue sky, Germans. I jump to the ground and it's sand! I am walking outside on sand but receive two whip lashes on my shoulders. I run, I take deep breaths. A Boche is filming our procession. What does it matter now – we're saved! Air, soon we'll have water. It's almost freedom!

Chapter 8: NEUENGAMME

A veritable armed detachment is awaiting us and strangely dressed people wearing armbands have stopped to watch us. Led to our old empty wagon, our clothes are thrown to us and without even time to dress, in ranks of 5 we pass through huge gates of barbed wire.

Cries, jostling tending towards panic, cowering over I advance under the blows administered to us by a group of madmen, who seemed to be waiting for us.

Bewildered by the light and space, I don't even notice where we are going but let myself be guided by the man in front. We are going down some steps. Under ground there is a huge cave with columns and various large rooms. There are many of us, several thousand maybe. I get dressed after having recovered most of my things, already being worn by someone else. My shirt, stained in blood, reminds me of the shots heard during the transportation. It's hot here and the ventilators are narrow and very widely spaced.

I'm thirsty. It's impossible to get water and yet it is running down the walls everywhere. One can hear it flowing somewhere but men in blue and white striped suits are guarding the way with truncheons. We'll be able to drink soon. Many have already sat down on the ground. Rounds of bread are strewn on the ground. I am not hungry and yet I force myself to eat a few lumps of sugar found in my jacket and dating from Compiègne! A warning is shouted! We will not be able to keep anything, clothing or food. That's why many are eating as much as they can, without drinking. This new situation, however bad it may be, is a real comfort. At least we are dressed. How many are there of us in these never ending underground rooms? Hundreds, Thousands – Nobody could say!

We will soon go out but the air is getting so thin that many are fainting. We carry them to the door where others try to bring them round. Hours go by. Is anyone bothering about us? My mouth is burning and I'm suffocated in the jostling each time a German appears. At last we are going. Outside, friends are laid out dead. Several naked (they were in my wagon) are taken away on stretchers. They are covered in blood. Freed from the infamous wagon, we are easily recognisable with our madmen's look, completely streaked with black marks, dark circles round our eyes, swollen lips and sometimes bleeding underneath the dirt. We stink. I've a sort of plaster on my head, for all my hair is stuck together. Pierre, who had gone off to find water, has found none.

We are being called. Will I be in the first hundred? We cross a yard, an immense square, all concreted. On each side are lines of large barracks, all numbered – Block 15, 16, etc.….. and painted dark green. There is barbed wire everywhere. Each block seems separated from the others. Nevertheless, everything is clean and seems calm, flower beds, small gardens in the foreground. We must be going to the showers. On our arrival in a small yard, we are made to throw everything edible in a large vat. I have nothing but that's not the case for everyone, and in passing, I see pieces of bread next to chocolate sugar and saucisson.

Still in ranks of 5, we advance outside. There, we have our hair cut. I am surprised by the speed at which everything happens. About 10 barbers are waiting for us. We will be shaved close. I sit down, lower my head, have placed on my knees a cardboard box already full with other men's hair, mine still wavy, falls amongst it, not without pain, for it is pulled out, as much as cut with shears.

A room, a desk and a clerk dressed in the same zebra-striped clothes, hands me an envelope in which I put all my valuables – 2 watches and a purse. I did not find my nice wallet which was stolen in the wagon. A number is written on the envelope. I am given a large piece of white card on which is printed in black 36.582.

A narrow cord is placed around my neck on which is hung a small disc. I undress a little further and have to take everything off, shoes, shirt right down to my rosary and mess book from Compiègne. I put down my printed card on top of the pile of clothes. A striped man, speaking German, pushes me further along. Everything happens quickly and in silence. On the wall are some German inscriptions, which I have no time to decipher.

Here one doesn't see soldiers any more – everything is organised, run by prisoners like us but whose striped clothes and armbands evidently indicate their rank. They also have numbers and coloured triangles with letters sewn onto their jackets and trousers. From these, I guess their nationality. There are no Frenchmen – P is for Polish, R for Russian. Those with no letters are German.

Now we are in a long corridor. We are inspected by a gang of fanatics, bare chests and covered in blue tattoos. One of them looks at our hands and removes the wedding ring from those who have kept them. Another makes us open our mouths and a third, with a pair of scissors, brutally removes the bandages from those wearing them. A fourth makes us walk with our legs apart. A fifth makes us remove our belts or the bandages some have around their middle. Another man looks at us again. I am allowed to keep my glasses. Instinctively, I look at the zinc disc round my neck – 36.582.

We come into a large airy room, with yellow mosaic walls, still in single file. We are shaved, not just beard and moustache but the whole body – one man scantily soaps our chest, under the arms, stomach, between the legs, back of the thighs etc.….. Then another man shaves us but each one is designated for a certain part of the body. Our barbers look like real toughs and have many scars. They are frightening. One says to me "Franzouse – Parisse?" (Are you French – from Paris?)

I tell him yes and ask him where he comes from.

"Warsaw." He answers. I move forward, walking on a pile of damp hair. It's my turn. One scratches me a little and draws blood. The same brush, the same razors for thousands of men. They don't even wash them but wipe them on our shoulders or thighs when they have finished. Beards, moustaches, all are irrevocably cut, right down to the hairs of our legs…. Then it's shower time, boiling hot, but at last one can drink. Rub as I might, the dirt doesn't come off. I am completely black and can't stand this boiling water. My mouth was just a solid paste. I spit, wipe my nose, clean my glasses which are no longer worthy of the name. While still under the jets, we walk, and then come to a large corridor where damp is running down the walls. Suddenly there is a strong current of cold air and cold water jets make us stagger. I shiver and my teeth chatter in spite of myself. We stay there for a quarter of an hour – the cold air dries us summarily. A Pole inspects us with the aid of a large electric lamp. Then we come to the dressing room – shirts, under pants, trousers, jackets, one shelf for each item.

Here we are aware of the organisation of the thing – what is this Germany which can absorb so quickly such a large number of men? Everything is either too big or too small but there is no fitting. The Russian distributors have an eye for it and can see at once what fits. The clothes are very damp. I have some Russian Cossack trousers, and Italian soldier's jacket and large Romanian hat. Then, at the exit, the Latvian in charge of shoes asks me and the others "Wie wiel" (How big?)

I tell him my size. I get a strange pair of sandals – two flat pieces of wood, crudely shaped and attached to the feet with a piece of material. They make me think of Turkish slippers but these are only like flip-flops. Impossible to raise one's foot without fear of loosing them! They have to be constantly dragged.

We go out, leaning forward, with small hesitant steps, twisting our feet at the least piece of clinker. We stumble frequently our flip-flops slipping everywhere. We come to tables and painters with their pots of yellow paint. The brush moves over our clothes – yellow crosses on our backs, on our trousers, on our sleeves and hat. Yellow stripes on both jacket tails.

We pass into another room. Here people are sewing. Clerks, at about 100 sewing machines are at work. There is a chief to command them. On his yellow armband I read the inscription "Kapo" (Overseer) two other ranks are called "Vorarbeiter" (foreman). We are all to be given a serial number. I give my jacket and trousers, show my number and move as quickly as my flip flops will allow (in pants and shirt).

At the exit, a man cries to us "Nummer" (Number) I say my number and at once I am given my things, on which has been sewn, on the left side of the jacket and right leg of the trousers, a red triangle, an F and my number F/36.582,

Olivier has number 36.413, and is dressed in a large sailor's costume of purplish red. He is unrecognisable and looks sad. Pierre dressed lightly and all in blue makes a joke of everything. In a general clacking of our soles on the cement, our group crosses the square again and disappears towards a large door surmounted by towers, two large poles, the flag bearing the swastika, next to it a black flag with the two white letters "SS".

Block 9, block 10 on the right, barbed wire separates us from the gardens of late beans, hardly yet in flower and on the left from a pavement hardly 4 metres wide, here is our building. Opposite, 50 m away, a big square wooden tower, surmounted by a large glass cabin is occupied by two sentries who miss nothing. They have twin machine guns on pivots, lamps and sirens.

We wait for hours in the full sun. We have been made to remove our hats and these, for no reason have been taken away. Our bare heads become scarlet and the faces of some men are swelling already. Policing is carried out by prisoners of varying rank:- Block leaders, Block cleaners, Interpreters, Soup distributors and others, designated by whom? Why? I don't know yet. Strange our "Blokalteste" (Block leader), short, thin, features drawn, bones protruding, bare-headed with long hair neatly parted from forehead to nape, always running about, moving with the random gestures of a man who has lost his reason.

At last he lets us come in. Four large tables each with some flowers, benches, chairs, all very clean. At the back it is dark. Beds in 3 tiers, simple and neatly aligned. Our man makes us cease our noise with a few loud blasts of his whistle. He wears, like us, the red triangle, but not the letter; he must be German. He explains camp life to us. He has been there 13 years, as a political prisoner!

"The life is hard but one gets used to it. Anyway, here you come in by the gate but go out only by the chimney. There is only one thing here if you want to live – you have to work.

Arbeit, Arbeit (Work, work)" he cries several times. He finishes by saying:

"There are no sick people here, everyone is counted, and therefore everyone has to be present at every Roll call (Headcount Parade) or else be punished. As soon as Roll call is called, we must all get quickly into ranks of five. Here, eight times a day, the living and the dead are counted. Whoever refuses a job, strikes a superior, tries to escape, will be hung or eaten by the dogs. Now, one last piece of advice, keep silent, carry out the orders, whatever they are and if someone hits you, don't turn around." Here's the soup. One litre of cabbage water. It is warming. Now we go to bed. A mattress and a blanket for two. I get in with Pierre, head to toe, for our shoulders are too wide and hang over the bed. What relaxation! Alas, all too short. "Alarm, Alarm" voices are crying. Sirens are blasting from everywhere – hou ou hou ou hou ou…..Everyone up, it's an air raid. What should one do? Shaded lamps make blue spots in the night. Quickly we put on jacket, trousers and the flip flops which served as a pillow. "Are you ready Pierre"?

"Yes."

Already the truncheon blows sound dully in the night. The slow ones are jostled, trampled on and clouted by the Block leaders. Where should we go? Everyone goes out. It's pitch black so we hold each other's arm – one always feels stronger in twos. Everywhere in the night there are howls and curses in German. We must hurry. The flak is already growling in the distance and search lights are sweeping the darkness. We follow the human tide. Are we going to the shelters? No – to the cellars. We must be careful as there is barbed wire on the left and rails on the right. Fortunately for me, Pierre has eyes like a cat. Olivier must be coming too but we seem to have lost him and the lamps hardly guide us. There is rubble and demolished buildings like piles of scaffolding. We go down some steps. There are planes about, which is so much the better as their whining is a real comfort to us. They must be British, or perhaps ours? The sirens begin their music again but this time the danger is nearer. Hamburg is not far away fortunately. There is a turn in the stairs and I pass by a narrow bay cut in the wall. Pierre and I stop. Far away in the darkness there is a rocket and red sparks slowly come down. Caught in a movement, we go forward. What a pity! Dogs are following us. In a nearby corridor, some madmen are brandishing batons, threateningly and also other objects, I cannot distinguish. They strike and strike, hitting anybody anywhere!

I recognise the cellars where it is suffocating. The damp gets into us and to my unpleasant surprise find myself walking in icy water. We stop. Shoved on all sides, we do not let go of each other. We wait. The dull thuds are getting nearer; the earth is shaking and at times seems to be rising. Why do we stay in these cellars, with hardly 2 meters of earth above us? The dogs keep guard. The chiefs have boots for standing in the water. I understand, they fear escapes. London often advised us thus "make the most of bombing raids."

We are stiflingly hot. The earth is trembling. Our feet are frozen by the cold and stagnant water. Many people are coughing and insulting each other, blaming their neighbours for such a night! We feel bodies fall down, and then get up again with difficulty. All clear!

There is a stampede and a crush in the corridors, at the exit or on the stairs. Flip flops in hand, we run barefoot, cross the yard to block 9 and go into our hut. The blankets and mattresses have disappeared. We have to fight, if we don't want to sleep on the boards. We wipe our feet with our jackets and overcome with fatigue, we fall asleep!

22nd July. Since we arrived, we've been in quarantine. No going out, except for air-raids and work! In the morning, at 4.00, woken by cold and hunger, we rise under rubber truncheon blows. We go to the washroom, compulsorily naked. The Poles and the Germans make their own laws. Of course, we have to queue – the water smells so bad, it would make you ill – a small amount of chlorine and unidentifiable chemical products. We wash, or at least pretend to, as hundreds of striped men are waiting behind us and there is only one tap for three hundred! There is a large towel to dry with but it is so black and time is short! We go back to dress after having passed before the inspectors. Too bad for any man who is not clean – the whip will make him rejoin the ranks to queue again. We can go to the WC if there are not too many people and if one has the courage to go and paddle in 10 cm of urine! It takes two minutes to shake the mattress and the room becomes a dust cloud! Those in the top bed have to stand on the other two mattresses all the time, which is why arguments are so frequent, between the occupants of each of the three tiers.

"Roll call, in fives, everyone outside. Zu funf"

Once again you have to be quick, quicker than our cursed wooden soles will allow. Quite often we take them off and barefoot is better! You mustn't be seen by the Jerries though. Damned Roll calls! (parades). Always the same thing – standing still, waiting impatiently. Once, twice, three times, we are counted ten times! First the little Pole in the black cap, then an interpreter, then the block leader, then the SS adjutant! We have to keep to attention. Still we wait! If the general count of the camp is correct, all is OK but if there is a mistake, like yesterday, we remain there in spite of the misty cold of the morning, until everything is right! After Roll call (the headcount parade), we can eat. One bowl of sliced beetroot in vinegar, between 10 of us, and a 1.2 kg loaf between 12. I don't say loaf of bread, for is it really bread? A thick paste, hard, heavy and black, with a lot of saw dust, pieces of straw and little bits of wood! The bitter taste is unknown in France. You have to bite it with vigour and in spite of a lot of saliva, it stays in small hard lumps which dry the mouth and scratch the throat if eaten too quickly. Only the crust appears to be good. Sometimes you find a whole grain of corn in it, or other seeds, whose names I don't know. I haven't been able to swallow it before but now it tastes good. Still outside, we pass round the little litre bowl of beetroot, seasoned with cumin. It is July but we are freezing cold. The fog is impenetrable and icy in its dampness. We have hardly finished, when the circus music starts up its tam-tam again. Nothing is wanting here in fact but, for us the music is not, as in France and other countries a source of joy, a way to forget your miseries! It's not even music while you work, as the SS so proudly proclaim….it's a bear dance, always the same so called "Halten Kameraden".

All outside, in the square in fives, in step with head straight, we walk in time to the cymbals and castanets. Attention, straighten your arms – if you swing them, the kapo will make you change your stance. The music carries on and the orchestra seems indefatigable. All the musicians, in striped clothes are very clean and seem very proud. The leader, standing on a stool, waves his arms like a devil, in order to conduct the morbid cacophony!

Each kapo counts his workers and chooses them according to their face or appearance, discarding the small and weak. Today, my group of 50, also has two Vorarbeiters.

Going through the main gate, the cold blows on my back and I march like the others, as stiff as possible, between the large kepis and shining decorations showing skulls. There is a special team to inspect and record the number of workers. The site is 3 km away. We have to clear away the rubble of demolished houses. It is 6.00 am. Until midday, we will sort out beams, plaster, stones and bricks. For six hours, non stop, we have to run carrying awkward loads to a distance of 500 metres. At about 10.00 the sun becomes burning hot. The work does not slow down and it's then, that the Vorarbeiters begin to hit us. On our right is a hole full of stagnant green water but it is forbidden to go and drink from it. Only at midday can we quench our thirst with the hot, filthy water, which will give us dysentery. A whistle blast, tells us that the trolley with the barrels of soup has arrived. Our group, once counted and recounted, awaits the soup. What is it today? What a question!.... Cabbage, as always! The soup looks good. A Pole gives out the bowls. There are only 10, so we have to wait. Of course, the Russians and the Poles go first. The soup smells good and we are so hungry. At last it's our turn. There is some left over, because we have only been given two thirds of it but the barrel is taken away to the kapo's barracks. Every day it's the same thing. Those who do damn all, those who hit us, those who make us run to do our work, make us die of fatigue, and steal from us the little soup that is left. If we could, we would rise up in protest but here we say nothing. An SS soldier watches us surreptitiously – the black flag flies at the top of the pole. Anyway, we have no time to think. The whistles announce that work is beginning again. Up until 7pm the same routine begins. How difficult it is to start work again at 1 pm. We haven't even time to eat, for each time there is a Roll call (parade). The air is heavy and it will be cold this evening. How long is the day of enforced labour! What time is it? We ask ourselves. What time do you make it? I don't know. Only the sun gives an idea and sometimes the changing of the SS guard which takes place every half an hour. Deliverance at last – it's 7 o'clock! A loud blast sounds. Roll call – again! Forward. The return to the camp is fairly long. I'm hungry and thirsty. The air is cool and makes me all the hungrier. The camp, the music – yet again. In step, we go in.

Oh! These square bases surmounted by skulls – do they really belong to men?

Ein, zwei, ein, zwei (one, two, one, two). The bass drum beats out the time, dull and indefatigable, whereas our flip flops can hardly keep up! At last we stop, after having made the usual and useless circuit. There are thousands of us and I can't see the end of our ranks.

Roll call lasts for hours again, for the count is never correct and the Boches can't count.

The elderly are sent to their huts but we have to remain and listen to a speech. A Belgian translates their jargon. They are asking for volunteers for a small transport, good food, easy work – if you speak German, you will command the others. Also, there will be shoes and clothes. There are not many volunteers – so they choose some.

The kapos pass among the ranks and point out at random about a hundred men who move away, still in step and in fives. Next, each trade is called – specialists, turners, cutters, panel beaters, mechanics, engineers, cooks, painters, masons, doctors, bakers, etc.

At each call, our ranks diminish in number. Night is falling. The lamps and search lights are coming on. How long it goes on. Old men become unwell and fall. We pick them up again. When the railwaymen are called, I remain still, so does Olivier and Pierre. We mistrust them. Then it's the turn of the locksmiths. Pierre hesitates, then after all moves out of the ranks. Is he going to leave us? No. We will see each other again soon. He is no more a locksmith than me. I stay with Olivier.

Now it's over. I'm so hungry and thirsty, I feel ill. I am tired of standing but will we be able to sleep tonight? Roll on the moment, when I can drink. It is forbidden to go to the washroom! I receive a slice of bread 100 g and 25 g of margarine. Now to bed. I move to go for a drink but the 2 Poles are there with their truncheons. They are enjoying a half-loaf of bread to themselves with plenty of margarine which they have stolen from us. I shall go and drink tonight. Pierre is thirsty too. My mouth is so dry that I can't bring myself to start on the bread. I spread the margarine on it. There is a hubbub and whispering. We can drink! The poles have fallen asleep. Quickly, we get up, without any noise. Already in the light of the blue lamps, chaps are coming back, damp all over and jostling each other, for they are afraid of being seen (watch out!).

Block leaders! The taps are full on but the whip is lashing out already at the end of the corridor. Too bad – Pierre drags me along. We drink deeply, in spite of the crowding. I moisten my bread. It will be less dry. Now I shall be able to sleep!

Days and nights follow on with no change in routine. The most varied and disconcerting rumours are circulating in the huts. The landing is said to have completely failed. The Russians are retreating. I don't believe it but am anxious, nevertheless. The Boches are still very powerful and just their attitude towards us give us plenty to think about.

There is, however, an information service where we also hear about numerous bombing raids. The frequent air-raid warnings are therefore quite genuine. While we wait, the work is harder and harder, the nights shorter and shorter. For us, the alerts are a veritable nightmare in which we don't sleep and are in fear of hearing the sirens for that means suffocation, blows, fatigue, cold, dampness, feet in water quite often for several hours. I don't complain though. Nobody complains here, not even the sick. I feel privileged when, during the night in the over hot dampness of the underground rooms, I hear chaps gasping and dying of disease, cold or starvation. Quarantine is over. We have been given back our hats and given sandals with fabric straps, crudely nailed on. I take size 41 but have at least size 45. Often, when work permits, I go barefoot. We have been given different clothes too. We are now like zebras, having striped outfits. Our outfit is now a uniform, fitting our lifestyle. Some are quite affected by wearing these clothes – they feel dishonoured. Others, on the other hand are proud. I personally couldn't care less! This pyjama suit of wood material is so light that I miss my former cosmopolitan costume, shabby and splashed with yellow paint. What causes me the most sorrow is the shoes! I cannot walk without twisting my ankles which are already rubbed sore. Pierre and Olivier, like many others, still have a swollen face, caused by prolonged exposure to the sun.

In fact, not having worked for the first few days, they stood in the boiling midday sun, hairless, on the little pavement in front of the hut unable either to sit on the ground or to get into the shade. Some have died already from this treatment for of course there was not a drop of water to be had. Yet, nearby was the swamp! Only the Poles are allowed to drink.

Chapter 9: KITCHEN CHORES

Twenty five volunteers are needed for a small paid chore in the kitchen. It's a tempting proposition for men still hungry after the soup. Pierre whispers to me not to move. Already 10 have been singled out because no-one has volunteered. A priest from Alsace, Stéphane, acts as interpreter and advises the young ones to go along. Interesting work....We've been picked. Well, we'll see! So we move towards the kitchen, only stopping to pick up large crates of stretcher boxes, one between two. We pass the limits of the watch towers and casements. I notice that our group is composed entirely of Frenchmen. Here are the tracks which brought us here. Some wagons, one of which is open and full of turnips, has to be emptied and the vegetables carried into the cellars. "It won't take long" say two small Bretons standing behind me. I look sadly at the label, on which is written in blue "15 tons". We only have 12 crates. Already the first men are running towards the cellars with their load. We have to cross four tracks, negotiate three heaps of sand and stones, circle two huts on the right hand side, go down stairs, pass one, two, three staggered doors, a corridor, one, two, three large rooms full of cabbages and potatoes. We arrive at the pile of turnips. As soon as our crate is empty then the cry comes:

"Los, los, schneller!" (Quicker) We must follow the direction indicated by the truncheon holders. A German, with a green triangle (wearers of the green triangle, pointed downwards, are common law prisoners, for theft, insulting behaviour. When the triangle has the point upwards, they are criminals), is waiting for us with his rubber pipe behind a pillar. Let's go past quickly. It's Pierre who gets the blow on his head, even though we ran. I lowered my head instinctively and hear blows strike out on those behind who were not paying attention. They are two old men, badly dressed and who don't yet know how to walk with these heavy stretchers.

We have been running with our loads for two hours. My feet are bleeding, my hands are blistered and even my sight is suffering. It's a veritable circus in which I am caught up and can see no end. Sometimes I go in front, sometimes Pierre. We count the turns. The crates are loaded even more quickly than we can run to unload them. Each time, we pass in front of the look-outs of the SS, who always armed with their whips, shout unceasingly: "Los, los!" Only my nerves and my will keep me from falling. Some of the old men can't take any more and collapse exhausted between the stretchers. Truncheon blows and kicks either make them rise again or faint for good. If they don't get up, a team of Poles is on hand to drag them by the feet, I don't know where to, and they ask for Frenchmen to replace them. I walk barefoot and am better that way. I experience alternately the dust and sun outside and the damp inside the cellars where there is just room for the stretchers at each turning and where one scrapes the back of ones hands. The SS had said "Only one pile" Not content with working us to death, they are making us do useless work. Now we have to climb onto the heap with the crates and empty them from up there. Each time we pass the look-outs, we increase our pace. I walk with head up, Pierre too. We hide our faces as much as we can. Some cannot help weeping. As soon as a group of carriers stops, there is a general bottleneck. "Filthy French,......" Sticks lash out and strike backs and faces until they get up and start running. Not a minute's respite. At last, it's finished! Are we going back? No! Another wagon, with sacks of wheat weighing 100 kilos. Again we make use of our crates. It would be so easy to take the large cart with tyres – after about 10 trips we would have finished.

A large comrade from Narbonne (Rumeau, an SNCF mechanic) doesn't want to do anything and is beaten like Pierre. He is forced to walk. Now we have to go as far as the warehouse. My shoulders are burning and I can no longer feel my hands. Sweat is running into my eyes and blinding me. I haven't even time to wipe the steam from my glasses. It is forbidden to stop to urinate or do anything else; otherwise one is accused of sabotage.

A Belgian passes and says to me:- "There's a great deal too much work here, little Frenchman" I understand that he can do nothing to help me, although he is a friend but I have not even the energy to answer him. I can no longer speak and march like an automaton. My pyjama suit is soaked in sweat. The thirst and fatigue I feel make me forget my role and even my work. I have as much trouble marching empty as loaded. I have never felt so harassed. The wagon is not empty yet. The cries of the Boche irritate me to such an extent that I don't know why I am still walking. They will never get to know of this in France! They really want to kill us and it's to us especially that they bear a grudge. Why are those Latvians looking at us and laughing? They have striped suits too. I don't know any more. I am done in. A siren sounds. Will we have the promised reward? I am too worked up to think about it.

Chapter 10: THE BARGE

I change Kommandos each day. All are just as bad as each other. The Kommando unloading rubble from Hamburg, is now arriving on barges. The arrogance, curt orders, deafening sounds and the guttural jargon of the kapos and Vorererbeiters never changes – and yet these are not the same men. They are not even German. Greeks, Dutch, Latvians, all speak a pidgin German, which everyone must understand, or rather guess. Here again, the grudge is with the French. The SS snigger in the distance. There are about 30 of us with spades and we must move debris to the edge of the canal. We pretend to work normally and put as little as possible on our spades. We must however, keep our eyes open so as not to be seen. I think it is just as tiring to work with the eyes as with the arms! Alas – the invigilators are swarming with their small canes which they love to bend between their hands. Our dodge has been spotted! Already some of the kapos are striking out around them anyone and anywhere. Even on a man of about 60 who was working diligently and struggling a great deal. I would judge that the kapo is not yet 20 but his shining eyes are so frightening that everyone fears him. The work is not going fast enough. One of us is caught having a short minute's rest. What will he do to him?

Here in fact, one must be constantly on the move, making a noise, being busy, whether or not serving any purpose matters little – one must pretend to work – Otherwise it's 25 strokes of the whip. On the deck of the barge, there is a small barrel specially reserved for whipping. The culprit is laid across it on his stomach. The kapo strikes. He rises into the air to his full height, the long piece of black rubber jumps and comes down after lowering his arm with all his might. The blows fall with regularity as loud as a mallet knocking a stake into the ground. Powerless, we watch this indescribable scene. Are we civilised people? Two Poles hold down our friend on the barrel, one by the head, the other by the feet. At the first strokes, he jumped without saying anything, then let out shrill cries which pained me. Then he said nothing more, after a last 'ah! He must have fainted? The blows continue. I count 18, 19, 20. The kapo takes his time but he is hot too for he is breathing hard. If he could strike harder, I think that …. 23, 24. The Poles have already released our poor compatriot. His arms, legs and head hang dreadfully on either side of the barrel. 25. The kapo still doesn't seem satisfied, for an indescribable hatred shows on his brutish face. He stops, however. We begin work again. Spades work, all at different paces. Our hands are clumsy and our arms weakened, our tired minds are discouraged by the spectacle we have just witnessed. I work with rage in my heart. We must live for vengeance. I work in a frenzy, without thinking, like an animal.

"Not so fast," Jean says to me.

I do as he says. He's right, one must not go quickly, otherwise, before an hour has elapsed, I will not be able to go on. One is caught between two alternatives: work enough to avoid reprisals as far as possible but not too much so as to avoid fatigue. If we could only recuperate, through a few hours sleep or a good serving of potatoes but there is no question of that!

The chiefs are not pleased with our slow motion work.

"Sabotage, sabotage, terrorists!" they often cry out. They argue for a moment. Spades dig into the sandy debris.....and pebbles and throw the stuff sometimes a long way, sometimes not so far onto the bank. A young Pole takes up a couple of mallets and beats 1-2. 1-2 on the barrel. On the first beat, our spades must be filled and on the second, must be emptied. Our team therefore doubles its pace but at this rate we will not last an hour! Already, old men have had enough and fall down on the bricks. They get up again, under the kicks of the Dutch Vorarbeiter, a tall idiot of at least 6ft 6", who soon, will go up two or three times to fill his soup bowl. Bang, bang, bang, bang, faster say the blows of the mallet. I can no longer see clearly, sometimes my spade is empty but I follow the rhythm. At last, the soup is here! It's still just as thin! I did find a piece of rotten potato in it. It smells very strong and makes you want to vomit but I'm so hungry that I instinctively put my mouth to it and swallow. The soup is usually served boiling hot which is why we sweat so much and are so depressed. Of course, we have no spoons and have to eat very quickly, in order to pass the bowl to the next man after having had to wait for it ourselves. The conrade who was whipped earlier, is not allowed to have soup. You have to be here to appreciate the interest that a man has in the soup, or what we call soup. Not only will he not taste the beverage but he is not allowed the hour's rest. He has to stand for an hour, crouching on tiptoe over the little barrel, arms out straight – a particularly painful posture, when you already have your buttocks bruised from the blows.

Work goes on but already many have fainted or have been dragged off, I don't know where.

Chapter 11: "TOM RUMPER" SLATE MINES

As I noticed on arrival, our camp "Neuengamme" or "New Earth" is built on marshy ground where a lot of work will have to be done if you want to drain it. Therefore, a large work force has been created to this effect and I was lucky enough to be in it. There is no lack of tools, picks, rakes, hoes, forks, trucks, etc.

Nobody chooses his job here and can be made to do any work. I am barefooted, not having been able to repair my flip-flops. Sometimes in water, often in mud, we are black with dirt. The trucks must be loaded with all speed and taken away at a run, even when the tracks go uphill. Often, we deliberately cause derailments preferably on the turning….but we risk being hung for this little game, which can only benefit the men for a short time. As soon as there is a derailment, those in charge rush towards those working on the trucks and hit them in the face with their fists, or kick them in the belly. The truck has to be picked up and put back on the rails without tipping out the earth and using only our shoulders. The rails are often suspended in mid air with the sleepers but we must not take our hands off the truck or do acrobatics on the sleepers. Therefore, there are frequent accidents. The SS don't want us to waste time repairing the tracks, for they are only temporary (this has been going on for a month however!). Coming out of the mine, there is a large downhill bend, the danger of which I am aware of and I warn the others each time. The truck, overflowing again, gathers speed by itself and at a join in the rails, there is often a sudden disaster. Two young men from Luxembourg disappear under a mass of mud. We rush to dig them out but the SS overseers shout to us – "Wagons", wagons" We pay no attention to them and so the kapo bounds over with his whip, makes us pick up the truck and put it back on the rails, which takes us a quarter of an hour. Two minutes later, we dig out our young friends, dead from suffocation and the two vorarbeiters follow us shouting: "Sales Franzouzes, bandits, bandits, alles kaput, alles, crematorium". On our return with another load, we witness the removal of our friends by the team of undertakers who take them to the oven.

Chapter 12: THE CREMATORY OVEN

It's an obsession more than anything! All our thoughts start and end with it. From now on it's the only logical end. Undressing of the dead bodies, teeth pulled out and especially any dentures which will be resold by the kapos, the camp leaders and the SS, some for bread or for meat, others for money…..

Then the bodies are piled up so the trip is worth the trouble.

Flames, sparks, smoke curling up from the fatal chimney. A sickening smell of burnt horn, which the wind hardly covers, that's all that will be left… No, for I sincerely hope there will be some survivors to tell the tale; the tale that not only the dead are taken to the oven but also the dying, especially the Jews. How many have passed through there, over the years? I dare not think about it. Moreover, I have questioned several veterans without success and have seen from their attitude that it is dangerous to speak of the "crematorium".

Chapter 13: "FERTIG UM STELLER"

Stéphane, the priest interpreter, has translated for us: "Finishing workshop".

In reality, we are demolishing large brick buildings to make a Motorway. Here the SS are enjoying demolition. Armed with large beams which we carry between 15 or 20 of us, we attack pieces of wall, not at the top but at the base. Often, men remain caught under the rubble and we are not allowed to go and help them. As soon as a wall is knocked down, one must run either to the spade depot or to the wheelbarrow store. The interminable sound of barrows to be loaded and emptied begins quickly, for we have to run and our warders often strike our backs with batons. If they think we are not going fast enough, they make us undress under the pretext that our clothes are hampering us! When it's fine, it's of no importance, we are used to it – but they don't stop there. Each time I pass with my wheelbarrow, I am blasted with a jet of icy water, directed from the spy hole which you have to go past. Even though I run, I get soaked each time. It takes your breath away and increases fatigue. If I only had a lighter and practical wheelbarrow – but mine is heavy and tiring, even when empty and I run like that for 12 hours, only stopping for a few seconds on each trip to load or unload. I watch with envy, the Dutch sitting on the ground engaged in sorting the bricks.

The slightest attempt to escape the infernal circle which takes us to the work site is punished by whipping and kicks. In addition, as soon as a Kapo has noted the serial number in his notebook, the unfortunate man can expect to be deprived of soup or be hung in the evening, in public, or quite simply in the hut from the large nails specially placed in the ceiling.

Die Lagerkapelle spielt zu einer Hinrichtung: Neuendamme
(Zeichnung von H.P. Sorensen)

Chapter 14: "INDUSTRIE HOFF"

I have a Belgian as Vorarbeiter. He has no whip and helps us with the work each time the going gets hard. We are given the most varied jobs: cleaning and paving a yard, transporting planks, unloading coaches, loading lorries, sorting out ironwork, etc. but though our Belgian may be a decent guy, the Kapo terrorises us, with his bull's head, frizzy hair parted in the middle by a razor, yellow and black armband, he's there with a piece of a plank and his hammer. Those are his favourite instruments, not to work with but to hit us with, or push us in the back to make us run, when we are carrying loads. We can hear him coming from afar, for his strident voice can be recognised, going from column to column. To run away from him, ignore him, disobey him, not care, is just impossible, for he is not a man to be approached with staggering steps and rounded back. You can see, just by looking at him close to, that his thuggish body has also known the first rigours of camp life. He passes. Icy silence. Has he gone? Terror still reigns, for he is watching us, always indefatigable. He has no pity for anybody and often makes the weakest ones do the hardest jobs. Fortunately, for us, he is very stupid and remembers nothing. I am singled out for transporting to a distance of 100 metres a pile of stove pipes. One has to run but they're not heavy. I slow down each time the Overseers turn their backs. When I've finished, I begin again and take the pipes back to where they were before. The Kapo, seeing me continuously busy with my pipes leaves me in peace and moves further on.

It is not a question here of having a soft job for that's impossible for the French but of passing unnoticed – then you are privileged. I am singled out for sawing work. One lot bring the timber, others pile up the planks. I find myself on the planks. "Look out Kapo! Watch out SS!" That's the warning whisper of danger which threatens us at every moment in this building full of draughts. One day, the kapo gets angry for no reason and threatens to throw us under the circular saw. We don't believe such a thing but a Pole carrying planks with me, whispers to me in German – "He's already done it, last year!"

Today, I am carrying bricks. Our team comprises 200 men. I have found Pierre and Olivier again. Pierre is an expert and I have only to follow him with complete confidence in order to work because he can keep an eye on the SS or Kapos. If he takes two bricks, I take two: if he puts on 8 or 10, I do the same. It only needs the appearance of an SS on the site to see hundreds of men rushing, as if caught in the wrong and as if work already accomplished didn't count.

The Russians, used to this ruse, only work if they have an SS on their backs; otherwise they do nothing, or pretend to go to work whilst strolling around the whole day with a hammer, a plank, brick or some other object. This dodge is not possible for us, who wear an F in the red triangle, for kapos, vorarbeiters, simple Poles or even the Russians, prisoners like us make us work in order to create movement on the site and to keep them out of sight.

Russians and Poles reserve easy jobs for themselves. They are the masters, load the barrows, pile up bricks in our arms, or just command us in the language in which we have to guess at everything. One hesitation or delay and they strike us. One young Pole, of about 15, amuses himself by loading our barrow of bricks as full as he can. He speaks a few works of French and constantly repeats: "Frenchmen, much eat, don't much work. Frenchmen, much eat, don't much work!" Nobody answers him but we grit our teeth and push our barrows.

Chapter 15: A FEW HAPPY MOMENTS

Sometimes we don't work. We are left outside. Consequently, we can talk and discuss things. Firstly, the military situation. We have no news but things are going round none the less and everything leads us to believe that victory is near. Groups form and we take part in interesting discussions held in good spirit, even among men of the most varied opinions.

Father Système is highly thought of and we hang on his every word. His Christian philosophy gives us back a great deal of courage and he is so kind. His friend, a freemason, is himself listened to.

Opposite us, on the other side of the barbed wire and the areas planted with beans, is the hut for the Prisoners of Honour, those from Camp C in Compiegne. They have retained their clothes and all their personal effects. The priests and bishops have their cassocks and can read their breviary. It is forbidden to go and speak to them but we make signs none the less. Here are M and C. They have extra soup. There is definitely a worn passage by a pipeline between blocks 9 and 11 but you have to go to 9.

I take advantage of a passing column and mingle with the hosts of that block, with my mess tin under my jacket. Here is the trench and the pipes which will take me to the other side of the barbed wire. I slip through, pick myself up – the man in the watch tower has not moved. I am afraid of being noticed in my suit, among the others dressed in civilian clothes. All goes well. M.M. gives me a sign. I run and follow him. I go into the block. They are all in civvies. What a life it is here! Piles of plates on the tables, a young man is washing up, another drying. M. takes my bowl and says: "We are making a sauté of it but it's not much. We must think of the end of September."

"You are having an easy time, so much the better chaps," I say to a man stretched out on his mattress and deep in the perusal of an "Assimil" in German.

Here is my bowl full of steaming cabbage and potatoes. "Thanks, M." We'll repay you. Don't mention it. Courage young man. I again cross the little yard of hut 9. Pierre is waiting at the door for me and has it opened by the Luxembourg warder. We share out the soup with Olivier.

I am moved to another hut before the departure which must be near. All my worldly goods are a wooden spoon which I made for myself and a small piece of metal which

I picked up at the Industrie Hoff, and which I call a knife. Unfortunately I shall not be able to take them with me, for we are going to change suits again. Pierre has stayed in No. 10. Until now he had managed to keep his wedding ring but I have advised him to leave it with a friend among the Prisoners of Honour. That is what he has done, throwing it over the barbed wire to a teacher from Autun.

Chapter 16: BLOCK 9

Our block leader, tall, fat, brutal, a real Boche, former NCO in the German Army, warns us on the first day that he doesn't like the French. He finds us too slow in getting into ranks and amuses himself sometimes by jumping on us and tipping us onto the barbed wire. He cannot count at all and as he often gets the total wrong, the SS are exasperated. Suddenly, a small man, tall as a youth, although the kepi makes him seem taller, appears, announced by the "Achtung" of the concierge. He goes straight up to Karl and begins to shout at him. Karl, standing to attention, appears to be apologising but the Boche gives him some punches in the face and kicks somewhere else with all his might but this didn't seem to affect him much! Seeing all that, I feel a real contentment!

Chapter 17: A MEDICAL INSPECTION

We have been standing in five ranks since the beginning of the day. Like every morning, although this time we are motionless, we feel the mist, the cold, the drizzle, the wind and always hungry. It is the 1st August and as soon as the sun comes out it is boiling hot. "Achtung" Five SS have just arrived. We are made to go into the huts. Tables and chairs, on which we were never allowed to sit on, are in one corner. In ranks of 10, we have to undress. The Boche officers are present. There is talk of a medical visit. The old hands say that this heralds a departure. Ten by ten, young, adolescent, old, all naked, we move forward. The Jerry Major looks us over from hand to toe, makes us hold out our hands, turn round. The infirm are weeded out. We are good enough for the departure. We put on our clothes again, happy at not being separated. Pierre is not going.

Chapter 18: A NEW DESTINATION

Under heavy escort, we have taken a train. Where are we going? Nobody knows. Not even the Boches who answer with that fatal word – Transport.

Swaying, bumping, jostled, shaken, in broken down wagons, we travel along, herded against each other, not speaking a word, our round caps with blue and white stripes pulled hard down over our ears. They say we are going to work in pine forests with a good Commander.

In fact, there are a great many fir trees along here and heather, deserted dunes, it's a poor region. Covered in coal dust, we pass for a good few miles under a building made of grilles and artificial foliage. We are camouflaged but that is because there are hundreds and hundreds of tanker wagons here. At last, we are there. Sand, heather, a few fir trees, huge piles of cabbages along the road, we pass small barbed wire, and further on some huts. A door, some SS, overseers, in striped clothes, we arrive and are counted as we pass. There are not many huts and from on top of the sandy dunes we look out over a deserted landscape. The few veterans look at us with curiosity, then move away. About 10 overseers are there. Lager Aleslater, Block Alteste, kapos with the green triangle are in the majority.

The watch towers are less obvious than in Neuengamme. Where are we? Here there are no forests, no saw mills, as we had been told. The strong cold wind rather takes our breath away and heightens our appetite. Roll on the soup!! Counted, recounted, put into groups of 100, for there must be about 2000 of us, we arrived at the centre which dominates the whole camp. In front of a narrow but high hut but made of planks and with no window or door, we go around it. It will never hold us all! At last a door!

Chapter 19: "THE BUNKER"

I go down some wooden steps. Everywhere is dark and I have to grope my way along, guided by the man in front. A few lights. A lot of noise, a varied assortment of sounds, blows of a hammer on spikes, shouts which I don't understand, weak electric lamps, a crowd of striped suits, noisy, with wooden clogs. Olivier is there. Huge pillars linked by enormous horizontal and cross beams of iron, make patterns on the walls. We are underground. Is it a Tunnel? Factory? — We'll see.

A huge cylinder with an oval base makes a continuous purring noise, deafening but appears not to disturb the Russians or the Poles, who have evidently already been there a long time. Two Frenchmen — there's a surprise! I move nearer and Olivier does too. They are already speaking to the new arrivals. One is Leconte, (from Finistere), small, fat, dirty, hands covered with warts, — the other one is tall and thin. "Bonjour, chaps, Hello sports. How's France? You're at the Bunker here….yes, underground. It's a reservoir where they want to put oil from Rumania. Meanwhile, we sleep here.

In fact, I can see the same three tier beds which we had at Neuengamme and the pallets. In a corner is some crumpled straw."

Our two Frenchmen are there, causing a gathering, for already men are forming a circle and they are pressed with questions from everyone.

"The name of the camp? Bremen-Farge. You have come from Neuengamme, I know about it. If I had stayed on the barges, I would have died there but now I have a soft job."

"What do you do? Is it hard? What's the food like?"

"I work at the base about 3 km from here, we're building it. I am a painter."

"And the work?"

"It depends, you have to get out of it or you're done for. In the last convoy from Neuengamme there were 52 Italians, last winter. There is only one survivor. He looks after the latrine buckets."

"But we were told about pine forests."

"No. no, You might as well say I'm from Brest, that I've been here for two years and have buried hundreds. It's for the submarine base that you have come."

"The grub, cabbage soup, marge, chemical soup. It's good sometimes. The food is better on Sundays and Sunday evening there is theatre for the Germans that we can watch.

There is in fact a stage, surrounded by panels depicting allegories."

"There are 5 huts in the Bunker but this is the first time I've seen so many arrive, especially Frenchmen. Maybe you won't get a mattress tonight."

Called in alphabetical order, I wind up in hut 1 with Maurice Bourdet, Maurice Clement, Roger Clarenc, Andre Chaumont, Jean Fougerat, M. de Flesselles, two Bretons who don't speak French, Fournier and some others.

The block leader is a young Pole in red shorts. Full of energy, he exudes good health. There are many tables and benches but just the same as at Neuengamme, no place for the French. At our table there are about 7 of us and 23 Poles. For us, the word table is just an expression and we remain standing. On the pillar from which hang the locked boxes belonging to the overseers, are the letters B A...T A 1... T A 2... We are given a blanket between two of us and after having eaten a small piece of bread, some substitute cheese, I go to bed with Maurice Clement. He is a railway man like myself and he talks to me about La Chapelle station, the Rue de Londres and about France in general. It's good to have a friend, when one is alone and it's cold....... Maurice is already more than a friend to me because before going to sleep, I tell him my life story and give him my address.

The straw is damp, the cement floor cold and I am happy as I am with Maurice. We have hardly known each other for two hours and already he wants me to address him as "tu!" It seems funny to me but in here, old and young, we are all in the same miserable boat. "Good job it's not for long" says Maurice to me. I am less afraid and with him, have high hopes.

A bell rings and whistles blow. "Aufstehen." Get up, quickly. We fold the blanket and then go towards the washroom. What a crowd. Block leaders and deputies are there with their whips and make us undress, by force, for it is forbidden to go up to the taps in our pyjama suits, even if you only want to wash your hands, moreover, the French have to wait until all the others have finished.

Amongst the Germans,(often ex sailors) there is competition as to who has the best tattoos, butterflies, anchors, birds, women's heads, inscriptions. Their bodies are quite blue and sometimes the drawings are so close, that everything becomes a mass of snakes, flowers, crosses or crowns. The wide square back of one German overseer even seems to have been used as a canvas for the work of one artist. We can see depicted a complete funeral ceremony with a priest, servants, coffin and mourners, nothing is missing, cross, candles, the book on the altar. We don't go too near because the man is twisting in his hands a large piece of rubber, with which he tries to hit us. Naked then, we go up one after the other, for it would be foolish not to have one's clothes looked after by a friend. Since everything is a one-way system, you have to choose between the WC and the washroom. I go to the WC – there are buckets there and since they quickly become full, two men have the job of emptying them, one of which is an Italian, the famous survivor. To empty them, they are attached to a chain, attached to a winch on the dunes and the pulley pulls each bucket to the top.

Here's the coffee, bread and margarine. The head of each table receives the rations and gives them out. One slice 2cm thick, a finger of marge. Then we queue up with our bowls for the coffee. If there is enough for everybody, we will get some. The cleaners reserve the best for themselves

Henrick is standing up. The day is beginning. We have hardly been served when a whistle blows, like the calling of an owl. Everyone – outside. It's a cavalcade of clogs and flip flops on the stairs.

"Raus, Raus". The block leader of Hut 4 (his black armband bore the letters B A IV), an incredible man with his fang-like teeth, is enjoying himself hitting us. Heads lower, clack, clack, I go by.

It is hardly light and the wind is cold. In fives, pushed, jostled, a general movement, the camp leader cries "Franzouses" and threatening, terrible, full of energy, he hits us as hard as he can in the face, in front of a young giggling SS. Now we have to walk in step, for they say the French soldiers cannot follow the rhythm. Ein, zwei, achtung, about turn, halt. Some don't understand, hesitate, make a mistake. I whisper to my neighbours what they have to do. An overseer takes those aside that are doing it wrong and for 2 or 3 hours, it's a continuous "stand up, lie down, stand up, run, etc…" It's enough to make you wonder if they don't intend to give us a green uniform.

3rd. August. I am working in the camp on the construction of 2 large huts of cement and mud. It is raining and I am counting the hours. There are too many of us working there but nevertheless, one must always be on the move, always running and pretending to work, for here everyone is in command except the French.

That's why we are constantly pursued by an unrelenting overseer. I take my chance and prefer to get several extra kicks, than to be dead from fatigue in the evening. I still feel very strong but I am wary, for the days are so long and the meals so meagre. I am working at a concrete mixer with Maurice, Roger and 3 Poles who stop us from talking.

With a spade, we go up to the sand and without a break, have to start shovelling it. Others carry bricks, planks, joists. There is no lack of these materials. Not far from here is the kitchen, run by the Germans and the Poles. The pleasant smell of cabbage reaches us but that's all. About 10 o'clock, a few Poles slip over to the kitchen, pass their bowls through the broken window and take it back full, doubtless thanks to a friend. I am hungry, Maurice is too but have we the right to be hungry? At midday, we return to the Bunker to eat, each one is in his hut. In the evening the hours seem interminable. Maurice speaks to me constantly on the strategy of the military plans, but we speak softly, for we have enemies everywhere. With two of you, the time passes more quickly and we forget the work and the fatigue in talking.

6th August. I still sleep with Maurice but now in two-tier beds, below Russians and Poles, at the side of Hut 2. Every evening, there is a fight for blankets. Mr. Bourdet is never lucky and if we weren't there, he would not even have a mattress. Here one has to have confidence only in one's few friends.

The Pole in red shorts makes his usual round to see if the French have really taken off their pyjamas before going to bed. He also looks to see if our feet are clean, makes us get up to look at our faces. If he is satisfied with us, all is well, if not the whip will chase us to the taps, even if there is no water! He would be better to count the blankets which his henchmen have stolen from us.

For two days, Maurice has been complaining about his ankle, which he has grazed. He has no dressing for it. Several times, I have heard it said that there is an infirmary but each time I try to talk of it to the Head of my table, I come up against a real brute. "Warum krank, warum, hier kein krank. Niemals krank" No sick, never any sickness.

7th August. Maurice is limping badly but does not complain and walks for as long as the others, just as often resting on his good foot as soon as he can stop. "Was macht du" The big Dutch kapo suddenly shouts to him with his face ravaged by scars and boils. Maurice does not answer. He repeats "Wie weil Jahr?". Maurice tells him his age and instinctively shows him his foot. "Ya, ich verstehe aber revier doctor ambulanz" Maurice makes it painfully through the day.

8th August. Maurice is working at pealing vegetables. He is pleased because he is sitting down but his ankle is very painful and is now a vile colour. Roger, Jean and I advise him to have it looked at since there is an infirmary. I see Olivier each evening. He has been put into Hut 3 and is already working at the base. My turn will doubtless not be long in coming.

10th August. The Roll call is terribly long this morning. We are sorted out into Kommandos. Maurice, unable to walk, is in the ranks of the sick. I would like to stay in the Lager Kommando, the camp commando but the cursed "arbeit dienst" always comes into our ranks to count the columns of his vorarbeiters. I am singled out with Fourneir, for the "Weiss et Freitag" Kommando.

Chapter 20: "BREMEN FARGE"

One by one in step, the commanders of zebra-striped men follow on, one after the other. Counted one last time, with rage in our hearts, we pass through the wide barbed wire boundary, in front of the bunker and huts of the SS. The damp sand is like a sponge under our feet. We are now outside the barbed wire. I am impatient to see this base of which there has been so much talk for the past few days. My clogs, three sizes too large, will not stay on my feet so I take them off and carry them in my hand. The little trucks of sand are 1 km away. As soon as we go out, a group of soldiers from the Kriegsmarine come to escort us, both old and young. For us they are no more sympathetic than the SS, only the badge has changed.

The trucks of sand are here. We climb onto them and piled in as many as 25 or 30 standing clinging to each other, we move towards the German countryside. There are about a dozen trains like ours following each other at a distance of a few metres and resembling a long angry snake surmounted by black smoke and sparks, from which we must take cover or else risk catching fire! You have to hang on in order not to fall overboard. The little trucks lurch from left to right, swaying with every jolt and often stop without warning.

A few dunes, sparse cultivation of kale for the cows, a few potatoes, a field of rye, huts of planks coloured for camouflage, guns with an anti-aircraft battery in the middle of the countryside, hole, ditches, wire, obviously scattered around from other camps, on the roads a crowd of prisoners of war, Russians with their large green fur capes, stamped "S.U." on the back, Italians recognisable from the hats and the "J" on the backs of their jackets. There are hundreds of thousands of them, coming from all directions and going to work at the base.

We arrive and stop between two immense heaps of sand. In five ranks we cross Farge, in step and under guard. Pretty little chalets of red brick, maisonettes with large windows and roofs covered with thatch. The civilians, men and women, look at us and threaten us with their batons, urchins hiding behind a house send a shower of stones, pieces of brick and bits of wood onto us, shouting "Bandits, Franzouses, Bandits, Ruski, terrorists alles kaput".

I curse the whole village! As for the chalets, we will burn them when victory comes! A lovely smell of toast reaches us, when we pass in front of a Bakers. It makes my mouth water. There is a little garden with apple trees laden with fruit. We turn away.

The mist is thicker and more penetrating. The wind doubles in strength. There is a din of lorries, of engines, tracks, trains passing at top speed and disappearing with their warning bell. In the fog, in the background, I make out with difficulty an enormous mass which rises up, fast and ghostly, surrounded by cranes and scaffolding, iron walls and huge staircases, immense ladders supporting enormous pipes and many more things still, which I have not time to see, for day has not yet come. Lost in a giant hail of which I cannot see the end, here is the kommando "Weiss et Freitag". In ranks of 5, we wait motionless; to be counted yet again before the work begins.

The kapo is a German. He doesn't hit much but we are afraid of him for he shouts all the time. We are not going up to the base but go to work not far from the Weser, digging enormous ditches and making terraces. Pick and spade work unceasingly for many hours. We don't talk very much and have to work with bare torsos. Towards midday, the sun becomes boiling hot and some of us have blisters all over our bodies. Many complain of thirst and manage to obtain some water near a cement mixer.

20th August. The work goes on, still as monotonous and crude as ever. Not only am I disgusted, discouraged at working with this cursed spade or the pick which is too heavy, not only am I tired from pushing this truck full of earth but I am weakened by the eternal cabbage juice and the crab-apple jam with the evening bread. We discuss the matter between ourselves and ask each other if this is going to last much longer.

Yesterday, throughout the day, we moved an entire meadow in order to create camouflage. I was cutting turfs with a spade or found myself in the chain of turf carriers. The insides of my hands are raw and bleeding and being barefoot, I had to put the tool in with my hands, with short thrusts. My lower and upper back is aching from the whiplashes received for breaking some of the grass turfs which should have arrived intact on the concrete shelter, to be camouflaged.

Today, I am on the trucks. I have the good fortune to be with five Frenchmen, amongst whom is the railwayman Fournier. When, by misfortunate, I find myself with Greeks and I am dead with fatigue at the end of the day. They are bone-idle, make the devil of a noise by showing off and always pretending to do more than the others but on the contrary, doing nothing. The truck must be kept moving and it's too bad if two or three are not pulling their weight so the others have to do the work for them. At soup time, we all receive the same share!

Jacques, a little Breton, is walking with difficulty. He is ill but there are too many people in the infirmary so he has not been admitted. He leans on the truck loaded with earth and walks, and occasionally, in spite of himself, he is letting out soft moans. He has dysentery and cannot go on. When the truck is empty, we put him in it to bring him back to the loading point, sparing him the effort of walking. This martyrdom will continue until the siren goes when the work is over. We make sure we're not seen. Poor Jacques – in France he would quickly recover but here he will die. At midday, "Mittagessen" as the Boches say, we eat outside standing up, the thin liquid often cold and so clear, that there is no need for a spoon. We then continue work again until the evening. Fournier speaks little. He explained to me however, why he was arrested. He had taken a room with a young colleague who must have been in the Resistance but he didn't know that. He regrets never having done anything against the Boche and his profile reminds me of Pierre Lhoste, left in Hut 10 at Neuengamme, who said at Compiegne: "If only they let us go so that we can go and derail what's left!"

In the evening, we go back to the camp in the little train, tired, done in, sweaty and covered in bruises. Men fight whilst clinging together in the trucks or trample around in them. There is always jostling to get out and they run in ranks of 5 to the door, then it's the cavalcade on the stairs! My feet, head, shoulders, everything has become hardened, unfeeling.

At last the taps! Here is some water but the Germans and Poles have their share first. I find Olivier, who is working at "Argue Nord Zwei". He is well and his morale is good but he has become so thin. I say nothing to him. He complains of hunger though. 100 grams of bread and 25g of substitute cheese, isn't much after 12 hours toil! I sit down next to him with Fournier on one of the iron planks overhanging a pillar. We talk of our country, of the railway but all that is so far away! Will we see it all again one day?

Olivier has been able to talk to a Belgian civilian on the site. He has also read the paper "L'echo de Nancy" but I don't believe all that. We have learnt of the liberation of Paris. We pass on the information. Good or bad, we cannot live without news and the resulting discussions keep us occupied.

Every evening, I try to go and talk to Maurice who has at last been admitted to the infirmary. That was good news. It is expressly forbidden to go near the windows, the light from the watch tower sweeps over the wide yard. The other search lamps light up the barbed wire every 10 m. and makes fixed shadows with the WC's and Hut 5. The violent wind is blowing lugubriously. Kapos and other people come and go towards the kitchen with a bowl or other objects under their arms.

I must see Maurice. They have made him suffer so much, twice opening his boil. He must be expecting me. The last commandos are arriving. I run quickly and find myself in the shadow of Hut 5 - one, two, three, fourth window. I go nearer, duck down, tap on the window-pane, after making sure that everything is quiet in this dressing room "Maurice! At last, everything OK? Yes, and you? Yes but it's hard and I'm starving. Stay there. Above all stay away from the base as long as you can!

"Don't worry - I can see you're holding out well. That's nice; you're not even getting thin!"

"Oh, but what about you, are you still in pain?"

"No, but I've had my share of it."

"What about the news have you got nothing to say?"

At that moment, the French sit up in their beds and listen, eagerly. How I would like to tell them about it. They talk of Paris, Orleans, of Belgium liberated and ..... What a bombing they're getting .....Did you hear it yesterday?

"Yes, the hut was shaking."

"Goodbye Maurice,"

"Goodbye, my little Maurice, it won't be long and we'll see Panama again. I'm off, there's a kapo coming. See you tomorrow, sleep well."

I move the length of the operating room, from whence I can hear howls and running I go back to the bunker.

22nd August. A convoy of French arrived yesterday. They all have hats, which distinguish them from our caps. I'm reunited with Douence, the Marquis of Moustiers, Bourgerelle, who comes from Montchanin, some Bretons and by chance a man from the Nièvre, Jacques Parent from Nevers, who also becomes a friend for there are none from the Nièvre in the kommando. All are in the huts higher up. The Marquis of Moustiers is still more and more optimistic. It's him who announces the important news. Thanks to him, we count the days and watch the time pass by with pleasure but unfortunately, the situation has not changed for us!

Some say there are 10 days to go before demob! Between 15 and 30, for the more prudent. I too had fixed a date for myself but I have had to postpone it several times. Olivier firmly believes the last rumour but I am firmly counting on the end of September, for my birthday! The Marquis often makes us laugh heartily and when possible, I love to hear him talk. He draws us a map in the sand with a piece of wood, indicates the first armoured American tanks which should arrive on the 4th September. M. Maupoil had talked to me about 15th October but I think he is too pessimistic! In October, it will be too cold here. We will be free before then.....

2nd September. Two days to go to demob. I smile and don't believe it. We are still eating the same filth and at the "base" life has not changed.

4th September. It's arrived but without the American tanks, without the stars and stripes and we will not sing the Marseillaise today. The Marquis is stubborn and does not change his opinion. "They will lose the war if they go on like this. They are heading for disaster. We must wait until this land of madmen is exterminated". Alas, will we hold out? I am still strong but the people from Murat in my hut were more robust than me and they are already pushing up the daises. Let's wait for the 22nd, it'll be my Saints day and perhaps there will be some news then.

10th September. I am happy, for I have found a few rags with which to wrap my hardened but blistered feet. Like every Sunday, I have my beard and hair shaved by the Polak, the head of Table 4 in Hut 1. Like every Sunday, the Todt organisation for which we work, pays us that is it gives out cigarettes to the kapos. The French receive five or six, sometimes none if they have not worked in the same column for the whole week. The soup was better today – I found three pieces of carrot and a bone – what lovely soup!

I am very tired because on Sundays there is no train going to the base and you have to walk there. We marched without shoes, without flip flops even because yesterday (Saturday) when I showed the Stubedienet what remained of my clogs, he seeing the F on my chest, shouted" Was? Shuh? Morgan keine Shuhe". He had a sack full of flip flops though but kept them for his friends. He will exchange them for soup, a piece of bread, 1 or 2 cigarettes!

I received 5 cigarettes but will not show them! I dare not approach that huge curved silhouette. As I don't smoke, I give 2 to Olivier and keep 3 for Maurice. The wind and rain make the Sunday even more desolate. Maurice is not worried I envy him his happy fate. His presence and friendship are very precious to me. I see him for a whole 2 minutes every day, but it's not much…

15th September. I am working at the "Platen Platz Kolonne". Every morning, on the dune, the nightmare begins again. 50 lashes of the whip for anyone who does not return to the ranks of his kommando of the day before. Like animals at a market, we are sorted, moved around to different columns with no motive other than the whim of the Arbeitsdienst, who we fear more than any other. Red, alcoholic (the overseers drink white spirit in the bunker, where we often find them stone drunk), small, muscled, flat face, he is always barking at us. This morning, therefore, with people I don't know – many Russians and Greeks – I went off to work, having changed columns without knowing why.

Wassily Dimitrianoff, the vorarbeiter, is not nasty but he is afraid of the kapo, and always makes us run when pushing the trucks full of concrete blocks. Fortunately, our work is varied and we also have to tip concrete onto a structure of iron bars to form a huge solid and portable block. It is not very warm in the morning and in the rain, with no shelter, soaked with the dampness, we wait in front of our blocks for the end of the day and the liberating siren blast, after which we can say – "another one over"! We watch the trucks while waiting, sometimes an hour or two until the count is correct and we can go!

22nd September. It's my saint's day! Alas, I think a great deal of that. In my little piece of box I had 3 cigarettes left, which the Russians did not manage to steal from me while I was asleep. They are my whole wealth! I want to take them to Maurice, for his own celebration. I am sad, for I know that he must be thinking of me over there. Here, the soup is even more filthy, made from cumin and chemical products. The Swedish jam nauseates me each time but Olivier swallows everything, as he is so hungry. I feel pity for Roger. He is so thin and the deprivation appears worse on those who are corpulent. Maurice is complaining about the soup too but keeps smiling as last night he again heard bombing on Bremen and even thought he could hear the guns (firing practice or just the front approaching?) A cannon? A real one? When will we hear it? In France, Belgium, Holland, Italy, Russia, everywhere, they can here the guns…..

30th September. It is my birthday! I'm 22. In 15 days time, maybe, I no longer dare to hope for an imminent end and the thought of winter frightens me, for it is already cold and our clothes are always damp on our backs. Maurice has had a third operation and has had such a lot of pain. I am frightened that he will remain crippled because the Polish doctor is only a trainee who only has makeshift instruments.

It's my birthday but Maurice is suffering too much and I don't stay long at his window. He will be at least another month in the infirmary.

This morning, I did not go to the base but unloaded coal and bricks all day. This evening I am picked for a new kommando: "Arc Nord" – Night work. The sky is always grey and the cold never stops. My shirt is in rags and my lime covered pyjama suit is torn all over and has no buttons left. I have to keep it together with a piece of wire. It is therefore quite a job for all of us to get dressed in the morning, with our rags and small piece of wire. I have a piece around my waist to which I attach the tin which serves as a bowl. My wrists and ankles are also wired up, to stop the wind a little, which goes right through me.

Now there is something much more dangerous if it was discovered. I have put a paper bag on my shoulders, underneath my suit. It has been cold now for several days. It's a nightmare when you are working near the sea, with no shelter and when you are too hungry. At the base where there is no lack of cement bags but the Boches collect them and it is sabotage to take them. The matter of the paper bag is crucial, for pleurisy and bronchitis and pneumonia are frequent. They entitle you to 12 days of rest and then you are sent back to work.

I would prefer inflammation or oedema, they say that doesn't hurt! I have really tried to drink a lot of water but up to now, I have been able to keep away from this sort of illness. I do not fear the cold but I am afraid it is going to last too long.

The wind and rain are raging and I am continually wet and in spite of torrential downpours we always have to work outside, without being able to dry off. That's why I have been running the risk of getting 25 lashes of the whip for the last 3 days. The Germans and their Polish henchmen have got wind of our dodge and search us morning and evening by feeling our backs and shoulders. Nothing happens! I go down the stairs with my bag in my trousers and will put it on later.

At the bunker, we are not searched when we come back, like the men in the huts below – that's why with Jean and Roger, we hide our friends' bags underneath our mattresses. That way we stave off illness. We must hold out until the end!...

I have become resigned now, when I am sad I recite prayers or verses by Vigny de Mussat or Virgil or I think about someone who has died in my family. I talk to him. Time passes. I do not think too much of my parents or my brothers, it hurts too much but I think about how things could be worse, sometimes, and in the midst of our profound misery, I continue to exist, confident, sometimes indifferent.

I have told Maurice of my departure for night work and my new separation from yesterday's friends. I will make new friends, of course but I can't go on. Six hours of unloading this morning and now here I am going off for the night. We are taking away the soup flasks and the bread box. The French are again chosen to take these loads to the little train. Seven flasks of 50 L for 400 men and a large box of bread cut for the midnight snacks.

We arrive at 18.00 when the day workers leave. At once, we are assigned a corner of the site to clear concrete which has spread in the wrong place. Pick and spade work away seemingly indefatigably and night falls. There are still 11 hours of work but let's not think about it. The lit lamps make large shadows in which we cannot even hide in order to rest a little.

I am transporting boxes of debris with another man, crossing via narrow planks and passing piles of bricks, beams bridging a deep gulley and finally a labyrinth of vertical iron bars, fixed to the ground like sticks. It's quite an art to run with a box amidst such obstacles. You must both be acrobatic and of Herculean strength but under the whip, because of the fear, the need to conserve yourself means that the clumsy and the weak must carry out this hard work just like the others. It is dark and cold but sweat is running down our faces.

I spit into my hands, breathe deeply, grit my teeth and this time avoid the hole full of water, in which I plunged just now. "Los, los," Pougault cries to us, he is the cursed vorarbeiter, green triangle, German "Los, los, schneller weiter, weiter" (come on, faster, carry on, carry on). They are all the same, whether they be ex-thugs, ex-thieves, ex-anti Nazis, ex-bad soldiers, they are all the same, with their whips and raucous orders.

They have good shoes, pullovers, 2 or 3 jackets, a striped coat, sometimes boots – they are allowed three helpings of soup, fall back on the bread they have stolen from us at the kitchen and which is getting mouldy in the padlocked box in the bunker. They reserve for themselves marked bottles in which their colleagues in the kitchen have put pieces of cabbage and all the potatoes, sometimes even bones.

As for us, we drink the liquid – washing up water. They don't work, know anything about the work, don't even know how to use a lever or avoid accidents to others – but they beat us. Their position is too good and like the Poles, they don't want to lose it. That's why they have forgotten everything, their reason for living, their ideals (if they ever had any), their life in the fresh air, their family; they have even forgotten they are men like us, since they kick us to death for the least disobedience.

Pougault is sinister, with a gait like a degenerate. At night he doesn't see the tears and the sweat he causes on the tired face of the old man who could be his father. Passing close to him, I sometimes would like to give him a shove on the shoulder so that he falls into the huge cemented hole at the base of the crane. Unfortunately, all men have the same value, all are worse than each other and sometimes I think sadly that in this hell, all men are bad.

All, from the sentry hardly visible in his boarded look out, to those who are loading my box every five minutes, to my co-worker, who either walks too quickly when we are in shadow, or too slowly when we are caught in the beam of a search light. Not only are the men against us, but everything gets us down. First it's the wind howling ominously and slyly with its gusts of cold water, then it's the noise of the crane and the concrete mixers opposite, the pick hammer, deafening, which jars on even the best nerves.

Lastly, it's the place where we are working: tree trunks, holes, bumpy ground, obstacles of all sorts, badly lit, hidden, and invisible but always there on every path you think is clear, horizontal bars to climb over, vertical ones to pass between, piles of planks, sheets of metal, boxes, and a jumble of objects.

Suddenly: "Vor Alarm". As at Neuengamme, the search lights flash on and off three times, then after a minute, during which time we must get into ranks of five, counted by the vorarbeiter, everything goes dark. The sirens blast. Good, that means no more work. You have to run to the Arc Nord underground because the SS fear there may be escapes. In the dark, I run with Roger behind Pougault, without however getting too near to him. He is no longer in control of himself and strikes with his truncheon. Planes! He is frightened. Oh, if only they could bomb! "Gross Alarm" We run in single file across bench forms, placed over large black holes. I can hardly see where I am putting my feet. We are in the underground, narrow but very deep. No ventilator, I stay close to Rene. For in the crowd I could lose him and I like to stay as much as possible with a Frenchman. We can no longer hear anything and it is very hot here. Instinctively, everyone is lying down and I have put my cap in the only pocket of my trousers, for it is always at night that the Russians and the Poles, expert at thieving, help themselves! Finding nothing to steal from the others, they often steal amongst themselves. The ground is damp but I rest a little and doze. Some are crushed under others already asleep, worn out with fatigue. I am hit by pebbles thrown by I know not whom and hide my face against the ground. Some shout and complain- when it's a foreigner, I don't care and even hide a smile but unfortunately, I mostly hear Frenchmen. I remain powerless, making myself as small as possible to avoid the blows and don't move, even if I am walked on. Some dull thuds – that's good. Is if flak? Bombing? It doesn't matter. I forget everything, pray a little and then, in spite of the air which is getting thin, fall asleep. I try to sleep but with such a crowd, sweat is running into my eyes and it's so hot. Fearful, I listen to see if the alert is coming to an end, for that means Pougault and work.

No, nothing! If only this could last! At Neuengamme, I cursed the alerts which deprived us of precious moments of rest. Every night there were two or three and when by chance we had not been disturbed, we still didn't sleep, for we were on the lookout for the cry of "Vor Alarm" on which we had to get dressed.

In the dark, kicks and punches are exchanged. Brutes! More stones! Ah, end of alert. Yes that's it…. The prolonged siren call is significant but is nobody going to move? "Raus, ramous, los, los" Poor legs, poor stiff knees. We go out and the cold of the night grips me, freezes me. The cement bag is stuck to my skin! We have to run between the guards' hedge, placed at two metre intervals and whose guns are trained at waist height! I find my box and its load. It is still dark, everything is covered by frost and ice. Several men suddenly fall. Congestion …. I am shivering but by walking quickly, I am warmer but day isn't here yet. What a long night!

At last the soup. We eat outside. Everything is cold. My bowl is quite dirty but there is no water in which to wash it. What a worry this encumbering bowl is for us! I have already changed mine several times, for mine has been stolen or borrowed and not returned but I found another on the site. I am hungry but I'm cold and say nothing about it. Even when the work forces me to stop, I walk about, jump up and down, and move around to keep warm. I go to fetch a barrel which I have attached to the crane. My frozen fingers are bleeding from undoing the cursed cable full of steel splinters. No worker avoids the threats of the "Kranefuhrer" (Crane Manager)

2nd October. Maurice is well, Olivier too. Roger is having a bad time and is depressed. Yet, the war cannot go on! It must come to an end. All the foreigners are pessimistic and are already thinking about a winter in Germany. The Poles are almost glad, for they have noticed that several Frenchmen are missing from our tables. The other day, I chanced asking one of them about the general animosity they have for us. Here again, I noticed the propaganda of the German machine! "French, bad soldier, bad work man, eat a lot, dance a lot in Paris with women while we, in Danzig, in Warsaw, we were at war – you did nothing for us. Deutsche gut soldat, Franzouses nicht gut Kameraden". I did not press the point. Anyway, for us all, they are real Bosche, assassins and thieves.

Some of the old lags are just the prison throw-outs from Poland. Most have been in concentration camps for 2 or 3 years. They have suffered and are dazed by the ill treatment. Why are they so eager to kill the French by kicking them, starving them, making them work, beating them, even when they are not foremen or block leaders, or of the least rank whatever?

Throughout the hierarchy of Bremen-Farge, as at Neuengamme, homosexuality is everywhere. Every German, especially the Overseers, has his "floozy", with whom he sleeps every night and dances with on Sunday nights to the music of a screeching old fashioned gramophone which keeps us awake. These kids, which serve as women, are not kept short of food (which they steal from us) or of clothes, which they can take from our backs. Like the overseers, they have the right of life and death over us, are in good health, do not work, ever. It's often they are the ones who throw the soup and bread at the head of the receiver, according to the letter in the triangle of our registration number. They are the skivvies, the harlots of the kapos, they do their washing, repair their shoes, iron their suits, make cakes and are allowed to make a fire. They sidle up to the Polish civilians on the site and obtain bread or other things. Moreover, when the kapos are away, it is these degenerates who come to beat us and who give us the impression that they are the masters and we the inferiors. Polish, Huns, a race of lords cursed 100 times, 1000 times! We are not even allowed to answer back. One gesture, one word against them and it's death for us!

The Arc Nord kapos woman, the "tart" as we call her, with his crimped hair parted in the middle and topped with the traditional little black cap of the homos, caught me with the paper bag on my back. He started to shout, to howl like a madman while tearing my bag, crying: "Twenty five blows. Twenty five blows of the whip". I grit my teeth; count the lashes landing on my back and shoulders. He won't kill me this time.

I still work at night with the Marquis of Moustiers, remarkable for his endurance and optimism. He has changed his hat into a cocked one which gives him a dignified look; his worn flip flops do not prevent his heels from touching the frozen ground itself. I don't pity him, for the cold and misery makes you selfish. I am astonished that I don't even have a cold! My nose is constantly running and my eyes water involuntarily. I am sleepy, for the work is crippling, on these frozen nights during which we experience a change in temperature at least twice, when we go to the underground. Sometimes in the shadow of the framework, men remain hidden. If the kapo does not notice their disappearance, they lie down and go to sleep. If they don't die of cold, they will wake up again but if they are discovered, they are lost.

I have learnt from Maurice Clement about the death of my friends Fournier and Flesselle. Their parents will not know. What about us? Will we have the luck to live long enough to remember and to give them the news?

10th October. Roger, Andre and 4 others are ill with Bronchitis, Dysentery and Coughing. Those from Murat have no luck at all and bear many trials. They suffer as much from the lack of tobacco as from the deprivation of food. They mostly have no will and my heart stops when I see them looking for a cigarette to exchange for a piece of bread or some soup.

Three "Bregavas" or two "Amadis" for some soup at midday, five ordinary ones for a large crust. The Poles, bottle washers, vorarbeiters or stubedienst are the kings of the market for they always have cigarettes. Woe to the smoker who lets himself slide down this sad slope! Smoking drinking water, and not eating any more! He is in great danger of remaining in the sand heap. I shout at him:- "You must do something, but no, there's nothing to be done, it's "swapping sickness." You have children, a family, you want to get back to and yet you sell your soup, bread, your life, you are not a man." There is nothing to be done! It doesn't even touch him to say he's not a man and he pulls on the miserable cigarette of hay, smiling, happy!

He seems happy. I am disgusted, for I know that he won't get far. Dam the tobacco which kills. If by chance an SS throws down a stub on the site, all eyes are fixed on it. Fingers point to it, hands fight for it. Former teachers, lawyers, all that is dead. Only one instinct remains under the round striped cap. All, or almost all, ensure their supply in this way. How proud the Bosche must be "Would we all, French, Russian, Belgian and others have lost the ultimate battle, that of civilised man against the savage?"

Triumphant, cigarette end in his lips, my friend continues to push his barrow of sand in the search for another stub which could light up his.

4

Chapter 21: "ZEMENT KOLONN"

13th October. I am no longer on nights but have joined the famous "Zement Kolonn" (Cement column.) There are about 100 of us, divided into teams of six. I am with a colleague from Reims, Francis Lajoie, one from Bethune, Louis Vichery, Mirabelle, an old barber from Montelimar and two Russians.

The train to be unloaded is here. Each team has its wagon, and must pile up the bags in the dusty hanger, in which hangs, in a constant and cold swirl, a cloud of cement dust. Here again we have to run, barefoot with 50 kg on our shoulders, for each team has a man in command who hits and jostles us even when we are loaded. I fetch up against rails, always hold myself stiff so as not to fall with my unmanageable and accursed bag, which is as heavy as lead. It's a race for whoever finishes his wagon first and white, dirty from head to toe, dark ringed eyes, impregnated with Portland cement, right down to our sweat, nose full of dust, we have not a moment respite. The 15 tons are piled up under cover. Then we have to sweep and shovel up the cement which has spilled from torn bags. During this time, the empty wagons are taken away and replaced by others. Two full trains arrive each day at Arc Nord, which is why we are never finished. In the cement column there are however, certain advantages. We are out of the rain and at midday we have some soup and eat in a barracks hut, with seats to sit on. Thanks to Louis Vichery who is very robust, very good, a real father to me and I learn how to work.

20th October. I am used to my job as a cement worker. My clumsy bureaucrat's hands handle the sack like small loaves. Green as I was to the job, Louis has shown me how to work with the minimum of fatigue. I have little courage left, for I am disgusted at having to serve the Boches. The cement, the rain, wind, cold, hunger, all that makes me sad and in order to carry out my tasks, to not lose too much hope, I have to reason with myself, develop a real taste for the work, take up the bags forcefully and put them down with energy, carry them, pile them up. Today I am put on loading the trucks and platforms, 134 sacks to a truck, 400 to a platform! You have to hurry and always go faster, for here it is mostly German civilians in command. They are just as bad as the SS. With their 2 or 3 jackets, one on top of the other, they come to eat bread and dripping, under our noses and mouths full of grub, shout : "Arbeit, arbeit, los, andere Wagonne, viel arbeit hiet"

As soon as we have finished, the locomotive is there and goes away with the loaded train, then returns with an empty one. Not a moment's pause. Mirabelle is no longer in team 7 fortunately – he could never have kept going. He is outside and is putting the empty sacks into bundles. We come across him sometimes when we have to load trucks of paper in which the whole team disappears in a real cloud of dust. I am constantly blowing my nose full of dust into my hand, for German hygiene forbids the use of a handkerchief or rag. My hands and my back are covered with cuts, which, in contact with the cement, do not heal. I can always feel them burning. The paper bag next to my skin is still protecting me but I have to change it frequently as it is stolen from me. Every evening, after work and Roll call, we have to stand and wait for the train outside in spite of the wind, often for many hours.

There are many sick. The cold dampness is one of the main causes but it's our misfortune in general which contributes to illness. I envy Maurice, Roger, Joseph and all those who are lucky enough to be in the infirmary. Before going back to the bunker, when I feel able, I go to see them behind their windows. Maurice advises me not to stay in this unhealthy cement. I cannot tarry, for I am hungry. They have already eaten in the Revier. Chemical soup and the hotch potch of vegetables and wild fruit in vinegar. I am so hungry that the sight of such a meagre meal discourages me. Faces are sad. Some are even weeping. Maurice Bourdet worries me.

Olivier is still working in his iron commando but has been suffering from a cough for three days. His thinness makes him appear even taller. How he has changed. What about me? How do I look? I have not the time to think about it. "Zement Kollonne" Cement column, cries the big Pole who looks after the showers. I have to go. Jean looks after my clothes for it would mean 30 strokes of the whip to obtain rags from the shop. As every evening, I run to the cold showers, compulsory for the cement workers. Big Paul Legrand, from Dreux is amazing, for he is indefatigable and holding out well. I never manage to wash myself completely. My teeth chatter, for I am still sweating from my last run after the train stopped. The water is icy. Fortunately, the shower does not last long and I return to my heap of clothes, shivering like the others. Without being able to dry myself, I dress.

22nd October. I am still working at the cement but I can't go on. My hands and back are itching from the cement. The water and pus smell bad and the wounds become deeper instead of mending. During the "Ambulanz" (inspection) some black ointment was put on my back and legs with paper dressings which do not stay in place. It is Sunday; the kapos are drunk again, for they have managed to obtain white spirit in abundance from a German civilian.

When the cigarettes are given out, the Arbeitsdienst rushed into the ranks with a broom handle which he brandishes around his head. I just missed it but many fell under the blows, knocked out, and trampled on. At 11 o'clock, the head of Hut 8 "Alfred the Terrible", devoid of pity, teeth like fangs, seized my bowl from my belt while I was crossing the yard of the camp. It's now midday and I have no tin. I venture to the door of Hut 8 – my bowl is in the corner.

Heres the overseer recognises me because I don't have the same hat as his men. Before I have had time to think, he kicks me with all his force, in the stomach. Doubled over and winded, I withdraw without a word into the ranks of those with no tin, to await my turn.

On Sunday afternoon, I work at unloading the supply wagons. Olivier has volunteered to go out in the rain to work at the silos, to try and bring back a beetroot, at the risk of 50 strokes of the whip. Six hours work for a beetroot! What a miserable Sunday! On our return, we must go to the general shaving session which takes place every month. This time the French are the barbers and are allowed extra soup! This operation goes on all night, for you have to wait your turn and queue up in front of each specialist, as at Neuengamme.

Everything is done in the twilight. What a sight for the uninitiated! It really is the devil's parlour for after that, the inspection of the shaved men is done, there will be a show on stage in which striped thugs will show off their talent as violinists or pianists. Then the whining and raucous gramophone, with worn records, will prevent us from sleeping and throughout the night, the half naked Boches and Poles will dance.......

30th October. The days are getting shorter. In the morning it is still dark when we leave the base and in the evening, night has already fallen, when we come back, especially if there is a discrepancy in our numbers when a man is missing.

At the Revier, Maurice watches his ankle heal in despair. On my advice, he moves his dressing each day to delay his leaving. It is so cold and it is so hard outside. He has given me, under cover, two slices of toast. I didn't want them, for fear....but I'm so hungry. Will I be able to repay him one day?

I have succeeded in changing columns by playing the idiot during the morning assembly time. I pretended not to remember who my kapo was and after a few baton blows on my back, I was put into other ranks.

Every morning before departure, the farce begins again. As soon as I have been able to slip a paper bag under my suit, I pray fervently for a long time for a member of my family, a friend, a comrade, for my communist chum who doesn't know any prayers who says poems to himself. There is a general humming of invocations of all types. Many keep silent however and you don't know exactly what is going on behind those sad faces, lined, ill and aged, many bearing scars. Some faces have retained their dignity and one can guess at an eventful past from this wide and energetic chin, from that shaved head with no cap, delicate features. What is the point of thinking about all this? The blue lamps of the kapos are so weak in this darkness and flicker in the squall. In the cloying mud, we must leave once again for the base!

1st November. We really should think of the dead, for we will soon be joining them. The news is not good and in spite of frequent alerts, the end of the nightmare does not seem near and yet we are alive. The better vorarbeiters have become bad because the SS have given formal orders since the evasion attempts of a few Russians. How is it going to end?

I am in the Karl column. We are draining a peat mine. We have to shovel the mud into long boxes with handles. It takes 12 men to lift them. The rain has already torn my fragile bag but I dare not look for my body feels moulded into my damp and dirty pyjamas. We have to climb 50 m up a slippery and bumpy slope with our load, which is too heavy and badly balanced. My companions are Russians. They are strong, do not fear the work but they are clumsy. One of them is commanding. Dogouri, Dogouri. Heave! The planks crack and the whole mass comes away from the adhering mud. I slip, fall, rise again, the rain drenches me again and drops of water, which sweat has made salty, continually run into my eyes and mouth. An obstacle, a more violent gust of wind and we stop. Karl has seen us and bounds over with his leather belt in his hand. He too slips, loses his temper and vents it by whipping us in turn with all his might. Weiter, weiter, come on, carry on, repeats our friend Nicolai. Exhausted by the rain which washes over us again, we come to the top of the ravine and empty our box. The caked spade is heavy, so heavy. The peat which must then be removed, sticks to it like wax.

My back is so painful, that I grit my teeth and bite my lip to stop crying out. You must never show any weakness here, otherwise all is lost. This evening, in an hour maybe, where will I be? It seems as though we will remain in this cursed cold mud which comes up to our knees and under which I can no longer see my trouser legs. There are men of all ages with me but not one speaks French. Some are Latvians. They are having trouble too but say nothing. It is the same fight for all of us, we must live. You have to hold out by self motivation!

Karl, 15 years penal servitude, meaning 3 more to do, is completely insensitive and would like to kill us all. Interminable minutes in repulsive filth, our hands and faces are blackened, as though varnished and polished by the rain mixed with snow, which is falling almost horizontally. I feel I am alone but if I reflect on my situation, I frighten myself.

Bad luck for the man who is alone! There are days like that, rainy days mostly, when

I don't pray, when I don't recite poetry, when I relive a moment from my childhood, when I was quite small, there in the Nievre, how far away it is! There are days when I live just like an animal, as though I had only my instincts, as though my body was just a machine and my brain and heart somewhere else, departed, I know not where. There are days when life can be summarised in three words: work, sleep, eat. Days when I forget everything, even France, even myself. Those are black days, yet one must make an effort to feel something. I still have will enough to escape this withdrawal, this noose drawing closer and which is called despair. What will there be at the end of this episode?

Liberation? It seems as unlikely to me now that it's maybe absurd to think about it. Death is liberation too. You can at least sleep, it's not cold, you are not hungry or thirsty. You no longer thirst for water, wine, justice, equality, pity, pardon. You no longer thirst after anything which we lack here and which perhaps we will never have again!

What is in fact left to us, in these rags, soaked to tearing point but formerly striped? Have I not always been like this, in the mud, barefoot in the rain? There is a shelter there but we never go to it. How happy they must be in the cement column. They cannot fear getting wet in the hanger.

Night - at last! The Nachtif are already here. The Vor Alarm siren....

Chapter 22: BETTON KOLONN

3rd November. My career on the railways had not taught me what cement was and I had not the smallest idea of what the construction of a marine base could mean. Here I am finding out.

I also see the immense human folly, directed towards the same goal, war. Hundreds of thousands of men, most of them reduced to the former slavery of the pyramids, dispensing incalculable quantities of cement, iron, materials of all kinds, plus their energy, health, their life, in order to build a shelter for submarines, whereas we could be building so many houses for peace time!

So I now belong to the cement column. This, or any other they are all the same. My cement itching has healed and I don't care about the rest. I have a new friend, Fernand Loret, from Brionze in Normandy. We talk a great deal about his region and of Lisieux. He is a Catholic and we promise ourselves to go there together one day. We also talk a great deal about food, because his parents have a hotel. He dreams only of fried eggs and his great speciality Scallops St. Jacques and of butter, cheese, rolls, when he was a baker!

Fernand is younger than me. If only we would stay together! Today we are working on the dome, or more simply, up high. The wind and storm goes through us and takes our breath away. Below us in the Weser, on the left, the heaving mass of slaves. Here there is a veritable esplanade cluttered with huts, materials, bars and crossed by the hose pipes, coming up from below and bringing the cement under pressure to prepared frameworks.

What is a man on such a site? And all this for Germany! Engineers and marine officers meet here and survey our painful toiling. The pipes which are too heavy for our shoulders are nevertheless carried on a man's back, cleaned and fixed together. It goes on for hours, with no respite, in spite of our swollen hands, frozen feet, legs covered with undressed wounds, our fatigue and ever increasing weakness. Suddenly, in the middle of the work, and without knowing why, the kapo takes us away. Where? Below! This is the central area with the cement mixers. Same scenario as at the cement column. Everything is of 'Portland' colour but in addition, there is an agitated, troubling, irritating noise from the 8 or 10 monsters at work called cement mixers. We have to keep them supplied. We never go fast enough, for they are greedy and swallow up their 10 sacks at one mouthful, not to mention the barrows of sand

and gravel. We run after one another on the boards, often benches, from the trucks to the shed, after having climbed two flights of very narrow steps, one of 7, the other of 22 worn and rickety steps. These stairs are a real nightmare for us all because we have to hurry with our bags. Pougault all too often hits us and a Pole stands continually at the top of the steps to correct those who are slow.

We run around like madmen in a veritable merry-go-round. Some have tears in their eyes. The stronger ones, in a hurry to arrive with their loads, shout at the slow ones who keep them hanging around, for we must not overtake each other. Sometimes, my head is spinning and our silence, in the hell of the hydraulic machine striking loudly on metal, wears us down.

I hardly have the will to wipe my glasses. I am lucky to be one of the few who has been able to keep them with all the beatings. I am covered in sweat and can feel my heart beating rapidly, while climbing these cursed crumbling steps, so as not to annoy Fernand, who is behind me and above all to avoid being hit by the board in the hands of the Pole, who is always sniggering. You must be for ever on the move, going down empty, running, and coming up again loaded and stumbling, gathering together your last strength. If a civilian, a foreman or Inspector arrives (everybody is one or the other) the Poles and Germans start to shout, to speed us up: Weiter, weiter, weiter, weiter. (The steps, the steps again, be careful) Number 5 is not holding any more, be careful, be careful, the last but one is broken)

All this passes through my head in a twinkling. Then mechanically, I think about something else, my thoughts run astray. There is no doubt, I must have committed a crime but no longer recall it. I am paying for a mistake – which one? Are there others too? How much longer will this go on? Why not die now? At once? Why go on waiting, for there is no way out of this situation and behind us the cylinders full of stones and cement are still turning and the bags are still arriving on the same trucks, pulled by the same numbered machines and the strongest are still running, running, until the moment when a relief comes to take over, when they have died.

4th November. Jacques Parent from Nevers is working with me, in the rain. This morning, I saw Andre Chaumont and Mougin from the Vosges and the lawyer from Murat but for two days I have not been able to go near the infirmary where Roger, Maurice, Gabriel and others are. I know Maurice is well, although he is forbidden to get up. He is walking on purpose so as not to get better. In the "Revier," everyone must always remain lying down 24 hours of the day.

We are at the foot of the huge concrete pipes rising almost vertically up to the fantastic mass of the base. Yesterday, some pipes exploded, tons of concrete were thrown around and we have to break it up and remove the already hardened concrete. There are seven of us, each armed with a pick axe. All of the others, including Jacques Parent, are lucky enough to have a spade. Here there is no possible place to hide, no little corner, no screening materials to hide us from time to time, to escape from the eyes of the Polish spies and other overseers. They are always on the look out for the pleasure of shouting and hitting us if we speak, if we are not fast enough in plunging our 20 wobbling kilos into the already hardened mass, or if our colleagues do not load their spades enough. "Warum nicht arbeit? Warum langsam? Scheize Franzouses, alles Scheize" they shout again. At the risk of beating us down with a revolver if an SS is not far away and demands some explanation.

My back is so sore that at times I would like to roll on the ground but instinctively I take up my tool, move the lever and the bar which I must guide, with all my might, into the mass which finally gives way. When I stand up again, the frightening humming stops. I would dearly like to wait a minute or two before starting again but one must make some noise, always the same noise, otherwise the silence, the cause of my stopping, of my desired nonchalance, would alert the enemy. The incessant jolt of the tool goes right through my body, from my wrists down to my heels. My head aches and I feel not only a slave of men but also of this unstable, noisy and infernal machine. Even the SS almost count for nothing now in my mind..... I shall remember this "Beton Kolonne". Until evening, until night falls, until the arrival of the "Nachtig Kommando", in the light of the lamps, I have to hold this heavy and cumbersome tool which I am not used to. The concrete breaks away, spades shovel it up, trucks take it away and down there, the "Transport Kolonne" formed with Russians, Ukrainians, chaps who are never ill and built like tanks, take it to an immense furnace to be melted.

The soup was good and hot today, for the beetroot and swede were sufficiently cooked and I was among the first served.

Already it seems a long time ago. What remains of the soup in my griping stomach, which thinks of nothing more, waits for nothing more and hopes for nothing more than this evening crust. What will there be with the bread? The piece of margarine, as long as a finger and as thick as a schoolboy's small ruler, 25 to 30 grams, made from the distilled oil or fat which runs from the crematorium at Neuengamme? The small sliver of cheese, of "Kase" or substitute cheese? The round of red or white sausage with no meat, wrapped in paper to look like a tube? A spoonful of honey, also substitute but good, because it's sweet? (We've only had that once so far!) Don't let's conjecture. We will learn the menu from the night workers who will come to relieve us. We will know what colour the soup is beforehand, in the ranks for Roll call, on the train, it will be as if we can smell it, can taste it, remembering the taste of the last lot which had the same colour.

The last hours are more and more difficult and worrying because of the cold and the gusts of wind which bring drops of rain. For a long time, the rain has been running over my cap, down my forehead, down the lenses of my glasses (one of which is broken in the middle) down my cheeks, temple, filtering through my striped rags, seeping through the cement bag which serves as my shirt and I can feel it running down to my feet, down my legs on which my trousers are fixed like gaiters with wire to stop the tears. My new clogs, covered with canvas uppers are worn down at the heel and the right one is slashed down the middle but they protect me from the stones and I feel at an advantage over the poor soul wearing flip flops as I did for so long. I am searching for rags and pieces of canvas but I have only found 2 which I am wearing like Russian socks not to protect myself from the water but at least a little from the mud!

19.00 hours. The work is over. Roll call at the site. Just as long a wait! What interminable moments, in a full draught in the corner of the base, standing in ranks of 5. My teeth are chattering, for the work had kept me a bit warm and I can only see the rounded and damp backs of those in front of me. Some of them, as protection against the rain, have donned bags suitably folded in a cape shape on their heads, thus protecting their backs. It's a dangerous exercise but useful as long as it lasts. The paper becomes damp and lets in water but it still protects. We have already been counted 3 or 4 times! First by a Pole, then a Russian, then a Yugoslavian, a Belgian a Frenchman and even a man "without a letter" who is a German! The results do not tally. The German gets angry and in the rain, tears roughly at the cape-bags, as if he had only just noticed them, or as if they were the cause of the discrepancy. Some of them watch him stoically, defiantly but the kapos have come up and bang, bang on heads and shoulders. One innocent man receives a real thump on the back of his head, intended for the one behind him who ducked down. Overcome, he is supported by two neighbours, for during Roll call, you must be standing, head up, eyes fixed on the cap of the man in front! Whether your feet are wet or dry, we have to stand there, talking little because of the beatings but often thinking of many things, murmuring a prayer or simply thinking of the count, which is not correct, of the usual neighbour who is no longer there, either asleep, dead or maybe he has escaped, also thinking of the train which does not come and which will no doubt be late, like yesterday. Here it is, it's here, and we can hear the engine bell... No, wrong – it's a train belonging to the base.....

We are told to advance to the middle of the track, encumbered with stones and planks, I lose a clog. I find it again by feeling around, in spite of the jostling. One of my feet is quite grazed and already swollen by the cold and the fatigue. I am losing patience, limping and jumping around, trying to get back into my rank and avoid being seen. Others more unlucky, fall into holes full of water, trip over the beams and are jostled. The Russians take advantage of this to steal their bowls, pick their pockets, take their capes and this happens each time you are in darkness. We have hardly anything but a few, like Melin have knapsacks. You are very lucky, if like me, you still have caps, bowls and a rag with which to blow your nose, a small wooden or iron spoon, hidden in the lining of your jacket with a small piece of metal which can serve as a knife to spread the margarine or cut the piece of bread into slices. If I lose these things or if they are stolen from me, it will be an almost irreparable loss for me, for they represent the equivalent of a cigarette, a portion of bread and 2 or 3 helpings of soup at the bunker market which is held every evening and especially on Sunday: Brot, Cigarettes? Brot? Bandshube? Cigarettes are the only currency in the camp but as I often change kommandos or columns, I don't get many. It doesn't matter as I would not smoke them and when I have some, I give them either to Olivier Melin or to Maurice Clement. They get by with them and sometimes come to my aid. In theory, all trade is forbidden by the SS, the law and the orders which come from Neuengamme. Whipping and hanging punish delinquents caught in the act, just as they punish thieves. The Russians and Poles are masters of trickery, theft and trade. The worst threats have no effect. Defiant, arrogant, denying the evidence, when they are caught eating from your tin or cutting your pockets, the Russians and the Polish Jews get to you again as they try to clear themselves and go away to begin again further on, two minutes later.

The French are great buyers of cigarettes and bread. Some are always looking for swaps on the site, during transportation, in the huts – it's a veritable sickness. They live, only for that, think only of it. I cannot bear to see them and think that anyone who buys the bread from a poor bugger is an assassin. Sometimes, but rarely, it's the kapos who offer food in exchange for tobacco and then you can risk your cigarettes as they will always have enough soup, which they have already stolen from us!

At last, here's the train. A large train, since the sand trucks no longer go back and forth. In the cattle trucks, we are better off and warm. The Jerries get in with us and don't speak. Sometimes, the Russians intone a song in sombre and heavy voices which has a despairing sound to it. I can't understand the words but guess nevertheless that the song must have been one they sang when they were free, out there in Kiev or Leningrad.

I know some Russians from Stalingrad or Vladivostok but they don't speak the same language and have their own interpreters. At times, I sought the friendship of certain

Russians in spite of the strangeness of their language but such friendship was short. They are thieves at heart, many are stupid, imbeciles and have no more sense than kids in spite of their advanced age. Many are worse off than me, having lost everything – at Minsk or Dniepropatrowsk, their families and their homes. Some are learned men and even seem very intelligent to me. I talked to them secretly about Stalin or communism. Then I saw their faces smile and mistrustful, like someone who has committed a fault, they whispered to me "Soon they are coming, comrades". Of course, German is the only means of communicating with these men who are so different, so foreign, so far removed from us. In my opinion, the Russian is egotistic but when he says the word "comrade" one can feel the sincere spirit of cooperation which unites them in doing good, just as in doing bad. They belong in truth, to a great people, although a very different one. They are patriots.

Chapter 23: OUR DAILY LIFE

On arrival at the camp, we jump out into mud. The cold grips us. We are counted again and wait to leave until each vorarbeiter has said to his kapo the word which brings relief and heralds departure – "Stimmt".

Then we run to the camp, along the road with follows a large curve and which is always lit by search lights. "Alert at the base! Hoot hoot hoot hoot". Quickly the light goes out. After three flashes, we are in complete darkness, with wind, rain, mud, a general jostling with my clogs – which I have to drag along, with my feet bruised from the wire which holds my clogs together.

The SS have camouflaged pocket lamps and you can only see the edge of a glistening cape and shining boots. "In haken" the cry, "In haken". We go from rank to rank (hold each other's arm!) "In haken zu funf" and in fives. It's better, for I remain with Jacques Paren from Nevers and Maurice Treillen from Aigueperse but the Russians, Poles and some others don't obey and will not debase themselves by holding arms with a stranger! The rank disintegrates. I recognise the place, we turn to the left, another 400 metres and there are the silos. In spite of the rush, I feel strong which astonishes me after such a day, working so hard! In 10 minutes we will be inside and then we will get the bread and soup… And they say it will be good……then we'll sleep in spite of the wind.

Now, still holding arms, we move forward. In places, some of our ranks have become a band of zigzagging, fleeing men. The rain is pouring down and it's streaming lights up the darkness. On the edge of the road, blades of untidy and stunted heather wave continuously. The sick that must be carried, delay the groups-then comes the whip, the blows. Los, los! cries, moaning. I narrowly avoid some object, probably a stone, for they often throw them. The door! Everybody stops. We move forward and are counted, anzig, anzig. We go by in fives, the inspectors mark us off.

Wild disbanding! I can't carry on, Fernand and Jacques give me their spare bag for tomorrow – they always have one folded in their trousers. It's so precious. Goodnight, Sleep well. A cavalcade on the stairs and tumult of our cosmopolitan crowd, I can't yet face going to see Maurice tonight. I am exhausted. Still water on this cemented floor but it's good. I am at home, I am all in. I run to see if my blanket has been moved. It's OK but Jean no longer has his, nor his friend Guy.

I greet Olivier in Hut III and give him my jacket and bags before going to wash, torso naked which is the rule. Then I return, glistening but just as dirty and then he takes his turn. Everything is done quickly, automatically, by habit. Then it's time for the soup…It's steaming!

I run to wash my bowl, on the bottom of which I can still see my finger marks. Jean is already in the queue. I go behind him. The brown soup looks good and we are given a half-litre. Already, those who have been served take it carefully away and try a sip whilst walking. It's "red shorts" who is serving and he is reasonably fair. It's my turn! Slosh, I am served! It's filthy but I swallow it. With despair, I think, gone already! Now for the bread.

The slices are lined up on the board of the Head of the Table. The crusts and bigger pieces are on one side in order of size. (Table 5). "Brot essen" cries the little Pole in charge of distribution, his sheaf of numbers in his hand. He calls us in German and I act as interpreter for the French and especially for the poor Breton, ignorant, frightened and stammering. I pity him, he is getting visibly thinner, too!

Of course, we receive the smallest share, the thinnest pieces, with a little piece of cheese, and gelatine. An infamous child's "tea time". Slowly, Olivier arrives at Hut I, hardly biting his cheese – as if he was afraid to touch it, as though keeping some for tomorrow. My piece of bread is small but I think his is even more meagre.

All right then?

Yes

Any news?

It's taking its course, but it's long!

Jean Faugaret is there and joins in our conversation without preamble. We are all brothers here.

It's long, long, too long!

His final 'too long' hides a real anxiousness, a doubt, a feeling even of unbelief in an imminent end. "They are fighting in France but will the Boche give in?"

There is the Siegfried line…… Oh, don't let's be pessimistic!

Lucien Poulet, from Hut 4 comes over, shakes hands and says:

"Anyone selling depression here"?

Being optimistic is all very fine but we need facts, results. Life has not changed here and I believe we must reckon on the end of December

You can stay if you like, but we are leaving!

Let's go to bed, I've had it. Goodnight!

5th November. I share a bed with Jean. He has funny habits! He prefers to eat in bed – to savour his food!

I point out to him that eating that way; he is taking in all the dust falling from the bed above. He insists. It's Sunday but we get up at the same time, i.e. about 3.30 or 4.00, after the bell has been rung by the BA/4 and amid the deafening rumbling of the ventilator intended to renew the air made fetid by the breathing of thousands of men. No water? Why not? We don't know. Chosen yesterday by the head of the table for the "Cafee Hol", I run to the kitchens with the elderly Breton. It's cold this morning!

In the huge red boilers, with lids half severed, I can see the soup ready for lunch – cabbage and potato. It will be good but there will be less of it. There are the flasks of coffee. Ours. We go back. I reduce speed, for I can sense my companion is tiring. In front of us, a "Kesse" has just tipped over and the 70 litres of steaming juice, falls down the stairs to the bottom of the bunker, accompanied by shouts and a general commotion – the whip again! It is not much of a loss but it was something hot. It is my hut which will go short! This morning, with the 150 g of bread, we are allowed a spoonful of sugared beetroot jam. It's good. The heads, in front of us, cut off the rounds and make red slices. They are gorging themselves. Their leek does not inspire pity though.

Not all the kommandos work. It's a question of luck. In any case, there are always camp fatigues, if you don't go to the base. The Poles and the Germans know which kommandos are chosen, which is why they almost always escape. Just like every morning, some catch chills because of the cold and wind which blows on top of the dune. Those who fall are lined up before us, on the mud, after receiving a bevy of blows or kicks, because according to the heads, they are shamming. How many times have I seen epileptics having an attack, killed in that way, believed to be feigning. Any moment we expect an order, to cripple us and increase our misery...

Aus zeichen. Clothes off for inspection. This is to see if you are hiding a paper bag or a jacket too many, of if you are wearing 2 pairs of trousers, hiding a knife, or weapons even! They are frightened of us, for several times they warn us that any revolt will be put down and that we must not be encouraged by outside rumours that look bad for them! Half naked, in the darkness, hardly lit by the kapo's lamps and police, I go for inspection but I'm not searched because, in passing, I murmur a few words of Polish, which always saves me in these sad moments. The inspector has not seen that I am French!

At midday, it's the "Tobre soups" from Sunday - but how little there is. It is excellent, for it tastes of meat and even contains some flour but there's not much of it. Just to give us an appetite and then it's gone. I am so hungry and we must return to the camp on foot because Sunday evening is reserved for shaving, cigarette distribution, theatre entertainment, selections for transport etc.…. Perhaps we will be able to sleep a little longer. It's hardly likely though. I have been to see the sick. Maurice is well. What a lucky chap! I have never gone near the window of the contagious cases, the tuberculosis dysentery cases – in any case, they cannot get up!

11th November. Still no change. I was able to read l'Echo de Nancy! Some civilian French workers had given it to one of us. V1's on London, German counter attacks. Our men are advancing then? I read between the lines. Although allowed to the civilians, this paper, if confiscated, would cost us dearly. It will serve to roll a few cigarettes!

15th November. Ein weg, ein weg. A Russian has gone. Where? Gone! The patrolling sentries exchange conventional signals, the kapos search the base with dogs, an operation which goes on for hours, during which we become chilled because of the cold air and being immobile. They'll not find him again!!

17th November. At Bremen, a Russian escapee is recaptured and has been hung. We don't believe it, because an escaped prisoner is always taken back to the prison he absconded from, even if he's only a bloody rag, with pieces of flesh torn by the Alsatians. I am working in the Tadek column with Maurice Bourdet, Maurice Traillow, Fernand Lorrel, Gaston Linier, Brassaidlly and Dimitriany a Greek student from Athens, transporting sheets of framework, before assembly or after disassembly and carrying iron bars for the concrete dome of the base. It's hard work, dangerous, fatal. To get there you have to climb up 7 flights of 30 steps, each in spite of the wind and the rain, of being above the Weiser, black and choppy and often crossed by steam boats and submarines. Often, you have to balance on narrow iron beams above the void and in our slippery clogs!

Two civilians, a Pole and Jerry are in command. They are terrible. Booted, gloved, leather jackets lined with fur, big velvet trousers, they smoke non stop and command 14 men per shift: "Ho hoch, ho hoch". Raise to shoulder height, advance, stop, backwards, on the ground. As not all of the team members speak German, there is confusion worthy of the Tower of Babel. Often, some who don't understand, pull when they should push, let go when they should hold on. The Overseers then indulge to their hearts' delight in hitting the innocent man who has not understood. Cut fingers, broken arms, or dislocated shoulders are frequent and the infirmary for the base is 2 km away…

The German, the "Pawler" as he is called, lay into the French. "Franzouses, Paris gut, Deutschland gut auch" He has started an entertainment for us. "Nur sieben" he cries. Seven only on each plank. Why seven, when the others are fourteen? We have to walk. Placing it on our shoulders almost breaks our backs and we have to cross a whole site encumbered with various materials. As for unloading, each time is a source of cries and insults. I am tired both mentally and physically, clumsiness, muddle and misunderstanding in the job, the blasting of the Jerry and his frequent threats. "Alles kaput" he often says and makes the action of pulling a trigger.

Maurice Bourdet is in difficulty as he is not strong. He never speaks about his weakness and thinks only of going home. He makes various plans for radio programmes with several of us who he will ask to speak into a microphone. He never has any luck, for he is too good and is not careful enough. He never has anything; all that he has is taken without him even noticing. The Russians are good at that! He says nothing but he is getting visibly thinner. He is in my team at the iron bars and I take the opportunity to talk to him, for although he sleeps not far from me in Hut 1, we are too tired to talk in the evenings. Here, when we can, it passes the time. He talks to me of the Resistance and it reminds me of the good times, gives me courage. We talk of Radio London, of Radio Belgium too. But alas, we are here in a concentration camp! The rusting bars of all sizes and bent and twisted into different shapes, are brought in by hand or on their shoulders, to the place for fixing, which is above the void between the enormous I-shaped beams, Careful! One shake, one wrong step, a loss of balance and you fall; below the emptiness full of tracks, wagons, locomotives, which ply up and down, cross each other, follow each other, with noise and smoke. The wind blows with incredible force and nothing protects us from it. The cold rain goes through me. The immensity of the job frightens me and I see veritable bunches of men suspended in the grey sky behind the bars of one of the pillars of Arc-Nord under construction, like animals in a cage. How can they hold on? Suddenly, vertigo or clumsiness grip hold of a striped man and he disappears. "Help!" That cry still rings in my ears. I did not recognise it, but it was a fellow countryman. Down below, I saw him crash down then ricochet in a ball and fall, limbs splayed out, flattened. I still tremble from it. The removal team from "Germania" takes charge and take the body away on a stretcher to the crematorium lorry.

18th November. A transport of sick has left for Neuengamme, where there is talk of black transport to the experiments, or other things. Maurice has gone. Another is already in his place. There are too many in the sick room beds. At 250, the Revier is at capacity and they are two or three to each 80 cm bunk. The departure has got rid of some but the general state of health is worsening with the bad weather and the bread which has become a paste, often mouldy. The pumpkins and the herbal conserve which burns the stomach with the mussels in mustard, which the Poles will not try. In each block, a German poster announces that inspections will only take

117

place twice a week and at fixed times.

24tth November. Roger, Andre, Olivier are in the Revier. I feel very weak. During the night I go to urinate up to ten times in a row. Lice are continually eating me up. I cannot rid myself of this curse. There are mice in the mattresses at the bunker and there is even a nest of them above my head, in which they are continually scratching. I don't disturb them, for I sleep alone since Jean left. I have no blanket any more and I lay on the boards themselves, under the mattress, my bowl upside-down under my head. Maurice Boudet, now ill, sleeps with me, under his half of a blanket. His teeth are chattering. They have kicked him so much this afternoon! The rain and the cursed wind! Fortunately there will be an ambulance call tomorrow evening and he has decided to go. He had kept a small piece of bread but the mice have got through his pocket and carried it off!

The general inspection of cleanliness is announced. We are forced to wash all over in ice-cold water. We are treated like pigs. I help Maurice who is very dirty, but weak and with a bad cold. The Germans mock us and root out the unruly with a torrent of words. Culture, Discipline. What a job to get out of rags held together by pieces of wire and then put everything back on again. All abuse mostly takes place at night because in the daytime, we are at the base. We fall asleep and suddenly the announcement "Blok Roll call, aufstehen aufstehen.

Already shattered, tears in our eyes, we crawl slowly from our boards. What is it? Inspection? Transport? Wo? Warum? All of us file past the SS doctor and the Pole. The thinnest of the men, the Muslims as they are called, are kept back. I stay, Maurice Boudet too! Although I'm not a pretty sight "Still too fat, not a Muslim, yet" is said as we pass by. "Gendarme" is kept back. I let fate take its course. Neuengamme, Bremen-Farge? The crematory oven? Experiments or the pile of sand? I would as soon stay in the small wood.

27th November. Maurice Boudet is at the Revier, in the contagious cases ward. He just had time to let me read his little book "The New Testament" – How did he get it? What a treasure here!

28th November. A Russian has been caught with a pullover and a civilian waistcoat under his jacket. Condemned to carry a beam beyond the limit, he was beaten down by the SS Feldwebel. Another, arriving too late for Roll call and accused of attempting to escape is tied to a table and given 50 strokes before lights out, letting out small sharp cries. Then the Russians have to file past, on tip-toe with arms outstretched one by one in front of a box in which one of their number is doubtless dead, while the other (the whipped man) remains sprawled over the table throughout the night.

29th November. A Frenchman, who had been making a knife secretly, is shot. A special authorisation is needed to go to the WC (a small green card signed by the vorarbeiter, which must be handed back afterwards) Ten minutes break, rest even, in the morning and evening but that's all. Too bad if you have dysentery! A Yugoslav was caught in the WC with no official papers. The German guard with green triangle, continually patrolling in front of the "Abort" notice, is there in fact to keep order and to send back the malingerers who remain more than 5 minutes seated on the piece of wood, or who chat amongst themselves on the military situation, on gastronomic matters, or just talk! The Slav was therefore called at midday and on tip-toe, arms in the air, legs bent, had to watch from the top of an iron tub all the others eating without him, while his soup was on the ground, steaming and getting cold in his bowl.

30th November. Reception of a crane. Still on the dome, I am working with Italian and Belgian P.O.W's. The bars arrive non-stop. My shoulders are torn and the rust has completely changed the colour of my clothes. From the shade of one's outfit, we can say — this one's working on cement, that one's on iron, he's a painter on the framework etc.

I don't like the Italians, although they are not unpleasant and it makes a change from hearing Jerry talk. Better than that! We come down to speaking German, even among Frenchmen, even among friends, as though we were already germanised. Fortunately, we have an F on our chests, an F which some were crafty enough to change into a P in order to obtain more soup!

December. The soup is more and more disgusting. Sometimes I don't eat it and give it to Olivier Melin or Jean Faugeres. I have got thinner. I can feel a hollow in my cheeks but do not have a mirror to chart its progress. My arms are so thin that I am astonished they can still do such work! I can feel my ribs, and my legs and back hurt so much that in the morning I can hardly walk.

With Fernand, who is wearing a week-old beard and who continually shrugs his shoulders to stop the cold in his back, we go about like hunted animals, no vertigo at several metres above the void, not speaking, carrying loads which are too heavy. Will they know of all this one day at home? No, they must think that we are dead. That is better. How lucky are the maquisards and the soldiers who die in an instant, weapons in their hands. Here one must live with the enemy, work for him, make weapons to be used against ourselves, against this France which the little F in the red triangle symbolises.

Up to now, what have I done? Nothing, or so little! Have I had a good life? I still have so much to do. Isn't that so, Fernand? We still have so much to see. I'm 22 years old! Is this life of forced labour to be our only future? No, we must just hold on. Pessimistic? Optimistic? We must hold on and therefore pray and think - think that people are praying for us back home. Think that they are free, that they go to the bakers and buy large loves and cakes and that General de Gaulle is building the France of tomorrow and that our Army is coming nearer.

The Germans may be strong but hundreds of thousands fell each day on all the fronts. It's us, those who are condemned to death who will survive. For no reason, we are sent from one end of the site to the other to look for something which can't be found, a tool which we will do without, or to keep the conveyor built to the sand machine supplied.

For the first time, the French have obtained a semblance of justice on the bread distribution. We have crusts and large pieces in turn. Thus, when two teams cross each other, one often hears "Who's on crusts?" "Me soon, or this evening?"

Constantly, the thought of a transport obsesses us. I don't know where the rumour is coming from. The Germans are good at the war of nerves. They even wage that one in the concentration camps. At Neuengamme, it was via the loud speaker of the hut that one received orders and news, but here, we are tipped off by whispers in one's ear! "The sick are going to the hospitals, where they are cared for" but be careful, don't say you are weak, otherwise you will be sent back to Neuengamme where they are doing experiments."

I am on the watch and with my friends, turn a deaf ear to the Frenchmen that we don't know. Some are sneaks. The other day, all of the French contingent had to march past before the SS, camp leaders, overseers at the base. Two were recognised and accused of having cut some wires. They were not seen again!

Yesterday, two Russians who tried to escape were betrayed for some soup by a 12-year-old little white Russian. The SS, NCO discharged his revolver on them in a barracks hut but returning some time later and finding that one of them was only injured, he ordered the Polish doctor to give him an injection. The latter refused, stating that he was not a murderer but a doctor. The NCO finished off the poor Russian. Olivier has had two days rest and then returned to work, to his same commando. He is still much hungrier than me and each time we are near the silos and the trucks of cabbage, carrots, beetroots and potatoes, he joins in the general rush, in spite of the beatings from gun butts, baton blows and sometimes shots. The kapos make us do a detour now but the attacks continue and often a Russian will prefer to be killed on the spot rather than relinquish the beetroot captured with great difficulty.

This Pole, damned Pole, what have I done to him? Why that kick? Why does he spit in my face? He's just a boy and it's better not to answer him for there would be 3, 4, 10 of them coming at me with punches and I have not got sufficient strength. Why do they all pray before they eat? Why these signs of the cross on their brutish foreheads, since this same hand robs us of our bread or our spoon if our back is turned. At night, it will withdraw from under the mattress with an iron hook, jacket, trousers, rags and clogs, without waking you up. The Russians are good at that. They even steal from the kapos, even the cigarettes from the pocket of the camp leader and without being seen the thieves disperse among us with their booty.

One morning, everything was taken from me and I had on my back only the rag which had been my shirt. I could have cried but pulled myself together and received the 15 whip lashes, necessary to obtain flip flops and pyjama suit. We won't mention the bowl and in any case, no one has one in the Spider column. The tall Jerry pours 10 ladles full of sauerkraut into a pail and it's every man for himself. Ten men, no spoons, it doesn't matter. We are hungry. Hands and mouth are not tired but it's boiling and kneeling on the ground, mouths full of dribble, sauerkraut running down their chins, the Russians swallow noisily, jostling the others. The bucket is already empty and the French who were at the back have not tasted anything!

There is a fire in the kapo's hut but it's rare that we can go near the welcoming flame to get warm. The shelter (made of daub) with no window, does not protect us from the huge draught. Some stayed outside in the snow. At the end of the service, there are pieces of ice around the buckets and bottles. This is a desert for starving men who lick them with their tongue, or pull them off with their dirty fingers, made blue with the cold.

Some at the site suddenly start to cough, to bleed from the nose and to spit up blood. They go on working for an hour at a significantly slower pace, then leaning on a spade, back bent over, head low down on their shoulders, they collapse with their tools. It's over for them, or almost. They will go to die at the Revier, if they can keep going to this evening. Pneumonia, pleurisy, tuberculosis, or just sheer misery. Maurice Bourdet is dead. The SS doctor wrote galloping consumption as a diagnosis. I did not think that kicks could produce that. He was reading the gospel when he breathed his last breath but nobody could go near him, not even his great friend and confidant, Roger Clarence. Alas, all the plans, all our common hopes have evaporated. It's sad news which goes round the huts and each Frenchman feels affected by this death. Thus the survivors live on with the memory of their comrades.

Winter is here with its snow. The Marquis de Moustiers is no longer listened to. I like him a lot though and he seems so convinced of his strategy and then, while talking of that, one doesn't think of anything else. It's so difficult to begin a new month, a week, a day, with the cold as enemy number 1. Isolation too, saps the morale. Parcels, letters, we will never receive any. The Boches though have some and receive large loaves, sometimes throwing us the mouldy crumbs. I sometimes get an onion too, a piece of sugar, an apple peeling. It's not often but, when it happens, morale which had sunk very low, goes up to its maximum.

Once, while unrolling a thick cable, several metres long and finding myself at the end of it with a Pole, I was practically taken away from all surveillance next to a hedge bordering a garden. Suddenly, in the air were 1, 2, 3 apples. One fell in the hedge and I caught two. I gave one to the Pole and ate the other. Never had an apple tasted so good and so juicy! I wanted to thank the generous hand but only saw an old woman who tried to hide herself.

Just as in Spider column, the Germans sometimes made us work in a violent draught which blows under the base. Transport full of huge masses of iron, steel sheets and enormous grills which need 50 men to carry them. Trucks, cranes, axle-cranes, we go from one to the other. Nothing is done to avoid accidents, in fact, quite the contrary! We set up a floor with trays in order to walk over the void, without feeling vertigo. We go over, one, twice, 50 times, then suddenly on coming back, notice that the planks have been removed and that only the beams 50 cm apart, remain. A moment's distraction or weakness and you could fall. Especially for me, short-sighted since the Russian kapo broke my glasses in my face. I am in a fog, half blinded now, discerning nothing in detail, mistaking a hole for a plank, not seeing the stones. I hate him to death that Russian. Nazatt, Nazatt, he cries behind him and Karacho, it's OK when the load has arrived safely.

The snowy drizzle continues to go through me. Fernand Lorret is sad. How good it must be by the fire! Does it still exist? It's such a long time since we knew warmth. When friends fall, it is forbidden to pick them up. Besides, one has neither the time nor the strength, or the courage to help them. Cold hardens the heart and makes you selfish. The civilian workers may well have lit fires here and there but it's the death penalty for anyone who goes near them. Sometimes, however, going past with bars, I can feel the heat coming to me and it does me good! One day I was even able to stop, under cover of darkness, by a stove pipe in which a fire was beginning to go out. I warmed my hands and looked for pieces of wood. I only found a pot of engine grease. Nobody saw me and whoosh, into the fire went the grease.

I was already far away with the bar, when a cloud of black smoke rose up with flames. I went back to warm myself with Fernard and others but the kapo saw the ruse and we went no further. We were however, warmed a little by looking at it!

It was there too, with the Germans, that I worked on the oxyacetylene cutting torch and the electric arc to install central heating but I didn't stay there.

Olivier is still on peeling. What a lucky chap! Roger Clarence is there, very tired and still feverish from his pneumonia. He is pale and has his ankle bandaged with a white paper dressing, already dirty and torn. I am surprised at not yet being ill but something tells me to play at being ill, before being really so. Roger's explanations about the Revier do nothing to reassure me about the care. What could I pretend to have? Epilepsy? They could kill me on the spot! Pleurisy, pneumonia? You need to have a fever of 39 or 38.5 degrees. Temperature is taken under the arm, in the morning – outside. I'll try to have oedema – they say it doesn't hurt and you are admitted at once. For two days, I have absorbed a large quantity of salt water but only got indigestion!!

Neither will inflammation have anything to do with me! Yet it's the perfect illness and you are admitted at once, Roger tells me. How do you get inflammation? It's so frequent here, with the boils. I still have a wound on my leg. I attached some potato peelings firmly to it, the moist part against the hurt. I would be hung if caught but I put the dressing on at night, under the blanket. It has no effect! I no longer want to work, for I can't carry on any more. Something must be done quickly otherwise the work at the base will kill me.

I still hesitate at getting my foot crushed under a truck. I do not have enough courage for that. I know that wounds are well thought of, so I try my luck one evening coming back from Germania and collapse in the mud. Someone tramples over me. I do not move. The Rumanian vorarbeiter is behind me. Suddenly, he catches hold of me, puts me on his back and carries me to the hut where inspection has begun. I took a big risk. My clothes are torn off. It is warm here. The Polish doctor listens to my heart and says to his clerk – "block scheunung, vier tage" Another man is giving injections. I am sent back to the hut with my little paper carrying my admittance number for "vier Tage" and the date. I put it carefully in my little round iron box. If I lose it or if it is stolen, I will have to go to work.

It even happens that in the morning, the arbeiterdienst to whom one shows one's "Kartoffens" tears it up and then one has nothing! All must then be postponed until the next visit, if you can keep going until then! That's why I have been careful and even with my most intimate friends, I play up a bit. Even so, I am aware of my weakness. Also, we had been given a striped winter coat, thicker than the pyjamas. One day, for no reason, they were taken away again. The overseers want for nothing. Some have 3 or 4 pullovers, one on top of the other.

Chapter 24: BLOK SCHEUNUNG

At last I can stay in the camp. I will be under cover while the commandos are departing, but you have to stay there in the snow! And nobody bothers about us. Three times we have had to show our papers and the Kapo has left us. Some are more to be pitied than me; their wicked coughs are painful to listen to.

At last we moved forward. Some are rushing. Why? Then I understand, there are only 5 benches in the rest hut and there are 100 of us patients. I came across Roger and Fernand. There are tables covered in strange debris. What is it? Brush wood: We have to make brooms! "Rest hut" we had been told. That's the rest, making brooms! Standing or sitting and with no fire in a cement and wooden hut. Is that all, only this? Hands feverish and trembling, the sick take hold of the blades of heather to be assembled. Output is certainly meagre for as soon as a broom has been made, it comes undone and one has to begin again... for 12 hours! We seldom speak, especially when the kapos are there. At last, I think they are going to light a fire. They brought a stove – yes, we have a fire! Just the thought of the flames warms me. But the stove is a long way away and one may not go near it: the German guard is terrible and kills without reason. He is called 'mad' Alfred. He takes it out especially on the French and the Greeks; he has already nearly killed me by kicking me in the stomach. He has his own domestics who cook him potatoes and carrots. It smells good. Sometimes, to amuse himself, he throws us one, causing a melee and a general jostling. Tables are turned over, patients hit each other, shout out 'my foot!' ,'my ankle!', 'my head!', 'my swelling', 'my boils!' Then the Boches run into the midst of you, trampling over everything which is a dressing or a wound, batter a leg which is swollen with oedema, squash a hand which is already black and blue from a inflammation or other illness. Cries, howls in answer, blows, fainting fits, bleeding, weeping wounds...it's a horror!

Sometimes, all is silent. Nevertheless, one converses in a low voice, from the most serious subjects to the most futile. Some talk about literature, cinema, theatre. Some are content to compose the most fantastic menus and write them down. Thus an ex-officer, a lawyer and a businessmen exchange recipes, the way to make a cream, a flan, a rum baba! Some have little notebooks and write it all down along with friend's addresses or French firms renowned for a certain nougat or gingerbread. It makes my mouth water to recollect and often, not content with making detailed explanations; some go even further with their cynicism! "What are we having today? Byrrh-cass? Port? Cognac?"

About 10 in the morning there is a good chore, well paid: double the soup ration, third of a loaf of bread, etc. It is to bury the dead. I do not move. Some go – the less weak and starving. 11 o'clock – the burial. There is no crematorium at Bremen-Farge. It is snowing and a white lace covers the barbed wire fence. The watch tower is completely white too, the guards, "Les Posten" strike the frozen ground with their hobnail boots. The team of workmen goes by with spades or pikes. Then comes the great convoy – a huge stretcher carried by four men. On the stretcher lays a huge mass in a bag. I cannot see clearly. Other diggers… a lump rises in my throat – so that's where they end up! All those that are missing, all those that die like that – my friends! Is this my fate too?

There is an eerie silence in the hut, both from respect for those that are passing away and those that have already passed away, yesterday and all of the other days, those one has known and strangers alike. The last green capes of the SS and their guns disappear to the left, behind the barbed wire, in a flurry of snow. Everything becomes quiet again. I look at all the heads bent over the heather and pity them. Some tremble and shiver through the cold whilst others are sunk into their shoulders, almost a protection from danger.

Four days rest and then what? I was able to have three frozen potatoes. It was a lot of trouble to cook them but what a delight, a real nectar. That cost me two blows for going near the stove but now I am warm again.

Roger, Frenand and I try not to be separated by the madman, for he is, at times, quite crazy. As soon as he finds himself a victim, he amuses himself by making him suffer, dipping his head into a pail of water, making him undress, wetting his clothes then throwing him outside, naked, in the snow. Then suddenly he lays into everyone forbidding us access to the toilet, even to those of us with diarrhoea. He is not interested in the brooms but he gets the idea of taking us with some 'posten' two kilometres away, in the snow, to look for twigs. Too bad for the man who cannot walk because of an infection; the feverish do not have feet that hurt and must help him. A little Russian, covered in red marks and continually sniffing back mucus which runs into his mouth, amuses himself too at giving kicks and jostling those who cannot stand. The walk is a nightmare for some and they miss the base. They were beaten less there.

Sometimes, out of fantasy or for no good reason, when it is snowing or when the wind is stronger, he cries "Mutzen ab." Take off your caps. For me it is done quickly but woe for those who have dressings, rags on their heads for they have to take them all off. One expects to see an SS chief arrive but he bursts out laughing and nobody comes. If, without thinking, I put a hand in my pocket, he bombards me with pieces of ice or snowballs, crying – "Raus die Tasche, hand raus die Tasche!" Hands out of your pockets.

We return and wait until evening. The madman is resting, dozing on his stool near the little stove in which the fire has gone out. No-one speaks any more, each keeps his misery to himself. You no longer even confide in your best friend, for we know that even if he does not have the same illness, he is suffering just as much.

What calm there is here, whereas at the base, our friends are in the white storm.... Here one can only hear a lugubrious noise, just the wind blowing from everywhere as if it wanted to take away the hut. I plunge therefore, into a deep examination of my conscience, trying to discover the fault we might have committed, me, my ancestors, my friends, this poor Greek, killed by the madman and even the chap from the Midi who has two swellings and who is here for black market activities on the demarcation line. Outside the sentry is still there and further off in the country, it is snowing – the underground reservoirs are invisible, although very near. Opposite, a few metres away, the placard "Warning: 6000 volts."

Chapter 25: CHRISTMAS

We have been thinking about it for weeks, speaking about it for months. No Christmas at Bremen Farge of course but there will be in France, among families. Christmas has come and in spite of the hopes, the "official" news, the surest grapevine, we are still here. We still work and the food is no better. Germany is having a ball! We have been promised three days rest, plenty of soup, sweetened half a loaf, a litre of beer and there are barrels with no label in the commando cellar!

The day, so long awaited has come. Our whole bodies have been shaved, in spite of the cold. We were given a small square of slate, called soap. On the base, there is a huge Christmas tree. Lit up at night and showing a swastika. In the huts and in the bunker, there are large green fir trees covered in tinsel but with no sweets, no barley sugar, no toys as in France, without even the half loaf we had been promised. The slices are just as thin as usual and the soup just as plain, with maybe a little more flour and a few noodles, not even equal to that famous white soup which we had once, on a Wednesday. Sweet, flavoured with vanilla and which made me dream so many times!

Instead of rest, we transported rails and planks which had to be prised up from the frozen ground and from the snow. We are alone at the base. The concrete mixers, the cranes, the sledge hammers are all silent. An immense sadness seemed to strangle my throat and I wept for a long while, because it was Christmas, because it was cold, because I was hungry and my friends a long way away from me. I feel so lonely. Yet the Russians, Germans and Greeks sang hymns throughout Christmas night. There was after all a ration of beer at midnight – a friend told me about it.

25th December. We get up later but we are going to work, at least some of us. At midday, the soup is good but we only get a litre. Two Germans have received a parcel and have placed it in their locked box. Seeing me, they come over. One tall, fat, full of strength, a former criminal, tattooed with the words "Keine Sonne" (No sun), the other, a thief with a naked woman on his chest surmounted by the three words "Meine erste Liebe" (My first love). They ask each other: "Should we give him some?" "Jawohl" They hand me a crust and some meat pate. Surprised, I thank them as best I can, but they move away as though embarrassed. I cannot get over it. Is it a present from God, given by the hand of a thief on the assent of a murderer? This gesture touches me. There are still good men around, even among the castigated!

The evening soup is not plentiful but very thick. It quickly disappears. That's why we make a circle around the flasks awaiting the Polish cleaners. Some are not empty and are still steaming. What a sad spectacle are these famished eyes and especially this van and useless waiting, caused by a disappointed Christmas. Christmas at Bremen Farge!

26th December. I have dysentery. Have I eaten too many peelings? I had told myself I wouldn't have any more but I am so hungry. Yet one risks being shot for searching among the barrels of rubbish behind the kitchen. The skins are wiped a little and I return furtively to the bunker to nibble this extra food, on my mattress. Sometimes when the overseers are asleep, we wash them, for Maurice Clement warned me that the kapo of the kitchens had the rubbish trampled on by the little Russians and that they spat on it and even defecated on it. As the water here is not drinkable and those who drink it become ill, I abstain from drinking.

28th December. It can't go on much longer. The days are long, endless. I feel drained of all the energy I had left, plus the gnawing in your belly, of which you are no longer in control! A time of sickness is beginning, nothing can be done and the colder it is, the worse it is. At the inspection, nothing was said to me – only "Kein soup, kein kaffe, kein wasser, kein margarine" What am I to eat then? Today the soup is so good, with carrots, I cannot leave it. The starving waited for my bowl, thinking I would give it to them. How many have I seen like that, profiting from the sickness of others for a short while, until one fine day, the curse grips them too, twists their bellies, empties them and transforms them into skeletons. They are accepted into the Revier and do not come out again. All that is just as much the result of the last mouthful as of all the soups, the peelings, all the horse-chestnut coffee, cucumbers, pumpkins, mustard and other filth of which they are sometimes so generous.

30th December. I still hoped that a transport, any transport, would take me away from Farge, for I know why we are so impoverished as regards clothing and medical supplies. All the stock comes from Hamburg, from Neuengamme and since they certainly don't have enough there, we receive nothing. I go back to the inspection and wait one hour, two hours, among the sick, in this small square room where there is not room for 10 men and where there are about 50 of us, some lying on the ground, others trembling, leaning against the walls. Some piled on top of each other, holding each others heads, raising a foot, with enormous hands ready to burst under a filthy bandage, eight days old, the nauseating odour of which makes you feel sick, others again kneeling on the ground in their suffering and their pain, some with a cane used as a walking stick or crutch

Gerard Bertin is on police duty. He is tall, fat, greasy, well dressed, and always smiling, speaking German badly with a northern accent. Some of his compatriots like him because he passes them bread, soup stolen from the sick or has found them a soft job in the Revier, as a sweeper or porter. Bertin is still there behind the door and outside, there are others who would like to come in but it's too late. Bertin is there and must obey the Pole. The job is too good. He doesn't know what it is to be cold, at least he no longer knows, for he is always saying he has been in the camps for three years – that's why he has a grade and makes use of it. The door opens and snow comes in with several sick men. Bertin has seen them and hits them, grabs them, throws them outside Behind the door bearing the little notice "Revier" they can be heard weeping, then there is silence. They remain there. We can imagine them behind the screen of planks, lying in the snow, in the wind, waiting for one of us to come out again and if Bertin does not see them, they will slip in among the others with a little luck, making themselves as small as possible!

I intend to go last. I lie down and go to sleep, while waiting. It smells awful here. It's so small, with the dressings, the pus and the rest but it is warm. I can hear howls in the room on the left where the doctor and his assistants and the SS are, without doubt. It will soon be my turn. I pretend to sleep. "Was ist los, was machst du?" (What's wrong, what are you doing?) I do not move. Somebody shakes me. I get up slowly. Seeing the state of my trousers "Cheise Rye," I answer, Ja, viel. I undress. Revier tomorrow fruh. At last I have been admitted! Tomorrow I will go into the Revier!

31st December. Having no blanket, I slept between 2 mattresses! I am frozen, for my trousers are quite damp.. I can't hold on any more. I have only one precious thing left, my little piece of paper which will open the door of the Revier (Infirmary) to me. On the dune, just like every morning at Roll call, those who suffer from congestion are lined or piled up next to the ventilation chimney of the bunker. They will be dealt with afterwards? Several times I take out my paper and my little box to show the camp leader, still just as greasy and proud of himself. I can no longer stay on my feet, all is grey with snow and with the darkness, the cold seems even more intense, the time longer, the Roll call more of a strain.

Suddenly the first kommandos get under way. The kapos have their gloves and even ear muffs on. As for us, we must have our hands outside our pockets and be motionless. The waiting goes on. The SS and the big chiefs have gone off to get warm I expect. Some are stamping their feet, others striking their shoulders with their hands. Taking courage, all fight and help each other against the cold, each rubbing his neighbour's back, while he does the same to another, or in turns.

Entrance to the Infirmary is not until 10.00. Whilst waiting, we have to make brooms.

Alles man krank. Revier. Schnell. (All the men who are ill, Infirmary, quickly)

I don't wait to be asked twice and get there by dragging myself rather than walking to the door. Nobody speaks. Each keeps to himself his suffering and mouths his curses in an imperceptible murmur against the cold, the snow, the closed door, his neighbour who annoys him or tramples on his feet without realising it. At last! We go in. No! We are pushed back again. There is a jostling and I can see nothing more. I lower my head and round my back so that the cold reaches me less. The door must have shut again for I heard an "Ah" of reproach and worried impatience. Still outside! Everything is against us, even the wind which envelops me, goes through me, strips me, blows up sleeves, up trouser legs, down my neck. Sometimes, one is lucky enough to be protected by a screen of sick people on the side the wind is coming from but these change places to come and stand behind us and so on.

At last I go in, show my paper. I wait again. One must undergo an examination. A young Frenchman takes me with him to the WC and says to me – "Here, do it in there, handing me a box.

You have dysentery?

Yes.

Seeing the state of my pants he says, "OK come on, it's all right, you are OK." He takes my number. We go back to the waiting room. The inspection is almost over. Just some temperatures to take. Fortunately when one has dysentery it is not taken. The state of things is enough.

Bertin takes us back to the bunker where the showers are. Once again we have to cross the dune. The shower is good, hot, then boiling. It does us good but does not last, for suddenly it becomes cold to make us get out. We each receive a short sleeved shirt which does not cover the legs. I put it on without drying myself. What could I do it with? Then a pair of flip flops and a blanket – we'll manage.

It is snowing but I am going to shelter. I pass yet again along this little corridor, called the waiting room, a door is on the right. I cross a large clean room with bunks along each side and blankets with blue squares on the mattresses. All the beds seem full – two men per board. To left and right, windows let in a good deal of light, thanks to the whiteness outside. In the centre is a stove. Now I understand why some were making small faggots of wood during the evening at the base and managed to exchange them for soup or a crust. I do not stop in this room, for the Pole says to Bertin – "That one, to the shits." On the left is a door. It opens and closes again on me. It's here!

Chapter 26: MONTESUMA'S REVENGE

I had often heard this room talked about but my imagination had not gone this far. The cold, the darkness and the infection dominates all. Five groups of bunk beds. One is empty. On my arrival, a patient whom I cannot see, says – "Russian? French? German? Polish?" I answer French. He says, "OK, me too!" What a smell and how cold it is! All is grey, dark, and dirty. Dirty straw spills over from the boards and is strewn over the tiled, sticky floor. Not a clean space anywhere. I approach the empty bed. The mattress, quite damp, disgusts me. It is flattened and stained with excrement and blood in the middle. Below there is no mattress. Comrade, Frenchman, are you alone? Do you want me to sleep with you? We will be warmer and my blanket is a good one.

I can hardly distinguish his face in the shadow, for there is only one window here. The other patients seem to be sleeping deeply. As he answers me, I approach this new friend, a companion in misery. It's so good to hear French spoken. It makes you less tired. "I am paralysed! I cannot get up any more and I have dysentery. You will sleep badly, try to lie down next to me, there is a bed!"

His shaky voice, so weak, frightens me but less so than his white face, so angular with bones sticking out of a broken jaw, hollow cheeks, eyes shining in two black holes and his pale forehead. Along with that head, I can see one of his hands holding the blanket, dirty, disgusting, covered in brown marks trying to hold it round his pointed shoulders and against his throat. What can his body be like underneath? It hardly seems to have any energy – and that hand, with knuckles too large for the rest of it, terrifies me.

I see all these sad things in a few seconds but I had to go very near because of my short sightedness. Then instinctively, I recoil.

Yes, I will try and sleep there.

I turn the mattress over to see if it is cleaner on the other side but it's a waste of effort – it is worse! It must already have been turned over several times and those who slept on it must have died long ago.

I'm cold. At last I will not work again for a while. How many are there here? How many French?

I lay down, rolled up with difficulty in my small blanket, feet in my hands, head on my knees, conserving all my heat and trying to sleep. The wind is blowing and howling outside. I dare not even put my head out. After a few hours immobility, I decide to look around a bit for I can hear a dull noise-han, han, han, hou, hou. It's somebody in here. Which one? I had not noticed the wash tub which serves as a toilet. Now, as I get used to the darkness, I can see the room and take in all the details. "Han, han, Frenchman, Frenchman" I say softly, for fear of waking the others and not knowing his name. "Is it you who is ill? What's the matter?" No answer. What a deathly silence and yet, I am already beginning to get used to the smell which reigns here. There are trails of diarrhoea all along the lines of beds up to the tub. Suddenly, somebody gets up in a rush and while getting out of bed, makes a mess which stains someone's blanket below. "Schwein!". Cries a feeble voice to which the blanket belongs. "Cheize.cheize.franl" answers the patient, who still does not get to the tub in time. All down his legs which are too long and too thin, tell-tale trails show me what stage the illness has got to with this man, for there is even some blood! Fortunately, I have not yet got to that stage. Will they look after me? They have just brought flasks for the next room. The door opens. Bertin comes in to count us but tells us that there will be no soup for me until tomorrow. No Sunday soup and no bread either? I cover my face and stop my ears so that I do not hear the others eating. "It's good," they are saying.

1st January. "Happy New Year, friend and Frenchman. Happy New Year" I say, shaking him under his blanket but his stiff form does not answer. I uncover his head a little. He is dead. Already? Yesterday he was speaking to me. What age could he have been, 20,30,40?

"Kaput?" the Russian asks me, who sleeps above him? "Ja, kaput". At once he bounds out of his bunk, turns the corpse over, searches the mattress, takes out 2 pieces of bread, still bearing teeth marks and goes back to bed, satisfied. I call him in vain. He turns a deaf ear and does not answer. Then, I hear him murmur to his neighbour – "Franzoski….." I do not understand him.

There are two Frenchmen in the next row. They are always arguing. "Get over a bit, lie down" hitting each other and starting to cry. One, very old, is very weak, the other, young and eaten up with dysentery, is always on the tub and disturbs his friend. Hearing them speak, I gather they are from the same part of Savoy. Some visitors suddenly come in and cannot keep back an "Ah" of disgust. They are the "Tod commando" or undertakers. "Wieviel man kaput?" How many men are dead? They lift the blanket and look to see if there are any dead to be taken away. They are Germans. "Nu rein". Without any respect at all, one of them pulls back the blanket, pulls the corpse by the feet, lets it roll onto the floor where its head crashes down so violently that I shudder. Without hesitating, they drag it along in the dirt and the stiffened limbs sweep the filth with them to the door. What savages! They look as though they have done that job all their lives!

There is no oven here. Therefore, once divested of its clothes, the corpse will be buried in a bag with 3 or 4 others, an entry in the camp register, a number and written opposite, died on 1st January from dysentery.

Every evening, a young Frenchman, Maurice Lelong, a student of medicine, kind and very devoted, goes round with his notebook and asks us how many times we have been to the tub. I say 12 times to be like the others, but fortunately, I am not as bad as that and since there is no control, want to make the pleasure last, despite only being given one litre of white soup at 4 in the afternoon and 2 pieces of bread, one in the morning, one in the evening.

I take a long time to savour these few mouth fulls and I can eat in bed, sheltered from the wind. The décor is not pretty but I would not like to change places with those at the base. In the evening, after Roll call (for we too are counted, on our mattresses) there is a distribution of medical supplies. The Polish nurse goes round with a little wooden box full of different coloured envelopes, pills! He announces. If you ask him for nothing, you get nothing. If you hold out a hand and say" cheese rye" he puts into it 1 or 2 tablets of coal or 1 grey tablet of tanalbine.

Not much for 24 hours. In spite of that, I am grateful for the "care" which I am receiving. I can feel that my dysentery has almost gone and at night I sleep well. One must always stay lying down, for we are not allowed to go out to wash in the basin – I therefore get the worst off by spitting in my hands. I am the least ill in the room but don't let the others see, or they might give me away. The little Russian sometimes manages to slip away to the basin on the left and brings back a tin of water which he will drink or sell for bread, for thirst and disease are masters in this little airless room, in which you can never open the window.

5th January. Twice a week, those with major wounds have them redressed, so it won't be my turn this time but a Latvian next to me, has a whole leg bound up and he will be taken care of. The nurse has to carry him, for he cannot move at all without howling. Sitting on a stool, his leg is plunged into a bucket of hot water. He twists up, grimaces, breathes hard. Under the bandage, the wound has no definite colour – green, yellowish, brown. It's putrid. The smell which emanates from it fills the whole room and the nurse moves away to get help in moving the unfortunate man to the operating table. The paper dressing hangs down throughout the journey, taking with it the smell and the pain. Half an hour later, the French nurse brings him back in his arms. He has a new paper dressing and seems to be suffering considerably. "Will he remain crippled that one?" "Oh, he could drag along for a fortnight, a month but he's done for. We only have a sort of ointment left and he has blood poisoning" It seems that at Bremen Farge, the word Revier means that the sick are cared for but not those who are too ill. There is neither ether, cupping glasses (that's forbidden), aspirin, antiseptics or fabric dressings. On top of that, there are the lice which run around the blankets, into the mattresses, suck our blood, eat us up, go from one mattress to another, wake us up and keep us from sleeping. How I pity those who have dressings.

6th January. I have a bunk companion, Maurice Leclerc, a garage man from Moutiers. By chance, he is not ill and is just pretending. So much the better, we will pretend together. We exchange confidences, tell each other the story of our lives. Mine is quickly told. His takes longer, for he is 50. With two of you, we are warmer and when Bertin throws us our bread, it's he who catches it, for he is on the right side. Sometimes he misses it and it falls on the ground, on the tiles still damp from urine. I am not put off. The Greek sweeper always goes round before the meals. Our right-hand neighbour is complaining oddly this evening. Yes, he is not even covering himself with his blanket any more, and you can see his long skeleton like legs, with hollows where his buttocks should be. Is he still alive?

Jacques, Jacques.

I'm thirsty, give me something to drink! Get me a tin of water; you can have my bread from yesterday and this morning's. I am not hungry. I'm thirsty – go on Maurice, you can walk. Go on, I'll give you my bread.

No Jacques, it will kill you and anyway, we can't go out, there's Bertin and the Pole. The Russian has understood and gives him a tin of water in exchange for the bread. Jacques has a long drink. If I dared, I would stop him, but above, the Russian is keeping watch. Jacques has finished drinking The empty tin falls to the ground and nothing more is heard. A Pole, jealous of the Russian. murmurs something like "kourva" then lays into the Frenchman, talks to him of the water which is not fit, gives his advice and proposes coffee in exchange for tomorrow's soup. He gets no answer.

7th January. The Pole and Jacques are dead. I would have thought they would last longer. Jacques spoke to me last night. This morning Bertin threw him his bread, as usual, when he must have already been cold under his blanket. The bread has gone! The undertakers took them away with as little care as on the other days. Maurice Leclerc cannot look. Then other patients arrive to take their empty places. I am able to see Olivier Melin who is in the other room with Roger Clarence. They are better off there. Olivier, seeing me with the people with the runs gives me words of courage: "Try to hold on Maurice, It's not for long." I reassure him about my health.

10th January. Once again there is talk of a transport of sick people, but since I was never entered on the lists, I will not have the chance to leave. Maurice Leclerc, Olivier Melin and Roger Clarence, whose names were taken ages ago, are joyous. I will be left alone. If only I could stay in the Revier – but won't they notice that I no longer have dysentery? Don't let's think of the future but just let's live from day to day. Outside, it's so cold, the snow frightens me so much that I pray a good deal to thank God for having given me shelter. Oh, Lord, shorten the length of the Roll calls and protect all those who are out there, near the Weser, in the snow storm! Nothing protects them from the wild elements. Poor Jean Fougerat, poor Lucien Poulet. How heavy the iron bars must be, how cold your fingers and feet must be, how the wind must blow!

11th January. Hubbub in the corridor! The Polish nurse is angry again. A patient has made a mess in the tiled room. He hits him as much as he can, like a savage, blows falling one after the other – our door opens, the man is brought in and collapses. The Pole does not stop even so and his kicks bring forth terrible cries from the victim. The door closes again. The new arrival is still there, on the ground. Nobody speaks to him. There is still an empty place next to the Russian. We shut ourselves in our selfishness and forget the incident. The sick man remains on the ground, his shirt hardly covering him. Bertin comes in. "Was machst du? Aufstehen! Los! ... He still does not move "Tod? Scheize".

Bertin goes out. Is the Pole dead? Fainted? He seems to have a broken arm. Here are the undertakers. They are for him. They take him away. The Pole had killed him.

14th January. The Polish doctor inspects our medical cards which are pinned to the boards of the bunks. He makes me get up and looks at me. "Write in this number" he says to his assistant! I show the zinc disc round my neck, the same cord I had at Neuengamme. I have been written down for the departure and go back to bed, hiding my delight. I will stay with my friends. "Block Roll call. Revier Roll call" I hear my number. I get up. It's true, we are going! I am thrown a pyjama suit which is too large for me but that does not matter. I am leaving but Maurice, Olivier and Roger have not been called. Why? There are 300 of us going. Olivier is sad. I do not know how to console him. We will see each other again. I say goodbye to them with some embarrassment. Bertin gives me some flip flops. We advance slowly. Block 5 is waiting to leave! Here, everything is damp. There is steam everywhere and I go to sleep with a Breton. Let's get to sleep quickly, while we can. What joy! I am leaving! What about the others? We are relatively free in this barracks, for the overseers are French and Greek. I am relieved!

Chapter 27: PREPARATIONS

15th January. The snow, the cold, the sickness, the suffering and with all that, the waiting! The wagons are coming and we are going to leave Farge. We have only one thought, one objective, one reason for continuing to live, to hope – that we are leaving, therefore everyone is happy! We are allowed to talk, to go and lie down on the mattresses, to go to the WC, to the washroom when we want to! We can even go up to the stove when there are not too many people! We must be going to Neuengamme, although no one tells us so. Hopefully, we will eat better there and down there are my medical supplies and we will doubtless be in the infirmary. They have tables and benches to sit at to eat the soup. Paul, a German from the bunker recognises me and oddly enough greets me. I reply "Hello and goodbye." "Yes!" he says "Neuengamme – beware of the crematorium". I tell him I don't care a damn. I have become a fatalist, while swearing to myself to hold on to the end. Is not victory certain? Whether we live or whether they kill us, makes no difference. Yet, we must go back, we must see France again. It is so far away but if we have come this far, why die now? Where has the war got to? Alas, nobody knows anything. It's so long, so long. I dare not think about it.

The most serious dressings are looked at. All the wounds are infected. Those who, like me, have no injuries, have to be counted. Through having no ether all the ailments have got worse and become infectious. We are shaved again, even though we were done recently! Suddenly a rumour goes round. It's incredible, inconceivable and impossible. "There are no wagons – there is no transport". Discouragement, doubt and uncertainty take hold of the various groups. It's a critical moment. The camp leader appears several times. He has the soup and bread given out. He tells us that we will have nothing more for 24 hours. So, are we going? We are going to have this half a loaf of bread which is given in one ration as soon as we go off, in a large convoy. Each man, motionless and dumb, remains pensive. We are all happy to be leaving. If only I had a cement bag under my pyjama suit, because the weather outside is dreadful! There again, I remain a fatalist. With nothing on our backs, nothing in our belly, we are still alive, all the same. If the Boche threaten us with death for the last rag which we may take as extra, why revolt, why be miserable? We still have an F on our chest, the relics of the workers who are sent back with dirty rags, to the Neuengamme dump or elsewhere! What are we complaining about?

Maybe our parents, our friends have died in France and us, here, are maybe survivors? Why seek to change one's destiny, when it is written? Just as it was written that we should come here, it was probably also written that we will leave. A few kind men from the Vosges talk of serious things: philosophy, religion and literature. It makes a change from the banal gastronomic enumerations which make my mouth water and my stomach work empty.

The wagons are here!

A shiver runs up and down my spine. "That's it, that's it, the camp leader is here!"

Aufstehen, alles achtung.

He comes in followed by the SS.

Zu funf! We are counted.

Is it the last time at Bremen Farge? Some, who cannot stand, remain in bed. At last we go out. In ranks of 5, naked, heads shaved, in the cold and wind, we wait; what for? I don't know and don't even turn to see what the others are doing but from the conversation, sometimes in Russian, sometimes in Polish, sometimes in bad German, I gather that some of the sick will not come out, fearing the cold outside. The nurses have to drag them and to my surprise, even carry them on their shoulders to the ranks. How long are we going to stand in the wind, which is blowing on our frozen and weak legs? I am behind an old captain from Hut 14, a tough nut who is constantly telling jokes. He cheers people up, overflowing with optimism but is more cautious than our Marquis. We are going to leave! The Polish doctor is with us. It's thanks to him if I am going, thanks to fate too. The captain shakes his hand and tells him "Au revoir and thanks on behalf of all the Frenchmen" The Marquis (Mayor) of Moustiers, recovered from an abscess on his throat, is better but did not want to leave in spite of his age. Off we go. Olivier is at the window of the Revier with Roger. I wave goodbye to therm. We turn into the Roll call area, stop at the clothing store by the exit. Distribution of round caps. So much the better – The door! Counted one last time, we are 600 metres from the wagons...

Chapter 28: RETURN TO NEUENGAMME

We are 50 to a cattle truck, the space between the two doors reserved for the guards. There is just room to sit cross-legged in fives, head down. I sat next to the captain at the back, next to the group of Spaniards. Even so, we had to fight to keep a bit of wood under our buttocks. It's like Siberia in here. The Jerries have put on all their winter clothing, right down to the coloured cloak, gloves and balaclava. The NCO looks like a ball held up by his gun. In front of him a little stove has been erected, making a lot of smoke but giving out a bit of heat, despite the door remaining open. Hardly have we moved off, than the Russians get together to demand bread. The German refuses. A good thing, for we don't know how long we will be travelling. Everyone is silent, the cold encouraging sleep, although we cannot lie down! The captain is already asleep; I do the same!

At midnight, bread and margarine are given out. Quite a large piece but as I can't see anything, I make a large slice with my fingers. I eat very fast, for in the darkness, stealing is already going on. One Frenchman cries out – My bread! I hear blows and jostling. The German murmurs something, order returns and only the sound of chewing and smacking of lips in the silence and cold of the night remains.

It is daylight and we are still moving. I am cornered between the Spaniard who is constantly moving and the captain. Outside, the flat countryside has no effect on me. We go through an almost totally derelict town, so much so, that the houses still standing look weird. The instability, the fatigue and the intolerance begin to make themselves seriously felt in our wagon of sick men. The Spaniards are bossy and want to lie down at all costs. Our captain, who always has plenty to say (what else do we have plenty of?) addresses them violently. "It's not your space here. You should have stayed where you were, if you don't like it!"

The foreigners insult him and threaten him. I am frightened of getting into the melee for my buttocks hurt from being in one position and my flip flops have disappeared under the wood shavings!

Will we get there before nightfall? How cold it is. I am quite stiff and do not raise my head any more. I am cold all over and an impossible smoke fills our wagon The Boche walk up and down but we have to remain seated, only being allowed to get up one by one, with permission to do one's business out of the door.

Night has fallen and nothing has changed. We have had nothing to eat all day and the food box is empty. Outside, a fine sleet is falling, mixed with the melting snow. We stop. Where are we?

"Raus, alles", cries a voice from outside, muffled by the distance. We have arrived! I have the devil of a job to find my flip flops. I am stiff and can neither walk nor stand up. I cannot feel my feet. How shall I be able to jump to the ground?

"Los, los, schneller". Somebody helps me down and in the rain which goes right through me, in the ice and mud, somebody supports me and leads me along. I cannot see anything. There are striped men in jackets and capes. Arc lamps, barbed wire, watch towers. It's Neuengamme!

It's the same old story; is the same comedy of the cellars going to start again? Yes, nothing has changed! I don't know what time it can be but we are in the cellars. Nobody takes any notice of me. Some, who can no longer stand, lie down on the ground. As for me, I stay where I was put, legs fixed and as though stuck to the ground, shaking involuntarily. I am quite damp, which is what worries me the most, for I feel the cold penetrating my entire body. This cold causes so many illnesses. Here are the guards with leather boots and raincoats. Block 17, block 24! I see my old Fritz again from block 10. We pass one by one before a control table on which are our cards. Then in groups of 100 we are put in rows of 5, the most serious patients together, your condition being judged from your walk. I have the luck to be put with the worst of them and will go with the first group. Off we go. We go out. The tornado still blowing, takes my breath away. One can't see a thing, all the lights of the camp are out. There must be a "gross alarm". We cross the assembly yard. Then, it's the undressing room, another shave and then the showers. I feel better but I'm hungry. A Pole, using a wooden spatula, puts a little yellow ointment under our arms, on our chest and between the legs. The same positions, the same movements, the same methodical organisation is here. There is also the draught, the clean clothes room, but the clothes are still damp because we were not expected, the flip flops and the cap. We come out in the light of the blue lamps amid moans, cries, jostling, stumbling and falling in the mud. We do not know where we are walking, nor which direction we are to take.

Block 11: We advance with disconcerting slowness and cannot see the SS. The cement promenade is just an ice rink. I slip all the time. My feet, warmed by the shower and now plunged again into cold mud, are giving terrible pain. Won't we get separated, lose each other? Somebody is holding my arm. Mind the rails! Here are the huts, the barbed wire, from which icicles are hanging shines in the darkness. This is it. I only ask one thing now and that is to have shelter in the hut, to lie down and sleep. Sleep to no longer think. Everything takes so long.

We stop again. We are put into rows of 5. We go in. It's block 11. A weak light illuminates the large room, at the back of which are some beds. Will they give out some soup? No, we can lie down. The smell of chlorine, of stagnant water and the latrine buckets, is enough to remind me where I am. Nothing has changed. The washroom, WC with bow windows, the layout is the same in all the huts, which means that once inside, you could go to any spot with your eyes shut without making a mistake. I climb onto an upper bunk with a young teacher from the north. Jostled by the Spaniards who want to throw us out, we lie down on our sides, for the beds are just as narrow as ever. I slept, but my feet are just as frozen. Near us, is Danielo (an Italian interpreter) journalist by trade, who brings us up to date a little about what will happen to us. No work. Rest for 7 weeks. Roll call in bed. Distribution of soup in bed. During the alarm, we don't go to the cellars. After and during inspection, there will be a distribution of medical supplies.

17th January. I have been for inspection but was not marked down for the infirmary. The Polish doctor just gave me 2 tablets of charcoal. The soup distribution is long and painful. The thieves take advantage of the slightest occasion to filch 10 or so full tins or a whole flask. The block leader does not appear. He is in his little room standing next to an empty tin and still greasy from margarine which has served to make chips, stuffing himself with bread and red jam. We may cry in vain – "Thief, block leader," but the Poles are the masters and the Italian interpreter, a brave man nevertheless, can do nothing. The Poles eat 2 or 3 tins straight off, before our eyes; they go in the washrooms or even in the WC. Each flask is watched by a whole band of starving men, Russian and French. The Pole prodigious with his whip does not discourage the soup thieves. Sometimes, the first… or Stubedienst, gets red with anger and hits out with the iron lash. Bodies fall, fainting, before the vat of soup which is taken away amid cries and vociferations. Too bad if the row opposite has had none. During all this noise, amid the appetising smell of cumin seasoning, in the rudimentary décor of 3-tier beds, piled up under a ceiling which is too low to be able to sit under it, separated by partitions, heads show themselves, eyes fixed on the tins of those who are eating, fixed on the flask hidden by a group of Russians who are talking, waiting for the tins to become empty in order to pass them to those who have not had their share.

All the noises which herald the approach of soup or bread build up in a man who is hungry and excite that hunger. The grinding of the vat being dragged, the sound of the ladle, the crack of the crate in which the loaves are cut in the kitchen, are carried, the rubbing of the basket – all these sounds which are known make the weakest man rise up on his elbows and provoke gastronomic discussions. One checks to see if he still has the instrument which serves as a knife, another spits in his spoon to clean it, because at soup time, water is cut off and access to the basin is forbidden. Danielo gives us the latest news

20th January. There is talk early on of a medical visit. The prospect of once again standing naked for many hours, irritates me considerably but I am even more afraid of being sent back to work. I saw two German clerks appear from the Arbeitstatistik, the men who will sort out, who will decide, with a doctor, the destination of the serial numbers. The order to get up is given but nobody moves. There is competition as to who takes longest to decide who is to go. The block leader howls and beats the mattresses with his belt. We get up! Already many are naked before the doctors who I can make out at the back of the room, towards the door. I join the ranks. Suddenly we are sent back again. "Over" somebody cries. All they wanted was 60 volunteers for a chore. A chore! Outside, too! Let's go to sleep.

21st January. Medical visit. This time, I am woken up by a hail of punches in my face and I am thrown on the ground. I must go, without delay, to the ranks for inspection. This time, I don't hang about. The visit goes on until midday and here are the bowls of soup! My number has been taken but I don't know if it's for work, for one is rarely warned in advance.

The wooden latrine buckets are steaming and in the liquid covered with brown and green froth, one can see a few potatoes at each dip of the Stubedienst ladle. We have earthenware bowls but no spoon. We burn our lips all the time. What does it matter! It's good and filling. There are yellow and pink reflections on the cabbage. I eat very quickly, hurried by a Russian who wants to dip in his fingers to try it. I feel sick and think I am not well but it passes, because I am able to sit in a corner!

We are outside again in the rain. The orchestra is playing its favourite piece, old hat to our accustomed ears. We are made to exercise a little on the promenade, along the rows of workers. We don't know where we are going and probably the block leader doesn't either. Is he waiting for an order? Today we eat before all the others. Passing by the small windows of the camp prison, covered with bars, I deeply pity the fate of the unfortunate men held there, without food. We go on, in turn, our flip flops throwing up the mud to our knees and me, already pleased that my pyjamas were almost dry, get my share, for everything must be done again and I feel feverish in this dampness…

Block 4: We are going into a new hut, situated in one of the new red brick buildings which we were building last summer and under which are the cellars, bad memories of the alerts which we have been spared since our return. Here everything is new, white and clean. I cannot believe my eyes. It looks like a hospital, if only because of the light which streams in through the large bay windows. We shall live like real princes here! How lucky to be ill, some think to themselves. "What luck to be crippled" says another.

Hut 4 is divided into two distinct "Stube" separated by a large double door. These two rooms, (I am in the first) are in reality two dormitories with 3 tier beds, 80 cm wide, in which we must sleep three to a bed, i.e. always on our sides and head to feet. Our mattresses are full of splinters of wood and we have two blankets between three of us. As opposed to the other blocks, the ceiling being fairly high, you can sit down if one of you is on a top bunk.

28th January. We do not work. We remain under cover but this well-being is made up for by the discipline by which we live. We are always on the look-out, fearing the medical visits which for us, mean first the whip to make us hurry up, then a wait in single file and in a draught, naked, barefoot on the tiles, shivering for hours by open windows, anxious and not knowing what will be decided about us.

"Gut luft" says the SS Major, laughing at our misfortune. To ascertain our state of health, we have to do gymnastics, stand up, lie down, sit on the ground, go on tip-toe, arms in the air, etc for five minutes, one after the other, the interpreter asks us what the matter is. Some don't know and don't answer. I say "pleurisy and dysentery". I am given a small pink card bearing my number and rejoin the ranks indicated by a Pole. The wait goes on, into eternity. Suddenly it's finished, we are sent back to our side and the crowd carries me back to my bed. I sleep with Joseph Dauverne from Gueugnon and I come across Jean Fougeret from Treignac. The Poles have searched everything during the visit. Blankets have gone, clothes, too, mattresses have even been overturned!

At last we are going to be able to warm ourselves and maybe sleep if neighbours will let us, for we are very squashed and we often receive in our faces the feet covered in filth and excrement of our co-sleeper. When we are not asleep, our mind is still working and we ponder the reasons for the inspection and the card.

29th January. When there is no inspection ordered by the SS, the block leaders, "stubedienst" or other henchmen, on the pretext of 'discipline culture', organise sessions even more painful, even more weakening and sometimes fatal, for our debilitated bodies. It's disinfection time, because we are covered in lice! The lack of soap, water, the promiscuity, weakness and the state of the blankets and mattresses, are the cause. What a curse these lice are! For not only do they constantly eat us up and carry diseases from one man to another, but they bring typhus. We fight them vigorously, even though it's impossible to overcome them when 600 sick men, who often have neither the will, nor the strength to wash themselves, live without ever changing their linen in a place where there would normally be space for only 250. So, the familiar session of nudity, accompanied with all kinds of brutality, begins again, while the cleaners armed with buckets and brooms, wash down mattresses, blankets and clothes with white liquid. The overseer shines a lamp right into our eyes, looks under our arms and over our whole bodies. He has dressings removed. If he discovers the presence of vermin, if there is the least suspicion, we have to go under the hose of the Pole doing the disinfecting. Of course, the Poles do not undergo this treatment but they keep watch, looking for any who try to escape it, either by hiding under a bed or by pretending to be paralysed. Therefore, each day, frozen, wet, full of vermin, dirty, ill, our bodies submit to harder and harder trials. Like many of the men, I have dysentery. From time to time, I get charcoal tablets, which have no effect but which I am happy to swallow. This way, I feel as though I am treating myself but by eating only very clear and oily cabbage soup, bread and margarine or red or pink fish pate, even more weakening, the dysentery doubles in severity and strength decreases. For most of the sick there is only one question: May we go to the Abort? (to the WC) There again in fact, we have to await the pleasure of the Polish. They may at any time forbid access to the WC by a guard built like a giant and armed with a broomstick. Sometimes, the excuse is cleaning but often there is no reason. Also, during soup time Roll call, access to the WC is forbidden. Such a regime imposed on intestines wracked by diarrhoea is therefore not only a nightmare but a disaster for the mattresses, blankets, passages, walls, everything. A filthy stench! Too bad for the man who has messed himself or who has been messed on by his bed buddy. Sometimes the sick wait and twist themselves for hours in the central passage, imploring the Pole in good health, cruel and dumb, to let them in to the WC. Sometimes, unable to hold on any longer and taking advantage of a lapse in surveillance, there is a general rush, encouraged by 1 or 2 successful attempts made with no crack of the whip. Then the Pole turns around, raises his stick and hits as much as he can, knocking men out.... It does not matter. In a moment he is over-powered, the latrine buckets are full; there is a bottle neck, hesitation and a general retreat. Other Poles who have gone to sleep arrive to give help and it's every man for himself, because already many have fallen, trampled on and knocked out. The best time to risk an attempt is to take advantage of the moment when a Pole goes to the WC for they always have a free passage. Soon access is allowed, there is a constant procession and somebody organises a one-way system. Several pans are condemned and shut off and three are reserved for the overseers and doctors. About 10 remain, often very dirty. You must queue for the urinal and queue for the pans. Often, many no longer need to go there, which is why the WC also serves as a washroom for pants already dirtied several times. Those with dysentery do their own washing. As if the sick, devoid of strength, like skeletons, clumsy, tottering, could rub and wash linen! But the wash room is not often open, that's why after flushing (the new huts, as opposed to the old ones, have this refinement) they can dip their rags timidly in the bowl, twist them, rub them gently, without conviction, without help, amid the jostling, still victims of the general selfishness, knowing for certain that it will take a week for the pyjama to dry, if it dries. Unless it disappears in the hands of a thief!

30th January. The nights are worse than the days when you are ill, feverish and must go to the WC at every moment, barefoot (the guard's whip quickly makes you take off your flip flops which could disturb the sleep of the overseers). At night the alleys become a sticky dung heap and since you can't see where you are putting your feet, you get back into your bunk in an indescribable state.

Medicines are almost non-existent. Bread is really difficult to chew. The French doctors, who do everything materially possible, advise us to toast it and even to burn it. How? There may be a stove but we are not allowed to go near it. The Danes and the Overseers occupy it continuously with bowls of water, soup and broth. How many cudgel blows would you have to risk to toast some bread? The beetroot, cabbage and swede soup is rarely cooked and always indigestible. On Sunday, we are allowed some sweet red cabbage, which I cannot eat completely, although there is only half a litre of it, it is so revolting. Also, there are 5 or 6 boiled potatoes in the water. When you have dysentery you should not eat soup or bead that has not been toasted, or peelings but are we condemned to die? As an alternative, the sick persist on a downward slide; letting themselves reach the bottom and drinking water; that is, if we can get some, because the washroom is almost always shut. Too bad, there is a tap in the WC where the Russians wash the soup bowls at midday! Curses, it has been padlocked. There is still the pipe in the urinals but it's unusable, because it is now hidden under a metal sheet. No more water! One man, with his little box, another with his bowl hidden in his pocket or under his jacket, goes prospecting. We need water, we need water, this glacial water which chills your whole body and removes its very substance… "Water? I can sell you some." So water has become something just as important as bread or soup. It is on the market. Water in exchange for bread. Water? but what water? From the WC pans, or the flushes? It's not very clean but they drink it all the same. I have not yet come to that and have no wish to die, the Jerries would be too happy! Some go on purpose to the WC at night, bowl under their jacket and if they are not searched by the watchman, they will give up their water to patients in exchange for their bread.

31st January. Dysentery is making ravages without precedent. The worst cases are relegated to the back room, in other words the rubbish tip. For greater commodity, the door separating the two rooms is locked and guarded. Latrines have been installed in the passages of those with dysentery and are emptied by the "Abort commando" composed of Russians. I remain in the first room, for my state is not serious.

February. No more medicines in the hut. The French doctors come by sometimes between the beds to listen to the more seriously ill and to try and get them into the infirmary. Sometimes a general review of dressings is announced. Then, ranks are formed, you take your place in the long and slow procession of the crippled, the infirm too weak to stand, leaning on the beds, sitting on the ground, bent over, unable to carry on. An incredible intolerance, which is understandable, results from this state of affairs. Many, like me, itch all over. For that, we are given some yellow oil, which we rub all over our bodies. In order to get rid of this ravaging completely, you have to repeat the operation at least 2 or 3 times in a row but the lack of will and strength to queue up in the cold, makes us keep the affliction. I can feel myself getting weaker little by little, each day, for I have considerable trouble climbing back into bed. Fortunately, Lepont, station master at Aigueperse helps me a lot. I am no longer hungry. The soup makes me sick. I can no longer swallow the bread and I am so thirsty that my lips are burning. Yet, I do not want to drink a drop of liquid. Each morning, I rinse out my mouth but swallow nothing. I force myself to eat the bread. I receive the most varied pieces of advice from friends or from those who roam continuously around the beds looking to steal or to swap something. One man offers to toast your bread in exchange for soup, or sometimes out of compassion but often you see nothing come back. Some keep pieces of bread accumulated over several days, wrapped carefully in a piece of rag. They nibble at them, a little bit at a time; then one day they are stolen. They cry, lament and take it out on their neighbours, often on their best friends. Then there is only argument and discouragement. I have joined in for I am materially obliged to make swaps with friends in my turn, those from Gueugnon, Murat, Aigueperse, Nancy, from the Nord, etc. Being unable to swallow the soup or the other food, I give them everything and they give me pieces of potato when they have some but I do not demand anything. Only one thing counts for me now and that is to gain time trying to get well and not be denounced as seriously ill, for the second room frightens me. Every morning, there is an endless procession of corpses dragged towards the outside by the undertakers

Outside the windows the countryside unfolds before us. The large watch towers, the barbed wire, the road, the fields with no hedges, no trees, lost in the snow and grey sky, as far as the eye can see. You witness, too, the comings and goings of the work kommandos. How cold they must be and yet their progress is impeccable, like the procession of a regular army, in which the officers are replaced by kapos with a whip and the soldiers by slaves. The wind is still blowing. Inside, the dampness is so bad that water runs from the ceiling and down the walls, as though it were raining. Those on the top bunk are sometimes quite wet although they take the precaution of wiping the walls with a rag.

Strains of music reach us. The musicians don't have an easy time either, for they must also work for 12 hours in the cellars, with the elderly, making ropes. It's not tiring work, but fastidious, impractical and unhealthy. There's the team of navvies passing, Russians pulling carts, there's a long line of Danes well dressed in blue, with caps. They have suitcases, so they must be going home. The Danes are not badly off for they receive parcels and are all fairly fat. We have also benefited once or twice from the bread they get from home. It tastes good and is made from rye flour but we have had so little of it! Yet, each improvement from the ordinary run of things reminds us that it is good to be alive, even in misery. It's after cold and hunger that you appreciate the well being of a garment, of untorn clothes, of a blanket, of a dry place to sleep, of a minute's calm, of a piece of bread, a little larger and less mouldy than usual! After having been alone, abandoned by all, lost in the middle of a crowd of enemies, one understands that there is no greater wealth than a friend and hope! I am very weak but if I help Jean to walk, I do him as much good as myself, for I feel that I am still good for something. I can still do some good, even quite a lot, when I have my strength back. This state of mind is a real support. It helps me to hold on. What good are all the great things, if nothing remains of them? Aren't we all dying here?

Jean was an Income Tax Inspector, Lepont a station master, Joseph Danvenne, a vet, the old man behind me was a colonel, the youth on my left a printer. There are infant teachers, priests and we are all abandoned here without care, isolated from the rest of the world, as if for us the world ended here. Out there in the snow with concrete look outs, with the road, the sentries, I forget about the barbed wire, the wire does not count; it's just white wires you never go near and that's all. Beyond, there is Germany, completely flat. It's white imensity hurts my short-sighted eyes, deprived of glasses and weakened by illness. Yet, I like to look outside, into the distance towards where the sun goes down. There are not many houses but that's the direction we'll take, us the French, to go home!

The visits take place just as often, each time I am lucky enough to be exempted. However, several of my group having gone, I am sent into the back room. It's a real dung heap and the dampness is incredible. I paddle around in water. There is excrement everywhere. All the beds are dirtied. I am obliged to sleep with a Pole, for there is no room elsewhere. I resign myself to it. He is an old man who starts a conversation straight away but seeing a chap from the north, whom I knew at Compiegne, I leave him.

I am much better, for my dysentery has almost passed and I feel more confident when I walk. I'm hungry. Remaining in bed for long periods you think less about eating, for the days are long and the gaps between the meals interminable. Up to now, we have had a spoonful of molasses on Sunday and Wednesday mornings. It was good! Now there is nothing with the bread and the acorn tea. Once we had fish soup, very clear with many bones and scales but excellent. Lucky was the man who found mussels. (Although they had, it seems a funny smell!)

One evening the block leader receives an order "Nobody may look out of the windows any more". At once, each man must get up and the beds are moved, far from the bays. Nobody will look outside again. It is forbidden to occupy the upper beds. We pile up in the lower ones which are the dirtiest, almost always occupied by the paralytic and those with dysentery. What does it matter? I will put up with anything as long as I am left here, under cover for I feel that if I leave, with so few clothes, I will die.

Chapter 29: A MEETING

15th February. "Where are you from?"

"From the North. I'm from the centre, from Saône-et -Loire!"

I jump on hearing the name of my Department, where I left so many memories. Incredulous, I continue to listen, while queuing for the WC.

Yes, from Etang.

Don't know it.

I touch the stranger on the shoulder and say to him "You're from Etang? Me too, what's your name?

Jean Rousseau

I'm Maurice Cordonnier.

Without recognising each other, we shake hands, hardly believing that the meeting is real!

Where are the others? How are you?

I'm OK. The others are in Dachau. I left Olivier Melin at Bremen Farge, while Pierre must have gone to Hamburg. I never saw him again.

What joy to be together!

Will we make it then?

Yes, we must not give in. Where do you sleep?

At the dysentery block!

Me too, right-hand row.

You are opposite me. We will see each other a lot. Are you very bad?

No but mum's the word! It's been going on a long time. Do the same.

That's what I'm doing but I prefer to pretend to be paralysed, that way, I'm not given less soup.

Yes, we get less than you. Too bad, I prefer dysentery. Goodnight!

A meeting like that is terribly good for morale and hardens you against the trials to come.

The medical inspections are more and more frequent. All blocks are full to bursting and millions are expected to arrive. From one minute to the next, you must expect to be thrown out.

Already, all those who are not too skinny have been sent in the transports to Hamburg to dig out bombs! There is even talk of making us dig trenches or of sending us to Meppen, on the Dutch border, to replace the dead in the commando in which George Cardon from Jivry is working and where they are sinking concrete tank traps.

Chapter 30: UNDER COVER

Sometimes, to frighten us, we are made to go outside to the Assembly yard, make one or two trips from the exit to the kitchens and back in the snow which is blown into drifts by the wind, and goes right through us. They say it's a little walk to get some fresh air. Fortunately, we come back again. The dying had stayed under cover. Aufstehen, alles!

In the middle of the night. What's going on? Of course nobody gets up. Let's wait and see first. The hut overseer hits those who have not moved. We don't know whether it's an inspection or if one must remain dressed. "Razieren." Already the barbers are at work and shave the hair which is hardly 1cm long, since every week or fortnight the operation begins again. This time, we have to stand around for hours at night waiting our turn. You must be surprised at nothing! One entertainment is as good as another to take your mind off things and stifle any illusions.

Sometimes in the evening, a musician comes to play the sax for us. The sax is pleasant and I would appreciate the Pole's talent even more if I could not, at the same time, hear the man lying below me, whose throat is rattling – he has been in a coma for several hours and must have a disease of the lungs, because sometimes he gasps as though he was choking. Maybe he has asthma? Or pneumonia? Nobody bothers about him, not even his neighbour, not even the Russian prowler who watches and waits for a weakness on his part or simply for him to be dead, in order to search him, rob him of his bread if there is any left and if possible, undress him to put on his pyjama suit!

Sometimes the block overseer gives us other entertainment. A giant black boxer gives exhibitions against 3 or 4 Russian chaps who are well built. Those who are in good health can watch but I have never liked that type of sport.

Washraum, alles! Heraus!

Everyone to the sinks! Out!

As we do not walk fast enough, in the opinion of the SS doctor who wants everyone to be clean before visiting the sick, the subordinates charge in with their whips, throw to the ground those who do not move, without waiting to see if they are dead, paralytic or just asleep. Now what are we going to do in the washroom? In an hour or two, everyone is standing, that is to say out of bed, in the passages. We pass naked once again before the SS who says nothing. We are looked at all over, with a large electric lamp. If you are dirty, the Pole says Schwein, washroom. If you are clean, he says with a blasé air, Gut, schlaffen and you go to wait in the corridor.

Often, he sends to the washroom those who are clean but whom he does not like. Completely naked, I wait in the corridor with about 30 others, shivering, while others are already stationed in the washroom in which the window is open! During this visit, striped-clad Boche, SS, Poles and doctors remain at a distance from us, for they dare not touch us because of our dirt and also because they really believe themselves to be superior.

Now, they are bringing the paralytic and the bad cases of dysentery, who can no longer stand as they are so weak. This procession of naked men carried by the arms and legs is something quite painful. Some are hardly moving and let themselves be led. They are so thin that they look as though they could only live two days. Their arms and legs evoke pity and you could count their ribs. On top of all that, their mess has left brown scabs on their white skin. The huge cylindrical tanks made of cement are full of water; the cold jets are blasting through. It is the Russian chaps who supervise this cleaning. The sick are dipped completely into the icy water and rubbed with brushes! They howl, gasp, feel faint and fall. The Russians take no notice, push them under the jets, and immerse them. When the Boche goes by, he seizes them and holds their heads under the water. Water runs everywhere and the cries, howls and supplications from the poor patients mix with the laughs of the overseers.

During this time, I look in, trying to appear indifferent too but my heart is full of rage and anger and I swear that I will have vengeance, that I will avenge them. I know there will be revenge. Yes, more than ever, we must live to avenge those who, before our eyes, are already in agony in the tanks or who, running with water, wait squashed against one another along the walls to be taken back to their mattress where they will be able to dry off, or die, in order to no longer be cold!

There is still a violent draught, which freezes my belly and brings on a new attack of diarrhoea. Is nature against us then? Is everything against us, right up to the end, and right up to our end? Yet the news is good. There is fighting along the Rhine. It's only a question of time now. We must hold on. Oh, if the Allies knew what was going on! Some are discouraged when you speak to them of troops arriving and yet they will come but in how many months time? In how many days? The French doctors are cautious and according to them we will not be home before Christmas. "Wohin?" cries the little Russian to a poor old man who goes out howling. He's only a boy and the old man is kicked. They have become monsters and us; we stay there like animals, only hoping for one thing, to go back to bed, to get back into our rags.

The poor unfortunates who have nothing with which to dry themselves – how many will die? They all look like corpses. I am hardly better than they but I can't see myself.

These days, the Tod commando is called every minute. Some are not even dead yet but in spite of the vigilance of the French doctors or nurses, they are undressed and carried outside. The corpses lie on the paving stones at the top of the stairs. While awaiting the return of the stretcher bearers, the porters, under cover of darkness, pull out their gold teeth when they have any, but secretly, because this operation is reserved for the SS.

I sleep with Mestres from Nogent-sur-Marne. Very nice but with no will. If I left him to himself, he would eat nothing and drink the water. By reminding him that he has children, I make him respond a little, in spite of his oedema and his dysentery. To forget our common misery, I make him talk of his work, of his region, which takes our minds a long way away and excites us to live. We even make plans for the future. We persuade each other that our absurd and inconceivable situation is just a passing illusion, just a trial which we will overcome.

In spite of the misery which we no longer even see, in spite of the bowl peddlers, in spite of the fury of the elements against man, in spite of the discomfort of this bed which is too narrow for three, in spite of the ban imposed on looking out of the window, in spite of these barrack roofs covered in snow, the camp, the wire all around and out there a long way away, in spite of Germany as a whole, we maintain our hope of being free men again one day.

I have seen Jean Rousseau again. He is well and holding out. We cheer each other up each time we meet. Joseph Beauverne has not changed either, he is holding on thanks to this superstitious idea that the fact of never having been ill is preserving him and guaranteeing good health. News appears to be excellent from each side but there are no details. The French Army is said to be taking part in the operations and there is even open talk of the Liberation, despite the threat of death. There are alerts, every night and it is said that the railways are being bombed. We will not be able to be evacuated if the Americans are coming but what will they do with us? We cannot do anything. Maybe there will be parachute drops and that must be why they don't want us to look outside.

Suddenly there are vibrant explosions and cries. They are bombing the camp. Spirits are so excited that there is a crowding and a terrible panic, despite the ardour of the "stubedienst! I do not move. Is it the end? There are some further explosions but in spite of a fire and a crowd of striped men with buckets and pumps, it is only an accident. They say the infirmary is on fire but it's not certain. Could it be the clothes store where the vats of grease are kept? Smoke is rising. Will we ever know what is happening exactly? The SS shout orders – the whole day is one of agitation.

The camp is short of clothes. There is a general check and we are left in just shirts, in order to clothe the workers who are going to leave. Shoes, clogs, sabots, even flip flops are taken away from those who still have them. For a week, Mestres and I have pretended to be paralysed and only get up in secret or at night. Therefore, during the visits, I do not move. We have had an extra and unexpected ration of mouldy bread. Many give it or swap it for water or a little soup.

The chap above me still worries us for his voice is stifled by tubercular laryngitis. Those opposite look very strange. Their gestures and movements are incoherent, their arms wave about like those of a mechanism which has become worn and upset through a strange and unknown cause. One man is constantly weeping, crying that his pillow has been taken, another would like to write but can no longer remember the address and another has his face deformed by a horrific grimace, he is very bad. Every morning, the smell of excreta which comes up from the ground is unbearable and the sweepers have quite a job getting along the passages crowded with the dysentery and paralytic cases who meet there.

Chapter 31: PROVIDENCE

Suddenly, a large transport is announced but we can hardly believe it, because it must be the 20th time it's been promised. There is a medical inspection. I do not move and remain next to Mestres who fears that we will be discovered by the Polish spies. We pretend to sleep while remaining alert to the sounds of the procession of sick men who are shivering with no clothes on. The French doctors urge us also to go to the inspection. Don't let's move! According to everybody, I am and remain paralytic. Transport? Leaving? – but where? Just when the Americans are about to arrive! I shall remain at all costs. The two rooms of the block are a hive of activity. This unstable situation tires and irritates us all. If only we knew what was going on by the exit. Are we going, yes or no? By train? On foot? It's not possible.

I am tired of lying down and have to get to the toilet without being seen. It is there, 3 or 4 yards from the wall but a Pole has forbidden access. Sometimes he moves off to chat. I take advantage of that moment but I am caught coming back and he shouts at me in his wicked way. "Passieren tu, aber Transport, schnell" and leads me to the queue, murmuring continuously "Discipline, discipline, nicht gut deutchland kamarade Franzouses". I can do nothing. I do not have the strength and I am caught in the one-way system of patients. It's impossible to go back. My turn comes. It's the first number check at the exit of our room. The same cards are still well filed in the overseers' little box. They are checking. I go out. Another queue waiting. I lean against the beds but lots of men are lying on the floor. There is more movement in this room and already I am regretting my imprudence which is once again making me lose my bunk companions. I crouch down on an empty bed. This inspection is longer than usual but we don't get undressed until the last moment. I try to slip into a bed but I am seen at once and beaten. The French doctors advise us to be sensible and I hate them for it. Why this obedience? Do they have no hope any more, or are they just pretending to command? Finally, I give in. We will see. We are made to hurry: "Get undressed!" Clothes under the right arm, naked men herded together in the WC. The SS are at the back of the room on the left. We move in single file. There are five of them, saying nothing and pointing out the way to go. I walk anywhere. There are SS in the corridor, gesticulating and asking questions. I am made to leave the block. I go down some stairs, arrive outside, still naked in front of hundreds of prisoners who are watching what is going on. I don't know where to go. A man in green points at a door, more stairs which I mount slowly. Same agitation I get dressed and they give out the soup in the disgusting bowls. I drink it standing up in the hustle. We have to wait for others who are arriving when I learn that we are down for Block 2. Departure seems to be imminent.

I am given new clothes and some women's stockings, silk ones. We can no longer stand. Suddenly, the SS camp leader appears lists in hand. Roll call begins in alphabetical order. Will I be going? To my great surprise, I see old friends from Bremen-Farge pass by — Andre Chaumont and Maurice Clement. They have not seen me. I could not say anything to them. Will I be called? Yes, that's it. Outside? I cannot believe my eyes.

There are lorries and coaches with red crosses on them and the Swedish flag. Our numbers are sewn onto our new clothes; prisoners are installed on the pavement with sewing machines. Is it really happening? Is the war over? There must be an exchange of prisoners. The Red Cross! It's been so long, we wondered if it still existed!

I try to rejoin my friends but how can one walk with legs so thin, which don't obey any more. No more cabbage soup or bad boards! Help is here. In small groups, we wait. The lorries come and go — some full of prisoners have already left. It's our turn. There are Swedish soldiers from the Freigamarine, still armed and smoking cigars. Off we go! We don't know where we are going but maybe towards the frontier.

Everyone is excited as can be but nobody says a word. The sick don't even think about their pain any more. We can only look out through the front window for all the others have been covered with planks. The benches are very hard on our pointed buttocks but I feel myself privileged, for about 10 are sitting on the floor. We cross countryside again, villages and streets with people well-dressed. We are free and they turn around as they see us go by. Did they know what has happened to us? They could certainly not see us from outside. We are going south. A stop to let out those who want to go. Fields, meadow, everywhere. A Swede even gives out toilet paper. We get in again and move off. It is dark. I sleep. We have arrived. I feel much moved, for without a doubt our trial is over. In spite of the total darkness, I make our barracks which we leave on our right, then others. We are not hurried. If we do not walk fast enough to keep up with the group, we are helped. I am terribly hungry and this lorry increases my fatigue even more. We look as though we have been abandoned and are wandering anywhere, carried by the wind which is just as cold. A building is lit up. Suddenly one of us says, I recognise it, it's Brunschwig, an old camp from 1914. This is Wattenschted.

Chapter 32: DISAPPOINTMENT

The wooden barracks is gloomy. You can make out a few beds, two storeys high. Is everything to begin again then? What was the Red Cross doing? Fobbing off? Playing the act? Fear of punishment? – And what about the Swedish soldiers, what were they doing? Complicity? I cannot understand any of it and there was not even any food. At least there are mattresses. We are going to sleep. We are given mugs for the soup ration. It's by the door but the order to serve has not been given! The better informed are already explaining that there is a large factory, making bombs. After drinking a mug of flour gruel, we give ourselves up to our mattresses.
Wattenstadt.
I am in the 7th row of Block 11 with paralytics and those with dysentery. I am neither one nor the other but continue to play the act before it's too late. Camp life is still the same, with interminable Roll calls for those who don't work. I have the luck to be noted down by my Belgian friend who is head of the row, as seriously ill, which spares me from going out. Therefore we remain constantly in this row, which I have sworn, come what may, never to leave until the Liberation. No more Roll calls! Just stay lying down, two steps from the barrels serving as toilets, not be too cold, eating in bed. I don't want to move from here. There is a washroom at the end of the yard on the left and I do not go there. I have not the strength.
My friends from the Vosges are here; Maurice Clement too, in the 6th row. I would like to go over but I would disturb him too much with my dysentery and he always goes out for Roll call. He would like to do what I do but his chief is a Dutch brute who sends everyone outside. To my great surprise, Olivier Malin and Jean Bousseau are here, in one of the next blocks. They often come to see me with Maurice Clement. "The Americans are coming," they tell me. In a fortnight they will be here, the main thing is not to move from here. In any case, where will they evacuate us to now, since they are surrounded on all sides? Had we stayed at Neuengamme, we would have been liberated two weeks earlier.
The bread is better here but we only get it once a day, in the evening, with margarine and some very oily and good dog pate, although green and spoiled. The soup is never cooked and the carrots are black but with stomach ache, you are less hungry. It's quite a comedy this hand-out, for there is no more method than at Neuengamme and the jostling is indescribable. Some have three helpings, others none at all.

"Miska, chissel!, is heard shouted at each moment. Sometimes a barrel is tipped over or when too roughly handled, falls to bits. The soup spills over. The starving Frenchmen and foreigners, rush to pick up the pieces of carrot which have fallen, with their fingers. They have forgotten everything. They just think about eating. I already saw that at Farge where Frenchmen blatantly picked up from the dust, some noodles which had fallen from a kapo's tin.

Behind me, Mirabelle from Montelimar, explains the confection of almond and hazelnut nougat to his neighbours, who hang on his every word and have the recipe repeated several times so as not to forget it, for they have nothing on which to write it down. The soup is sometimes very late coming, because there is no punctuality any more. The SS make rare appearances and never say anything. The block leader no longer even announces them by the cry "Achtung" (attention, SS, attention, silence).

There are frequent alerts, for at Brunschwig the sirens are sounding all day long. We have been ordered never to leave the barracks during an alert, otherwise the search towers will open fire but there are always people late or roaming around. It is forbidden to be seen at the windows but there are always some who manage to creep up and look outside. "Planes hum. Guns are booming in the distance but is it flak or artillery? Nobody works any more at the bomb factory, for it has been destroyed but sweeping up must be done in spite of the weather. Our predecessors, who though they would have nothing more to do after the English has passed over, now have an even more difficult job, for they are no longer under cover. They even miss the hard job they had before at the ovens!

Every day is longer and longer as we wait for the end. We begin to wonder if it is possible that the Boche will let us live in the hands of the Liberators. I am already working out all sorts of escape routes. Hide in a mattress, under the floor of the block, under a bed, under a tub. With a bit of luck, all will be well. One thing intrigues me however. Can the war end without gas being used? It's not possible. The Boche will use it and then we are done for.

Gross alarm! Hou, ou hou, ou.... All the sirens are going. The Americans are said to be only a few miles away. Do they know the camp? Will they recognise us? Planes! Here they are! Many run outside, look out of the windows. Already there are gun shots, a shower of bombs, cannon fire, German flak and in the camp between the barracks, the very air is vibrating, the earth shaking, the windows of the block are blown out! I curl up on my mattress. It must be a squadron, for we can hear the planes whistling as they dive and pass overhead. Boom, boom! Suddenly, it is dark. Bombed! A general panic..... Beds are tipped over; patients fall, run like madmen.

The bombs fell not far from here. The American tanks must be near. Then order is restored in an astonishing calm. Any dead? Any buried alive? Any injured? A large bomb fell 100 yards from the block which is still burning. I would like to see what is happening too but can only wait for the details which friends bring me. We only think of one thing. Where are the Liberators? The dull shots of the cannon bring us a joy without precedent. At last the war is coming nearer; we are going to take part in it! An order is given which we cannot believe. Total evacuation. Everyone is going, even the sick! They are capable of anything. Leave? How? With what? Some are certain that we are going to have large-scale reinforcements. There is general disorder. Nobody works any more. There is one Roll call after another, never ending. The most contradictory ideas and sounds excite imaginations and you can sense the Americans coming when the Boche move away. The kapos and other top brass are dressed as civilians, with new boots and suits. Even the SS may have a civilian suit in their case. "Transport", always transport. They only have that word on their minds, as though Germany had no limits and was as vast as Russia!

A dense cloud of smoke rises in the sky. Some say – "It's Brunschwig, which the Americans are burning before evacuating". I don't know if that's true. The thick smoke gets nearer and from my bunk, I have the impression that it's asphyxiating gas, then reassure myself.

We are going to have a loaf – a whole one! What luck! We can't stop thinking of it. How long will it have to last? I only have one woman's stocking and no flip flops any more. I am sorry to leave but too bad, we'll see. There is no longer talk of departure but I am eaten up with impatience, uncertainty, the silence, even the guns which you can no longer hear.

I see Olivier and Jean again. Maurice is no longer here. He must have changed blocks. Olivier is constantly roaming around the camp. We will go back to France together! Rendez-vous in my block because I dare not walk. The habit of being in bed has sapped my remaining strength!

Suddenly, there is a loud cry – "Brot holen." The bread bearers have in fact arrived. From a lorry running a shuttle service, the bread is given out. Blankets are needed to carry it to each block. Large blankets, the biggest, the least dirty – and the loaves are whole! The general animation is incredible and one can clearly sense the preparations for a transport. Unless the SS are going and leaving us reinforcements but the rumour is that there is nothing to make soup with. The kitchens are closed. The cooks have gone.

We each receive a large 500gr loaf, 100gr of margarine and some dog pate. Some too ill, too emontional, cannot eat. I am ravenous and fortunately a friend still has his knife. The pate is excellent but I didn't taste it because I swallowed it without even chewing! I put the margarine in my mug and the bread in my rag. I shall remain in bed until the end. An order is given. It's the departure, for everyone. I do not move. The stubedienst get us out of bed by force. If I have to walk, I am lost. In fives, we are counted before getting on the train. It is very big too, this camp, and we pass several gates covered in barbed wire. Nothing interests me any more. All my friends are dispersed elsewhere and I shut myself up within my selfishness. We have to walk barefoot in the mud and I think again of Bremen Farge but there, I was strong, whereas here, I am ill and simply exhausted.

I pay no attention to anything. I notice the sun however, so rare in this cursed country which is always grey. It comforts me a little, I am astonished at being able to walk but can only take small steps. Others who are suffering more than me are being carried. The road is long and in vain I look for the trucks!

The Boche exhort us with words, as do the kapos. Are they frightened? What could we do if parachutists came? My feet are quite grazed on the stones and my head aches terribly. As I have no string as a belt any more, I have to hold up my trousers which are too big. With my arm, I hold with difficulty my bread and my mug full of margarine, already dirty. Some are trailing loose bandages but I try to thread along without too much trouble in the middle of this troop of misery. Suddenly we stop! It must be the trucks. Yes, I can see some prisoners! "There are women" says a voice. Yes, and some even have the striped habit. Suddenly there are lorries on the road which will pass us. More women. There is no doubt, they are evacuating everybody – but why is their convoy coming from the station? They cry out – "French? French? Yes, French" we answer. "La Nievre, Burgundy, Nevers". Yes, yes, I cry. It's such a long time since I saw some women, women from home but the lorry has gone.

"Nazate, nazate" the Russians command. What? Backwards? Kein transport. "That's it, we're going back". I find courage from somewhere. This time we have won the game. Lines must be cut off. I am so happy! While walking, I nibble my bread. Too bad for tomorrow. Tomorrow, 'They' might be there. I no longer feel the fatigue which bears down on me, nor my tortured feet on the stones. We are going back, we are staying. It's marvellous. Just the thought of the tomb-like trucks was frightening me! I feel as though our slowness saved us! At various spots, corpses are stretched out on the ground, abandoned. Many from my group already have hardly any bread left and are trying to steal some. Starving men are arguing over something left under a mattress but I go back to bed, I am happy, I can wait.

"Transport" somebody cries outside, during the night. Maybe I dreamt it? It's not possible! I pray to God yet again that he lets me stay on this mattress. "Transport, alles raus". Another transport. The gravely ill stay put it seems, with the doctors, so I don't move. We're not staying long, all is quiet. There is not even an alert – at least I can't hear the sirens. The yard opposite is deserted, then there is a loud clamour from far off – they are coming back. Nobody can leave now. Nobody knows exactly any more, what is happening and the darkness increases the mystery even more!

We hardly ever see, even from time to time, any SS with their lamps. Nobody sleeps much. All just wander about, dream, chat between the beds. The block leader has gone off to a big meeting of all the top brass of the camp. We will have precise details, maybe some orders. I still have half my bread and my margarine. I am looking for shoes but don't find any, even though there was a hand-out at midday. This time that's it, we're all going, the sick and the dying. They say "those who hide will be shot." The SS will visit the huts with their revolvers to finish off any who remain. Contrary to just now, when we were threatened with death for taking away a blanket, we are allowed to take one now. I make up my mind, because you have to. The French doctors themselves implore us to go, our only chance of being saved. Those who have already made the trip to the station and back twice, cannot go on and one cannot see clearly.

Suddenly the camp is lit up. We are counted at each door. I can no longer see any kapos. Everyone is in civilian dress. They even have suitcases. We move forward for 50 yards and then the column stops and we have to wait. Many lie down and they are left alone, they are not beaten but nobody bothers about them. I would like to lie down too but something in me stops me from doing so for I am cold and frightened. Frightened of that cold earth, this is why I want to wait before lying down. Some of them deliberately break ranks and wait standing up or crouched down, not quite knowing how to fight against the wind, fatigue and sleep!

An extraordinary thing is that I no longer have dysentery at all! I see several unfortunates who have to sit down anywhere and who often don't have time to do it. Many, stricken with an unknown illness and doubtless incurable, cannot walk a step. I no longer have any friends. My short sightedness robs me of any hope of recognising them and I no longer look for them. I am constantly a witness to the most tragic scenes. A son carries his father on his back but the father doesn't want him to for he cannot go on. He wants to sleep, he is cold and orders him to leave him in the ditch or next to a barrack, out of the wind. Two brothers take leave of each other – one is leaving the other dying, without saying goodbye, without embracing him, without even trying to comfort him. As I ask him if he is going to die, he answers me in a slight accent of the Auvergne "What do you want him to do, it had to happen." During the procession which goes on for ever, it's a battle as to who can complain the most and display, in the darkness, the greatest possible proof of his weakness. Amongst the more able-bodied, the competition is for who can walk the slowest, who will arrive among the last, you must stroll, drag behind as slowly as possible. A few gun shots can be heard and the intermittent rat-tat of a machine gun. Some, walking in groups, hold each other's arms, others advance for 50 yards then come back. Some cry and moan, imploring someone to help them but we don't know if it's a Russian, a Pole or anyone else who is begging. Still others, fairly strong, take advantage of the confusion to play the very worst trick. They pretend to be the kindly soul, full of compassion, supporting an unfortunate as he walks, picks him up and takes him far up the road. The patient feels reassured, takes courage but there is no doubt that his new friend has his eye on any bread he has left. He gets a small piece first then since the rest is in the way, takes it under his protection and takes advantage of the jostling to make off!

Those who remained on the edge of the road are now carried by the stronger ones on pulled carts. The idea of being carried incites the weak ones to exaggerate their weakness, they literally let themselves fall in front of the porters who mumble something and load them on with no attention or consideration, in spite of the complaints and curses. I prefer to continue walking, but we are flagging – the road is long and our legs are weak. I am afraid mine will fold up under me. The last gate, the last wire, the last arc lamps which sweep the countryside continuously. We go out but to my great surprise we take the opposite direction from that of the station. My neighbour thinks that we may be going on foot. We are made to stop after 100 yards, then turn round. We must wait for the camp to be empty. We will take the last ones, no need to be discouraged – you must resign yourself and pray that in an hour or two, we will be gone, hoping that we will remain standing! I still have my woman's stocking but it no longer has a foot. Somebody is stretched out at the edge of the road and I notice his flip flops but have not got the strength to bend down, nor the will to go up to him. Will I have the strength to steal from a dead man? I no longer want to think of his unused flip flops which another person will take without any doubt.

Some lit-up lorries pass by us and it's quite a job to move when your feet are stuck in mud and your legs are giving way. We move forward. I sigh involuntarily and I am not the only one. What does it matter where we are going? We are moving, all I can see is the darkness and the bent backs in front which guide me. Like them, I walk leaning forward, head down. It's a habit which comes naturally and without realising it. An locomotive coughs ominously. Where are the trucks? Nobody knows anything and there are hundreds of thousands of us. At last, a rolling of iron tells me....

Some presume that we will not get in until tomorrow. Discouraged, many lie down, then the whole of my group does so, including my two neighbours. So, I do the same! The cement is very cold but it is good to rest a little and you feel the wind less. We draw near to each other. I take the opportunity to eat a little and finish my margarine full of pieces of glass. The night is very starry. Planes, flak, bombs, dull thuds! I don't care. I sleep. What a fine night!

Suddenly the line of trucks begins shunting. It's our turn. We have to get up but how cold it is when you're standing up! They are open carts. I foresee at once the terrible fate which we are going to endure. Men press forward. People jostle. I go nearer and as I hesitate, I am pushed up like a parcel. I roll onto something hard. An SS detailed to loading finishes counting, 68, 69, 70. A clash of iron, we are shut in with the night sky as a roof!

Chapter 33: MEDUSA'S RAFT

Since we have left, only one thing is important to me — sleep! Anywhere, anyhow, but to sleep. All my energy is focused towards that end but what a rocky position, what a tangle. My head is resting on a piece of wood which must be a cross-piece. I am well off, for I like to sleep with my head high but my legs are wedged as though in a vice, between the clogs of one friend and the head of another. The swaying motion sends me to sleep but without bringing me any rest, for I feel as though my bones are sticking through my skin, each bump, and each jolt makes me wake up in pain. I recall the truck with 103 men in it in which we were so hot but with no air. I thank God to have put us in open trucks, since like this we will not die of suffocation. The violent draught which tears into my poor blanket of damp wood-wool, too worn to protect me, means that I am frozen. I neither know who I am with or if they are French, for tonight, a difficult one but with plenty of rest all the same, has seemed short to me. Already there are signs indicating daybreak… We are still travelling… I remain with my head hidden under my blanket so as not to see anything, hear anything, trying to forget, to feel nothing. You are better at night. You do not think as you do during the daylight, always there to show us things which are not pretty. I have become like an animal who thinks that when his head is hidden he is safe but isn't it a bit like that? When I can't see anything, I close my eyes, forget reality, dream of other places… During this time, the hours go by and we travel on and then …we will arrive.

It is full daylight, heads gradually emerge from the blankets. Tired heads, hollow, filthy with the mask of death. The men at the back are asleep. Nobody moves! We must already be a long way away. Frenchmen! — They are saying good morning. I am between the two doors. The best places are undoubtedly along the walls but I have the cross-piece and it gives me great help to sleep. Above is the cloudy sky and sometimes the tops of a few trees, fir trees, which once again disappear. I eat two mouthfuls of bread but I am neither hungry nor thirsty. I have one crust left, which I hide carefully under my jacket. It is day — when will we arrive? My hands disgust me with their filthy blackness of grime and coal. I can feel that my face must be in the same state! We cannot be far from the engine because we are covered in coal dust. It is dark again. The train has stopped 2 or 3 times in stations, obviously. I did not see anything as I cannot get up. In any case, this or that station, it doesn't matter but one thing is certain, that we are going towards the east. There is nothing interesting in this cursed country in which I fear I shall leave my bones. Everything leaves me indifferent now. I am confident that we will have to get out of this train but I am terribly tired of this truck which is too narrow, in which I can neither stretch my legs or turn around when I am tired of staying in one position too long, so much so, that I am bent over and covered with bruises as if I had been showered with blows. Exasperation, intolerance, selfishness and violence, therefore begin to take hold of minds and bodies already worn out. There are frequent kicks and the strongest man is always right. Woe on the man whose legs are too long, or who has not found a place to rest his head or lean his shoulder when night comes, he will only be able to do so after hundreds of attempts to push a foot out of the way, a leg which is too long, a body with no will and after receiving punches or kicks in his face. In the middle of the general crush, I remain stoical. I put up with everything in silence and sometimes manage to sleep.

Dawn is coming, gradually uncovering the sinister ravages of the night. Two corpses, half naked are stretched out on my right – a Frenchman and a Russian. What will be done with them? Suddenly the train stops. A Boche appears, standing on the buffers – "Wieviel man kaput"? Nobody answers him. He gets down again, comes back and brings 7 glass containers of red beetroot. Some get up and take them. "Ein Flasche, zehn man" The German Jews and the Poles take on the role of kapos and distribute the beetroot in slices. Every Black Hand is stretched out. It is good but there is so little of it and the Boche have had a good helping. Moreover, they kept the dead men's share!

Five days later, we are still travelling. There are only 48 of us left, counting the 5 dead which we have not yet been allowed to throw out because the Germans and the Poles don't want to acknowledge them, in order to keep their share of beetroot, water and bread – when there is some.

The succession of days and nights increases our fatigue, thirst, the incredible filth which encourages vermin and the smell of the corpses. Our destination is still unknown – sometimes we travel north, sometimes south or west. The uncertainty grips us and I have as little appetite as I have courage. I give myself up to the mercy of God. I had to give up my last crust of bread, almost whole, so as not to be lynched by the Pole who, thinking I was dead, tried to undress me. Now I give him my beetroot so that he lets me sleep between him and the German Jew. The Jew too, interferes because he has seen that I have a crust left. I don't want to give it to him in front of the other, otherwise I am lost. He proposes the last of a full tin of water he was able to get during a stop. Seeing my hesitation, he seizes my blanket. I resign myself to giving him the bread. He gives me back the blanket and gives me a little book which he sometimes looks at. Curious, I try to read it. Books are so scarce but I can only see signs and symbols. It's in Hebrew…

The middle beam has been removed and I now try to sleep on the floor, one half of my head on a shoe, the other on my tin. I made an unexpected encounter. A chap from my home area, Gaston Brossard from Artenay, a regimental chum of Lucian Lagnay the baker from Chateauneuf, big Lulu as he is called. We talk about the area and I notice from his look that he is still strong, for he gets up often to try and see the countryside and during stops to try and get water. A terrible thirst takes hold of all of us. As soon as the train stops the strongest get up, in spite of the stones which are thrown at us, by those people who are near the fountains. They tie on anything which will hold water, mugs, tins, bottles, jars, pails which serve as toilets and pass them over the side with great difficulty. Sometimes they are filled up but that's rare for it's the same problem at all the trucks, the same cries, the same calls and one hears water asked for in all languages. As soon as the container is filled, the holder pulls it to him despite the jostle and drinks if he can. Therefore, as soon as someone holds a bucket of water out towards the truck, the melee begins again and I am trampled on. Though I cry out, beat with my fists to get free, people walk all over me.

Gastin Brossard is still sturdy, fights well and defends me sometimes, although friends no longer exist – it's just a fight against dying at once. The Poles and the Boches are bad but the French are too!

So, the large battle for containers begins. I still have my mug but as I can't get up, the Polish Jew uses it each time and never gives me water in exchange. Many who have neither tin nor bottle, try to get some by any means. Gaston has carefully kept his jar – some Frenchmen claim it belongs to them – punches and kicks are exchanged over my head, which I cannot lower any more because it is touching the floor. A Boche joins in and a blanket and jacket are torn. Gaston defends himself and would rather break the bottle than give it to them. This little incident amuses me. In our mobile prison, another anxiety is therefore added to that of thirst – how to answer the call of nature? In the beginning we had a bucket which we emptied during the march and a bottle to act as a urinal, which we could pass around but now the bucket is used to store water! Sometimes, several go in turns on the same piece of material and the last man throws it away. For urinating, the situation is just as bad if not worse. Some use their mugs or jars which they then wipe as best they can with a rag. Others go against the iron door but the urine runs as much inside as outside and even reaches us!

We are living in a filthy mess. My dry lips are bloody and stuck together by a crust of dust and coal. I can feel something thick stuck around my eyes and to my nose. Our fingernails are longer than claws and our hands are covered with hardened cracks. I no longer even have a sense of time and don't know whether we've been gone for several days, nor if I've slept for one hour or for 14. In this box, open to the wind and cold rain, often unsteady, sometimes motionless from dawn to dusk, dead and dying crouched over, piled up, sprawled, I feel as though we are living the very worst kind of horror.

Are we not in fact lost and almost condemned, those which Gericault told of so well? The beatitude of the dying, troubled eyes of those who stare fixedly, the astonishing whiteness of the flattened stomach of an undressed corpse, shapeless heaps where nothing is definable under the blankets, the smell of urine, of sweat and an indescribable mixture of coal dust, vomit and excrement, the tragedy continues to unfold, although some of those responsible remain hidden behind the scenes.

Each day passes slowly and we live without knowing why we force ourselves to live. I wonder too why the man on my left is always falling on top of me. He's a Russian. He never speaks but this time I sense that he is dead.

At Neuengamme, I had this strange feeling of being next to a corpse but there at least, they were taken away. Here, how long am I going to have him leaning against me and I am so weak, I cannot even push him away for he is already stiff and shrivelled. Also, I feel as if it was a contagious disease. I also notice that all the fleas have left it and are going to invade me, doubtless happy to have found a new prey. Then, my ideas no longer remain clear. I would like to talk to Gaston Brossard, who is asleep opposite me. I'm thirsty. I still hope that all this will end and that I will touch ground again, walk on solid earth, find water, finally leave forever these damned hard boards, so uncomfortable and which in a way are like a hearse.

Sometimes we stop for hours and I manage to get up when Gaston can help me. Sometimes, it's a station, a marshalling yard or just in the countryside, in the middle of the track. Some Germans, who know the area, say that we have retraced our steps. It's heart breaking! At one stop "Wittenberg" we were allowed to get out to do the necessary and the prisoner nurses, subjected to the same rules as ourselves, were able to re-do a few dressings, treat the worst cases of abscess, the wounds complicated by gangrene which at first sight look fatal. The nurses are swamped and have very little time but their presence has done a lot for morale. Those who remain without treatment and see that nobody is bothering about them beg: "Doctor, Doctor." There are calls from all, over, some showing a frightful leg, swollen and blotchy, some a deformed hand, a bare back covered with poisonous wounds, pointed hips covered with brown pustules, a face whose skin is shiny with oedema, some asking for the 10th, 100th time: "Water, give me a drink doctor. Give me a drink, I have a fever" or just "I'm thirsty." I will never be able to thank God enough for not having boils, abscesses or dysentery. I have several fairly large wounds on both of my legs but all that is nothing compared to the hideous wounds which surround me. Some of the poor sick with dysentery, like skeletons, weep softly. They look completely emptied and thirst eats them even more than it does me.

During this stop, Gaston helped me get down by carrying me as much as he could but as soon as I no longer have something to lean against, my legs give way beneath me. I feel as though paralysis is beginning. We take advantage of the stop to lift down our dead and the same thing is going on all along the train. We have noticed a brook a few yards away but you have to cross several tracks where trucks are lined up. It is forbidden to move away and above all to go that far, where you could drink. The Russians chance it however and carefully bring back their tin filled with dirty water! An SS notices, takes out his revolver and fires. We are made to get back in again, quickly. Some Boche soldiers receive a ration of beer, before our very eyes! Two Russians rush over, plunge their tin into the barrel, avoid the butt-blows which would have knocked them out and run off drinking. The incident is at once dominated by whistle blasts. We are moving again. I approach the truck with Gaston but the SS, deciding that we are not quick enough, rewards us with a violent butt-blow in the back. It makes me stagger, I tense up to stop myself falling but cannot get in. I am therefore, thrown inside with violence and fall again in the midst of the others. That escapade, if I may say, has brought me back to life, for it is good to touch firm ground when you are not used to it. At times, I ask myself: How long could I hold out with such a regime? The beetroot is no good to me, because I pass it out just as quickly as I absorb it. My throat, tongue, teeth, lips are horribly dry and irritated by the coal dust.

We are still travelling. It is another night. The side of the truck, where I am is favoured, for we are all hidden under blankets. The others have had theirs taken away by the Germans and the Poles, who, huddled close to one another, use them as pillows. With both hands under my head, I sleep between two clogs. Suddenly waking, I notice the sky above us is strangely crossed by red wisps.

What awful coal can they be burning in the engine? It is no surprise that we often get cinders on us and feel covered by thick coal! The speed of our crate increases still more and again I doze. Suddenly, I feel something burning my leg. At the same moment, the men next to me seem to be getting up. Immediately, there are cries of Fire, mind the blankets, there's a fire on board! Our blankets, made of wooden material, like the rags which remain on our backs, are covered with a 1 cm layer of ash, still hot and even red. A strong smell of burnt cloth comes off our clothes. I do not move. "Fire, Fire". Small flames appear. Some men get up and put them our near where they are but cannot go everywhere. "Fire, Fire, Fire!" They cry outside in German, in the faint hope that they will be heard and that something will be done. In the black sky, red stripes and sparks continue to rise above us. Then, all at once, with a long sigh and a noise of water falling, I feel myself being dowsed. A jet of water has spurted from the engine. The flames have gone but now we are soaked. In a smell of damp cloth combined to that of smoke, I fall asleep again and forget the incident which could have been our downfall.

At daybreak, we are covered with black ash and have to put out a small pocket of flames. My trousers and blanket have been eaten up in the fire but why move? The morning freshness sticks my rags all along my damp body. My cap, too big, pulled down over my eyes, gives me a feeling of warmth and I secretly thank God for the calm which reigns in our truck. I manage to realise that we are being given something to drink; I am afraid of being walked on. The whole of my left side is bruised and during last night, I received so many blows that I can no longer feel my leg.

During a stop in a marshalling yard, we stop beside a train carrying vegetables. The Jerries watch us and show no emotion whatever at the sight of the misery of our convoy. We are certainly not the first that they've seen in this situation. Suddenly to amuse themselves, they cry: "How many are you? Do you want some cabbages? What, 40?" The train leaves. They threw just one cabbage which is at once devoured by the more adroit and the more robust, who finish it in a few mouthfuls! The movement of the cabbage eaters makes a general commotion for their places are at once taken by legs and bodies which are stretched out. The Pole, furious with the imposter who has taken his place, breaks his ribs by kicking him. The unfortunate howls for some time without moving, and in spite of the kicks which sound in his back, remains motionless and silent. The Pole picks him up, throws him on top of the others who reply with curses - One more dead!

In this devilish and always uncertain race, the miles add to the miles. I only got up twice to look at the countryside but nothing is interesting and often the view is limited for many miles to the artificial green curtain which runs along the track and without doubt hides a bombed industrial region or some military buildings which it is forbidden to look at.

We are travelling on a main line, with double tracks and all the trains of prisoners and soldiers go in the same direction, just like the train-loads of guns, tanks, materials, covered in nets and foliage. One wonders what is really happening and how the war is going. We have been flown over several times and even machine gunned. Americans? British? Russian? German? God knows. We stop for at least an hour in a marshalling yard, which seems blocked. On the other line, a train-load of guns is escorted by women soldiers, dressed like the SS with the same shield. One of them calls out to one of our Kriegsmarine guards and says;

Why are you taking so much trouble over that vermin? The SS will take care of getting rid of them!

Then, as the train moves off, the old Boche with the moustache answers something like:

"Be quiet. In a fortnight, you may be happy to sleep with them!"

Eight days! This must be our ninth night and nothing indicates an imminent goal. Sometimes, I feel as though I am stuck to these cursed moving boards which never cease to shake us up. I have finally managed to stretch out one leg and, although one of my arms is stiff, I am OK. Again we stop. When we are travelling it seems really as though we are dreaming and time passes so much more quickly. Have we arrived? "Heraus, alles." The locks, bars of the left-hand door suddenly move. Electric lamps, a coming and going of boots in the night. "Los, los." Several men are standing and get out. I can no longer count on Gaston, too weak himself. I do not move, although I try to raise myself up on my arms. Others, remain lying down. I do the same but there are several dead among them. "Los, los, schnell." Jostling, trampling, I fold myself within my blanket. Somebody grabs me and standing, I fall outside pushed by the Boche. In the light of the pocket torches, one of them, seeing me move, seizes me by the shoulder and stands me up, then disappears. It is dark. Many groups wander around in a thick and cold fog. In the midst of this crowd, I am alone, walking wherever the wind and bumpy ground takes me, towards the haven of rest, the camp, another camp which I can't see yet.....

Chapter 34: RAVENSBRUCK

Damnation on this night! I have lost all my friends. The whole convoy seems dispersed, left to its own. I find it extraordinary that we are not counted, that we are not put into ranks. I am surprised not to hear the familiar order "Zu funf." Despite the cold, I would like a drink – but where? My bare and numbed feet have so much trouble in taking small steps on the hard, cold road… I know not where I am going amid groups which call to each other, question each other: "Is that you Henry? Is that you, Jean? And who, often disappointed, move away. Some hold each others arms to help themselves. Others like blind men walk bent forward, arms outstretched in order to avoid obstacles, then suddenly about turn as if they had forgotten something, looking for a friend, a relative whose absence they suddenly notice. On the sides of the road, some of the poor patients are dying; some get up, advance a little and collapse again. Others, sitting, crouched, wait for the help which does not come. I cannot help them, because I shall fall down too if there is much further to go. My wet feet hurt me terribly. If only I could sit down!… But it is so cold. As soon as I stop, my body shakes with a shiver of fever. I bump into guards who shout to me "Los, los, nach Lager! Viel Wasser, gut soup!" (Quickly, quickly, to the camp, there is plenty of water and good soup). I can in fact see nothing of a camp or barbed wire. What part of Germany am I in? What about those women who were pushing piles of suitcases on carts? It's such a long time since I heard women's voices, it has given me courage. They must have been Polish women. Are we going to a women's camp? All these questions run through my mind as I go through a village.

In spite of the darkness, I can make out pretty houses, surrounded by little gardens. How happy the people must be who live there! Oh, if only they could guess behind their closed shutters and without a ray of light! If only they knew! But I must be mad…! I'm considered as vermin to be disposed of! Am I not half free on this road where there is neither garden, dog, or search light? Freedom, What can I do with it, weakened, sick, famished, thirsty, barefoot and wearing a such thin pyjama which has become like lace in several places? How I regret the paper bags with which I dressed myself at Farge! Where can I go? At a cross-road, I try my luck and knock on a door. On my right? No, there is a ditch and unwelcoming looking gates. On the left? A ray of light in a yard! Let's go. I have already left the road. Normally, I would already have been shot… I knock but nobody answers. I go in – a hangar, a lit doorway on the left, a young German, an SS. The camp? It's here. He shows me the way as simply as he would have pointed out the road to a car driver. Forward… All these houses and barracks are just enemies and all this German soil, wherever you go, is just one huge concentration camp, even if you cannot see the barbed wire. Where are they, Pierre Lhoste, Maurice Clement, Fernand Lorret? Where is Gaston, Maxime Gerard and my little Breton friend, the Muratais, the postman whose name I forget, Roger Clarence, all those who gave me their addresses, repeated over and over again so as not to forget therm, so as to write to them later? I gave them mine too, in Etang! It's easier to remember. That way, if I don't go back, they will be able to talk of me a little at my home. "Only 2 km more" says a German. Here's a little bridge. On my right is a black expanse which must be a lake. I am too weak and can make nothing out. We follow the frozen and winding road. Despite my slowness, I catch up a group who have stopped. Electric lamps light up the road now, here and there.

A potato on the ground – they have seen it and taken it from me even before I tried to bend down. It must have been frozen but good all the same. I shall follow this group now for they are speaking French. Nevertheless thirst, hunger and fatigue do not make us talkative. At last – barbed wire, gates, a half buried watch tower, lit blocks, the barracks are invaded. I stumble into the barbed wire fixed 20 cm above the ground. Don't let's go in here; there are already too many people! Further on, more barracks. A guard, muffled in a huge balaclava and green-grey hood passes without speaking to us. "Wasser?" one of us asks him. "Kein Wasser!" he says, going away.

Since we cannot drink, let's go to sleep! Here's a barracks, a door, a step: a great effort for me. Quick! A mattress, a bed. I go past a half-open cupboard. Curious, I glance inside; because I have noticed that each man searches everywhere, turning the mattresses, looking under the beds. I find a small shoe which must have belonged to a woman, a red tin bearing a serial number and initials in white paint, a mug, packets of powdered insecticide, and the empty box of a Canadian Red Cross parcel – and in the dust, a small crust, 3 mouthfuls of hard mouldy bread. I carry off all my treasure under a mattress and lie down. It's such a long time since I searched in a cupboard! I am so hungry and thirsty that I can't swallow this crust without a drink!

All of a sudden the hut is in commotion. A Russian has found a parcel containing powdered sugar and some flour and he is suffocating without being able to swallow everything. Some walk around with boxes, searching among papers and arguing.

Others are too ill, have lain down where they could and are now in a deep sleep, which the noises do not disturb. Others again arrive worn out, stumble and remain stretched out by the door, blocking the way. A Frenchman, at my request, comes to lie down next to me, because I don't like to be next to foreigners whose language I don't understand, especially Greeks who chatter constantly.

Joy suddenly breaks out at the sight of several tins of water brought in by the Russians and the French who had gone to prospect the area. Of course we cannot count on a water ration and have no currency with which to buy some! My neighbour, who can still walk easily, decides to go and get some with my tin and brings me back a little. I drink… at length… as much as I can, I was so thirsty! Then between us, we eat the mouldy crust after having soaked it. Then I rest my head on my tin, since I now have the luck to have one. Andre, my new companion, has a box for a pillow. Insensitive to the cold and to all that is going on, or that could go on around us, caring not for the unfortunates who will never make it to the hut, who will not reach the mattresses and who will die on the road, not knowing how I got this far and drank some water. I give myself up to bestial slumber.

Roll call! General Roll call! Block Roll call! I am awakened by these cries, rested but still very tired! My limbs are heavy as lead and I have hardly opened my eyes than I want to go to sleep, to sleep again. I am neither hungry nor thirsty. I realise that it is daylight, but as we arrived very late in the night, our sleep has been curtailed. Already many have gone out. Only the thought of going outside frightens me, because fever is beating at my temples and my ears thump constantly.

In the row opposite, the others are not getting up either but they must all be alive for they have not been undressed. I do not move. A prisoner, with a surly look, shouts at us to go outside. He has no armband or distinctive mark but he must be a former kapo or block leader. He hits the walls and the boards of the beds with a leash to intimidate us but I still don't move for that and I pretend to sleep. He doesn't insist. Moreover, seeing the state of the alleys between the beds, which have been soiled with filth of all kinds, he dare not come into my corner. Seeing that his threats have had no effect, he shouts "Brot essen – viel Brot essen mit wasser!" Trying to tempt us and stimulate us.

If I move, I will have to go outside. I adopt as my watchword "Stay put". Moreover, I notice that my dysentery came back last night and my trousers are completely soiled. My neighbour has gone outside, because he is hungry. I will go without, too bad! Suddenly an SS and a LA come in and count us, those occupying beds, including the dead, then go away without a word. The block leader returns with little slices of oatmeal bread and beetroot and gives one to everybody. How dry it is! I cannot eat more than two mouthfuls of it. I will wait until I have some water.

The morning seems long. Outside, the others in rows of five are murmuring. Some have sat down in the sand, head down, hunched into themselves, waiting anxiously for the end of the Roll call, or to be told to get up for the SS who counts and recounts the groups. Many SS have donned the uniforms of the Kriegsmarine, with shields and yellow anchors, which is why you must be careful of everybody now, although they seem less fierce, as if they wanted to treat us with respect! It's a good sign but as we know nothing of the military situation and have no confirmation of the rumours, we live with the idea that each day the Allies are coming nearer, killing many SS and many Germans and maybe, liberating the camps in which there are still some living 'stripeys'! The Roll call is over at last. There is no talk of work commandos, although the old hands worked at navvying for many months, when everything was frozen and covered with snow.

I manage at last to find out approximately where we are, Himmelstod, next to the village of Furstenberg, 84 km north of Berlin. South of the Baltic coast, the camp is said to spread deep into the fir trees, or there are maybe 1000 women in the neighbouring barracks, plus a crematory oven. We are said to be in a small camp formerly occupied by women. Others, better informed by the Germans, say that Himmler has a property not far from here and will sometimes come to visit. The name of the camp? I have often asked. Many don't know yet and are not worried. I was finally told but have so little memory that I have forgotten it, I ask the German who came before to propose to the paralytics an exchange of water for bread: "It's Ravensbruck"...

I learn that we are not going to remain in this barracks and that there is an infirmary not far from here. Before going, we have an inspection. I am afraid of not being admitted, in spite of my general malaise, the semi-paralysis of my legs, my dysentery and the trembling of my whole body. Polish diarrhoea they call it when you are passing blood but I don't think I've come to that. Lice still eat me alive and I don't have the strength to even scratch myself. I feel as though I have billions of them, my rags are impregnated with them. They are of all colours – grey, white, pink, green, yellow, all the lice in creation have a rendezvous here! They crawl over the mattresses and boards, climb up the bed legs, come down from the upper bunk whose occupier must have been dead two days and who we have not been able to bring down. Fleas? They stick to your skin, to your back, to your chest. You think you have got rid of them and then a swarm comes up from somewhere else. They are monsters these creatures and only abandon their prey when it is dead.

So, we are going to the infirmary – but how? This time, French acting as doctors and nurses, gently exhort us to make a bit of an effort. It's not far and they will help us, because we can't stay here. I decide to get up but my head spins around. A German, exasperated by the slowness of the patients, begins to throw them to the ground from the top of the bunks. Some cry out, others say nothing; others find some strength and remain standing despite their thin legs. My neighbour above, who is dead, falls heavily to the ground before I can tell the Boche that he is "kaput". The sound of his head hitting the board of the box bed pains me and I am surprised at still being able to pity a corpse.

I walk, holding on to the wall. I go outside. The light surprises me, for although the weather is cloudy, the sun is often hidden. I cannot walk close to the hut, because barbed wire is fixed all around, only allowing access through the door. Carrying my tin and mug, my piece of bread in my only pocket, I go as quickly as I can, following the French nurse, stopping here and there, around corpses in the sand, soiled everywhere by filth. The infirmary is near but we are told to wait opposite a building enclosed by barbed wire. I lie down.

The reassuring sun comes out sometimes. Many, not knowing what to do, are already stretched out and waiting. To make the time seem shorter, I go to sleep, head resting on what remains of my blanket. When I wake up, I watch what is happening above on the sandy slope, between the huge barracks which must be on the right, the kitchens on the left "Abort, un Wasch-raum." There is a general Roll call of the men who are not ill, to send them to the blocks reserved for them. This interminable dividing up makes me suffer for all those poor unfortunates, as ill as I am, who at each moment are made to get up and walk while they are jostled.

A few organisers still have whips but don't seem to be using them any more. The SS, dressed in naval uniforms, amuse themselves by bending a little cane in their hands. Groups are already occupying the new blocks and file past before their chief, who with the help of interpreters writes their numbers on a card. Some come back from the washroom carrying buckets, bowls and tins full of water which glisten in the sun. When they pass near us, we beg for a drop of water from them. I too hold out my tin but as they are all Poles or Latvians, the French do not benefit from the distribution.

Suddenly there is a Frenchman. He stops, puts his bucket down on the ground, gives some water to everybody, filling all tins and mugs without worrying about nationality. Some French even reproach him for giving water to foreigners who have already drunk several times. A few jealous ones exchange blows and a tin is tipped over. The Frenchman, overpowered, returns to the washroom and we are unpleasantly surprised to see that the water carriers no longer use the same route.

Nobody bothers about us any more. I like that just as well. I appreciate my fate when I compare it to that of the unfortunate patients obliged to remain standing up for hours to have their numbers taken. We drag along for two or three hundred yards to reach the position where the inspection takes place. Some are carried before the three nurses and are laid out next to each other, waiting for the doctors! Many, too heavily afflicted, do not reply to the questions asked by the nurses. Others, not being thin enough, are not accepted, in spite of all their supplications and sometimes in spite of pneumonia or the beginning of an abscess. Some are even heavily jostled by a Polish doctor who doesn't recognise epileptics until they have an attack. The man whose pants are full of mess is accepted without examination as a "Scheize Reye" and goes to Revier 2. The man who is worn out and eaten up with already advanced T.B. goes to Revier 1. As for the paralytic, they are sent to No.2. Gradually the ranks clear and the less ill are admitted. Suddenly "Revier 1 is full". Too bad for the T.B. cases, translates a French nurse, tired of writing numbers since daybreak and with nothing to eat, "they'll go with those with dysentery" but there are lots of dysentery cases and the beds must be very full. My turn has passed and nobody is interested in me. I am worried. Will I be left here? I do not move.

Am I not paralysed? In front of me, a man with syphilis is not accepted either. The German doctor smiled at him without saying a word. I notice with fear that there will soon be no room. Already a Polish youth, doubtless a porter at the Revier shouts non stop "Fertig, fertig". I call out to a passing Dutch nurse whom I knew at Wattensted and who recognises me. He wasn't very kind over there but to my great surprise, takes me in his arms and carries me to Revier 2, pressed by the questions of the little Polish guards at the door. At last, I'm inside, put on the floor! A pole takes me to the left, at the far end. "Hier!" he cries, showing me a board already occupied. I end up next to a Latvian. Sleep, at last!

When I am awake, I spend my time dreaming, to forget the bed which is too narrow, the boards which are too hard, the Latvian and the German who chatter non-stop and shake each other so much I cannot rest, the lice and all the fleas who continue to eat me, my legs, so heavy and cumbersome although skeletal, my thirst, my extreme need to get up and take off my rags, the dying below whose faces one cannot even see because it is so dark. This narrowness impresses me, the general crowding which stifles me and the air made fetid by fever, the indescribable atmosphere which takes hold of your throat but to which you become accustomed, after a time.

A few Frenchmen, very devoted although deprived of everything, take care of us. Each evening, temperatures are taken with one thermometer for 100 men! I am only

38.5 and am afraid of being sent back, for there are others more ill than me waiting outside. Some even, must have been found dead during the night, stretched out in the sand by the door, dead with no succour, no consolation, and no friend. I have reported my dysentery and my paralysis but am still afraid. I am not one of the thinnest and when you are not a "muslim" you risk being sent back.

Sometimes, medicines are given out. "Tabletten" says the Polish doctor, passing down the rows. There are only 3 sorts of pills, black ones (charcoal) for the dysentery cases; white ones for the feverish (pneumonia, pleurisy, allergies and other serious illnesses. It's certainly pyramidon) as for the brown pills, we are given them to try when the others have had no effect and when the nurse doesn't know exactly what the patient is suffering from. "Was du krank? Krank, viel mein kopf?" Very often, he gives a pill, any one. It doesn't matter anyway but pills are rare and often many are put aside for friends, or exchanged for some bread or soup among the patients; that's why pills are not given every day and there are hardly any in the little envelopes lined up in the box!

A change of dressings is announced. For the five days we have been there, no talk had yet been made of that. Many therefore, not able to get up any more, resign themselves to keeping their wounds with no dressing. They retract into a ferocious despair, even refusing to listen to the advice of their friends. My leg wounds hurt a great deal but the ointment similar to machine oil and the paper bandages don't attract me when one is covered in grime, lice and fleas.

Morover, the suffering caused by the last terrible transport sometimes makes me feel as though I am going to die too, without a word, or go to sleep never to wake up again. I am stuck to these boards and there is no Frenchman anywhere around. Therefore, since I don't talk, I think a good deal about all that surrounds me and the hallucinatory scene sometimes makes me think that there is no other way of life and all of us, Europeans mixed up on the same straw. Is it really true that we have lived, worked and fought to come to this? Already all memories of home are wiped out and so far away that one wonders if we haven't been dreaming, our family, our friends, our job, our village, the Resistance and the cause of this punishment, our homeland even?

Craftsmen, unskilled workers, intellectuals, the elite, the poor, confused, unrecognisable, sunk to nothing in our bodies and in spite of ourselves, dominated by our animal instinct. However, this instinct still has something human in it, since it commands our body, forbids us drinking water, selling soup, of thinking also that we were once men, that we once bought round loaves of golden bread at a bakers shop and above all that, over there in France, there are hospitals, clean trains bearing red crosses, beds, white sheets and nurses. You have to harden yourself, control your sick body so as not to die of sorrow, to despair at the frightening contrast made by the idea of possible well-being and the sad reality.

Days are never ending and the modest piece of oatmeal bread, often mouldy, is not a regular thing. Only the litre of soup, made from rotten cabbage, peppered and thickened with earth, serves as our staple diet. Many, no longer eat and exchange their little bit of food for water when they have some. Since it has been raining, the more mobile go outside to fill their bowls waiting patiently under the gutter until enough yellowish water is collected to quench their thirst, or to try and obtain a little bread which has become so scarce.

I eat little but I don't want to drink at any price. Since there are many who can't get up, the water vendors supply their patients in bed or pass cans through the windows whose shutters are open.

There are also the body-bearers and sweepers for this trade, the man detailed to cleaning the sick and to the bed pan service. Very few think of their function and prefer to barter. For hours, you hear therefore, Mandolina, Mandolina (bed pans for the paralytics). Patients beg their neighbours, implore the man to whom they give their bread, ask 10, 20 or 100 times in a row for that which serves as a bed pan but nobody moves. Everyone remains deaf and indifferent as if our ears were tired of complaints, too used to suffering.

If by chance, someone knuckles down and goes in search of the object, he rarely finds it, for it is occupied, hidden in a corner or overflowing with excrement. There is only one for 500 men. Fortunately, I can still walk, although I feel as though I no longer have any flesh on my femurs. I can still drag myself along the beds by leaning on the partition. I even sometimes go outside, to the latrine buckets, next to the pile of dead. I rarely risk going to the washroom, for the doors are always guarded and padlocked and the water taps are blocked. When they are turned on, there is a flood, because the Poles drench everything for cleaning while outside, despite the cold. Groups of men, thirsty and filthy, shivering and impatient contemplate like starving ghosts, this water which runs uselessly and is lost down the drain.

I have been able to wash my hands and face a little, which does me good considering I have been without a drop of water for 2 months, for such an operation but unfortunately, it does not kill the lice. Sometimes, men severely ill with dysentery or TB, go to the latrine buckets and drink the water in which a whole load of dying men have already washed themselves. I can see that the icy and fatal water drowns their throat, their stomach, their intestines and chills their already weak and puny bodies. It runs, runs – how good it must be! They intoxicate themselves with it, without stopping to breathe, drinking as much as they can, fearful of being disturbed by the Polish overseers who have been given the order to beat them and stop them from drinking. The latter are not content with carrying out the orders and tease the poor unfortunates who cannot defend themselves. "Do you want some water?" They shower them then with hoses and buckets. I can still flee but some of them are subjected, trembling and begging them to stop this torture and go away drenched, chilled to the bone, and in despair.

Opposite the WC and the washroom, there is the kitchen but nobody may go near it. I cross the yard again, greet an old friend whose name I have forgotten and who does not recognise me, go around the naked corpses piled up in front of the latrine buckets reserved for the serious cases of dysentery again and go back beside the Latvian who is still just as surly but who gets on well with the fat old Boche, my long-standing worst enemy.

Discipline, although softened for the sick, still exists and there are many Roll-calls. We are counted in bed and it is therefore forbidden to leave our boards – even for one's needs for hours, under pain of a beating, a jostling, being clawed, bitten even by the young Polish homosexuals.

The temperature chart and the remarks of the doctors in charge are pinned above the bed of each patient and the SS sometimes make brief appearances, take a few numbers, for what reason we know not! Intuition tells me that my turn is imminent. My dysentery has not got worse, I even feel much better although I have become very thin and I'm still very weak, sometimes going 48 hours without getting up.

You must go; you are on the list a young Frenchman may say to me one day, looking at my number.

My stomach seams to drop out.

Go? Where?

I don't know but go quickly to the door to be shaved, you will not be alone!

Freshly shaved, chin smooth, I await orders, gripped by a great anxiety. I look one last time at this block of paralytics, the calm of which I am missing already. The patients hardly ever talk amongst themselves, they wait too, seeming to ignore that they may only have a few hours left to live and implore once again to have water or the Mandolina. On going out, the air wakes me up and refreshes my face.

There are about 15 of us – "Go to Revier 3"

Chapter 35: THE DUMP

I go to these new quarters with both satisfaction, because it is not far away, and with apprehension, because this cursed place from which 50 corpses are brought out each morning, horrifies us with unspeakable terror. Until now, we had only heard talk of it but now we are going to live there!

Everything is even more gloomy here, blacker than in any of the other blocks in which I have been. Newly undressed corpses are strewn on the ground in an indescribable state of putrefaction. The tired undertakers and the man detailed for statistics of serial numbers are overloaded with work. The latter, writes the numbers in big letters on our chests with a special pencil and puts them down in one of his two notebooks, the second being reserved for the departing dead. We cannot advance without stepping over them or bumping into the stretchers. We have to wait for a place, for all the dead of the preceding night have not yet been taken away. We cause a real traffic jam in this place which is too narrow, where the dying from several blocks are queuing up trying to find a place, a corner, a spot to lie down. The fetid air which fills the room adds to the horror of the situation. I do not yet fully appreciate the state of the dying who are lying on the boards but the sight of the occupants of the central alley in the middle makes me envisage the worst.

I accompany Joseph Ronchot from Allier, himself very thin too and we will not leave each other. We install ourselves in an upper bunk, so as to be a little removed from the mire of the ground floor. It's a Herculean task for our limbs without muscles to reach the third storey and we would not go any slower if we had a lead bag on our backs. Our mattress is rotten and still damp from the excrement of our predecessors but in view of our weakness and the lack of space, we lie down without worrying about such detail, under a ceiling which is so low that we fear we might suffocate. The lice, the diarrhoea and the lack of air keep us from sleeping. Everything is against us in this sort of stable full of dying men and all the ills which can afflict human beings seem to be assembled there.

Death is everywhere, on the bodies which are forgotten, in the alleys, in the latrine buckets placed inside, in our beds, in our boards running with urine, in our mattresses soaked a thousand times, in the ceiling which crushes us, on the floor covered with thick mud, in our communal tins, never washed and which each man licks so as to lose nothing of the last pieces of rotten cabbage, peppered, debilitating and in which the lice sometimes fall from our shaven heads.

Death is in the air, all around us, in the least effort which we make to go to the latrine buckets, it is in the barbed wire which runs the length of the block and on which I have often scratched myself, because I am short-sighted. It is in the rare tins of water which the starving sell for bread, it is in the putrid bandages and the cavernous eyes of our fellows, it is in the man who gets up urinating and defecating on the beds below. It is behind us, in the bunks of the Germans which have at their head a bowl of urine from which I nearly drank last night, thinking that it was salted water, it is in the eyes of the Russians who covet the bread I am eating.

Death is in the feet of Joseph from which I must endure the smell of manure, it is on me, in my rotting and lousy rags, in my hands, on my emaciated fingers whose thick layer of grime does not hide the deathly whiteness. It is in the saliva which covers my face when I wake up, it is the ignorance which we have of the future, in our general lethargy, in our abandonment, in our despair, in the cries of the dying, the arguments among thieves, the advice of false friends, the vociferations of madmen, the language of the Pole which I don't understand and which exasperates me to the utmost degree.

Death is even in the calmness, in the moments of absolute silence, in which ears buzz, bells ring, in which minds no longer register, it is the silent immobility of Joseph who does not answer me, who sleeps, oblivious of all my thoughts and of whom I am even jealous, for he seems to be teasing me, it is also in this vermin which surrounds both of us.

Happy are the soldiers, the sailors, the aviators who rub against death too but in different circumstances, for them, once the danger is passed there is a release, a going back, the certainty of living normally. Happy too is the man who knows that his time has come, that the execution squad is waiting. There is nothing of that here, not only is our turn imminent, after having sunk little by little to the very depth of misery in the face of the German taunts but I also feel a certain worry at the sight of the treatment to which the corpses themselves are subjected, these corpses which were men, which were life itself and who are no longer even that "je ne suis quoi" of which Bossuet speaks, who no longer have a name in any language!

They are not even respected. Outside, at the door, along the block, in the street, in the square, above all behind the Reviers, they are there. Men go round them, move away when they suddenly see them on their way to the WC or the washroom but they cannot be avoided, for the latrine buckets are outside, some even overflow onto them. I prefer to go outside, for inside the two buckets are reserved for the German and Polish sick and I have already been chased off with baton blows. Outside, just as inside, we live with corpses. A nightmare, an obsession, a Dante-like vision of which no description can give the least idea. What sorrow when you recognise a chum, a friend, a relative, even if on this skeleton's breast there is a letter other than an F next to the indelible serial number. Hands clenched as though still trying to hold something, faces fixed in the last spasms of a death which is too slow in coming, eyes wide open, skin swollen by an old oedema, distended stomachs, empty, beaten down, bearing deep stripes, signs of dysentery, discoloured skin tinged with yellow and green is marked, stretched, torn in places, ridged by the ills from which pus is still seeping, stiffened limbs, mixed all up together to such an extent that you no longer know to whom they belong, skeleton-like limbs in which the whole bone formation can be seen, often still wrapped in an old paper dressing.

Arms out-stretched, heads looking towards the sky as if to implore, to call for succour, young, old, all are mixed up, bearing the same mask of unspeakable suffering and death; a death which is not like other men's deaths, for they seem still to want to resist it. "Once again", said Bossuet, "what are we?"

Joseph is still very sad and much afflicted by dysentery, each day the dead are replaced by new patients, ever more numerous. The undertakers have quite a task in doing their job, throwing bodies down from the beds and dragging them outside to the heap, sometimes without using the stretchers. Over there, another team loads them onto trucks as you would load dead animals but in Revier 3, men die too quickly and although the teams of cleaners have been doubled, the pile increases, spreads out, soon covers quite an area, overflows into the barbed wire, comes nearer the latrine buckets. In the rain, some metres away a few striped men sweep and rake the sand. I am obliged, bare footed and wearing a shirt too old to cover me sufficiently, to step painfully over them to get to the barrels which are not emptied any more.

For a few days, the rumour has been going round that a transport is imminent for the men who are still strong. They are to go on foot or by lorry. I hide my fear and take care to say nothing of it to Joseph, whose morale is very low and who weeps sometimes. I do not want to alarm him and despite my dysentery which is causing me serious worry, I still want to seem strong and to put up with it. We must hold on and together we will go back, we will live, as long as the battle which we have been fighting for so long already does not come to an end through lack of fighters! In the meanwhile, amid great effervescence and to everyone's surprise, a distribution of Red Cross parcels is said to have started in certain blocks. Discussions are in full swing and joy breaks out. We almost forget that for a week we have had no bread and hardly a half litre of cabbage gruel per day.

The parcels arrive; they are big, 5 kilos apparently! There is one between 3 men. It's really true! The distribution is reasonably fair. Have the SS understood? Are they already afraid of punishment? At last we are going to eat something. The French still try to stick together and I rejoin friends from Saone-et-Loire.

With Joseph and our Belgian neighbour, we get along together very well and as we cannot share the tins of food, they leave me to guard them with the box. I sleep between my two friends, the box wrapped in a piece of cloth for fear of theft. There is everything in this redeeming parcel – sugar, biscuits, under my head some vitamin sweets, prunes, oat flakes, some oleo margarine, peanut butter, chocolate, liver pate, vegetable salad. I take pleasure in translating to my friends the directions for use written in English on this or that product.

Many eat like savages, emptying box after box with insatiable appetite. Some fill themselves with margarine, some make Russian mixtures, jam, butter and corned beef. Others stuff themselves with powdered milk or regale themselves with condensed milk. Many are afraid of being robbed and force themselves to eat, scooping out the tins with pointed tools or spending hours trying to prise off the lid with pieces of steel, taken from I know not which hidey hole!

A French doctor goes around with a tin-opener but he has a lot of work. Sugar, biscuits, chocolate, vitamins. Is it a dream? The décor has not changed however and among us there are dying men who are not eating. They are not hungry, so they are deprived of their cases or exchange their parcel by bribes for a little water. Now, hardly is one of them dead than the stronger ones, the starving, hurl themselves on their parcel and even fight over the corpse. It's a battle for who will get the sugar and all the other foods which guarantee life, when the dead man no longer has anything edible left he is stripped by the survivors. Has he some shorts, a shirt, a shoe? In a couple of minutes he is naked!

What does all that matter, you have to eat, you have to live! Ungrateful! I notice that I have not even thanked God for sending us, poor miserable men who have become wicked, all these good things, so clean, so full of life. How ungrateful men are! I say as much to Joseph, although I don't know his beliefs but here it is not necessary to be a Catholic to pray – that comes naturally, since the communists themselves pray in their own way and share with us in the same sacrifice!

I eat little but I soon feel the well being brought about by this food. Nobody can imagine the physical and mental comfort of such a parcel for three men, when one has come this far. It's more than a ray of hope, more than comfort – it's a link with the outside world and you no longer feel abandoned! They have thought about us, a bridge has been built between us and those we call "the free men"!

Chapter 36: "KEIN WASSER"

"Kein Wasser." How many times do you hear those sad words? The SS amuse themselves by turning off the taps, sometimes for several days at a time but this time we hear that the supply has been cut off by bombing or sabotage. If this news is correct, I can already envisage the disaster. What use is this parcel if we cannot drink? Probably, there will be no more food seen.

Thirst, therefore takes a terrible hold of the camp and of Revier 3, the infirmary for the dysentery cases and the incurables; from Revier 3 there are lots of complaints. If only it could rain, but despite the grey damp weather, our throats remain dry, burning with fever just like the rest of our body, dehydrated and racked with dysentery.

Like everyone else, I have come down to doing the necessary in an old tin which I empty afterwards into the alley. You must therefore, be very careful when getting up to go a few steps because you risk being covered by one of these missiles. Consequently, all the lower area is just a mire where those of the first tier live, their only valuable item being the almost empty Red Cross parcel. Fatigues are organised to fetch water from a nearby pond, because there is still some cabbage in the soup. They are asking for volunteers. The late-comers are detailed automatically and they carry a few flasks still dirty from yesterday's soup. The SS take them away under heavy escort.

I would like to go too, with my tin, to drink over there and to bring back some water for Joseph but it is 2 km away! On their return, the flask carriers, although defended by the SS, are attacked, the containers tipped over, there are arguments and butt blows but nothing has any effect. I witness this whole scene without going near and I am not alone in hoping timidly, empty tin in hand but in vain.

One flask is taken away by two men. They stop, tear off the lid, plunge their whole head into the black water at the risk of drowning in it and get up saying: "Oh! I am no longer thirsty." One of them sighs, at the moment when the butt of an SS gun surprises him and lays him out in the sand, before his companion, who runs away with me.

I drag myself painfully to the kitchens but it is impossible to approach them. Several of us escort a flask which is coming in. A passing Frenchman asks me if I work in the kitchens and as I don't answer but show him my empty tin with an eloquent gesture, he seizes it and two minutes later gives it back. It is full! I drink, one, two, three mouthfuls then stop, so cold is the water which smells foul. I fear, that stricken with dysentery as I am, it will make things worse. I take my tin to Joseph who does not know how to thank me.

Careful, Joseph, don't drink too much.

Don't worry, it cheers me up.

We make plans for the future. We will go home together. It will be good, so good! Joseph repeats three times in a row – "It will be good". The first time as if it was just a cry from the heart, spontaneous, the second time, I catch a hint of doubt in his shaky voice. The third time, I have the sad feeling that Joseph does not mean it, that he thinks it is not feasible, it's impossible. "Who has some water, in exchange for sugar, biscuits and food tins?" The poor patients who no longer have friend, support, courage or strength, sell their parcel for water. The most shameful bargains take place. There are 13 pieces of sugar and two biscuits each in the parcels. Often a little water in the bottom of a tin becomes a buyer of 5 or 6 cubes of sugar or a vitamin biscuit. Although the temptation is very strong, I swear to myself that I will turn a deaf ear to all these offers and anyway, I only get up once a day and yet I am thirsty too.

20th April. Roll-call begins early in the morning and goes on until the afternoon, because the count is still not correct. Escapes? Mistakes? Serial numbers of the dead not having been noted? Nobody knows what is happening and the SS have come back several times to ask the Stubedienst doctor how many dead there are, each time the second figure increases as the other falls but the total remains the same. Outside, hundreds of thousands of men, standing in ranks of five, wait. How I pity them!...

Suddenly there is a commotion. "Alles Raus." The absurdity of such an order, intended for creatures who in a few hours time will maybe just corpses, is beyond us. As incredible as it may seem, the order is carried out and the gravely ill are carried outside, beds moved, mattresses turned over, searched to see if any dead or living may still be hidden there!

In the general confusion and tumult, I persuade Joseph to go out. The area between the 3 Reviers and the block opposite is full of patients who wait, lying on the ground, 5 by 5 and the sun plays games by lighting up this sad scene from time to time. Emaciated men come out, carried by nurses who put them down in the sand. I would never have thought there were so many of us under this small roof. Mattresses, blankets, rags, pyjamas, various objects.... the cleaners, armed with spades and forks, throw everything outside. The 3-tier beds are tipped over but the filth accumulated underneath is such that it is impossible to remove it in so short a time, for the general Roll-call is sounded and everyone must be in rank. Counted and recounted by a dozen SS men and a few block leaders, we wait but still the total does not tally! The dead who are piled up and who the trucks have not been able to remove, must be counted again. A few Frenchmen are detailed for this task. They line up the bodies, carrying them by their arms and legs. There are many of them underneath in a sad state, because they may have been there for a long time! Sometimes a hand, a foot, or a whole limb comes away from the trunk. What of it? The indifferent Boche count and recount, lost in this number which it is impossible to establish with exactitude. Convinced of their failure, they finally go away. Roll-call is over but for us the sick, nothing has changed — we must stay there, for there is a general clean-up going on. I recognise an Algerian, the interpreter from the truck of 103. He leaves me because he is hungry and in his block they are giving out soup. A nurse goes along the ranks and asks me my name and my address in France. I do not know the purpose of this scene. Joseph's face seems indifferent in daylight but we go back inside and my efforts to walk stop me from thinking.

23rd April. I'm thirsty. Water! We must have some at all costs. Without eating you can live. Without drinking, you die, especially when your only food is soup made from earth, heavily peppered and which burns our stomachs. Yesterday, I bought two mouthfuls of water from a Pole in exchange for my share of liver pate from a parcel but the water was filthy and in spite of the temptation, I had the presence of mind to spit it out again. I go out on safari, despite my weakened state and rags sticking to my skin with excrement. I am only really disgusted when I put my feet on a corpse, and that often happens getting out of bed, because those below me have been dead for two days. There must be a corpse blocking the alley too, opposite the bed of the vet from Grandchamp, who in his turn has been gripped by dysentery. A brutal order has just arrived: "Inspection of the lousy!" "Everyone undressed!" So, here I am naked once again, and outside! I pass in front of the Pole, as rude as he is bestial, who sends me to the washroom.

Outside, it's always the same. You are no longer allowed to go near the wooden buckets, putrid, smashed or tipped over, the sand in the square covered, soaked in excrement. I go around the pile slowly, without looking, turn to the right towards the washroom. They are guarded as before by the Poles. I go inside, nobody there. I turn on a tap without success. The tanks are dry. Disappointed, I go to the "abort" (WC). It's disgusting. Some Russians are scraping the bottom of the tub with their tin. I go there but there is only mud. I do not stop at the WC where many are queuing up.

Outside, the temperature has become milder. I notice a former colleague and excellent friend from the cement column, Louis Vichery from La Bourse, near Bethune, where he is a mechanic. How thin he has also become, once so strong, so fat. We shake hands. He is waiting to leave and is walking alone in the yard, up and down, as though a free man, under the eye of the watch towers, still being watched. He is leaving on foot! The misery has no effect on guys of that type. I leave him. He shakes my hand a last time and gives me a final piece of advice: "Above all, don't drink anything!" That meeting has given me comfort and confidence. Further on I come across Jean Mongin with his shattered, patched-up spectacles. With him, memories are nearer home – we talk naturally of friends, comrades, of all those we both knew.

With a weary gesture, Jean tells me he knows nothing, no news but as I press him with questions, he admits that he thinks they are all dead or almost. What about Jean Rousseau then? Haven't seen him again.

What about Olivier? Olivier, you can see him if you want… I thought you knew What? I don't know anything.

There, look, he is there on the heap – can you see? The one who is all curled up. They took him out of Revier 3 this morning. He must have died in the night. It's this dysentery.

I am short-sighted and cannot go near the sorry place. I question him further

He was in my block and I didn't know? He died right next to me?

Obviously, old man, so many of them die in the dump! I recognised him from his tattoo. You know, the woman's head he had on his chest.

-Yes but what was his serial number?

-Wait.

Taking from his pocket a little iron box which he carefully opens, he takes out a dirty piece of paper, covered with writing done in pencil and I read my friends serial number: 36.413.

I am dumbstruck by this death and with constricted throat, back bent as though looking for a lost object, without turning to wave farewell to the man who will have no tomb, I go back to the dump to get dressed again and to find a little comfort from my friend Joseph.

28th and 29th April. The fit men have all gone on the road, nobody knows where, on foot or by lorry. Guns are sounding very nearby. Friend? Enemy? No details. I no longer move but content myself with the remains of the parcel, i.e. a little cleo-margarine and 2 to 3 prunes per day. Nobody bothers about us any more, as far as medicines go. We continue to live, doubtless because that is our destiny, without knowing why we are living, or even how. Is Liberation possible? Have we not been warned that those who do not follow the transport would be sacrificed? No water, no soup and there are still so many of us! Some have whispered "Mass executions" by flaming torches, by fire grenade. Guns! So much the better. Americans? English? Canadian? Would it be possible? Are we going to die before they get here, die in this damned country? The guns are getting nearer, everyone is quiet, listening, gasping, Joseph is very agitated – the uncertainty annoys him.

I pray a great deal and entrust myself to the will of God. At times, the barracks tremble and I expect to see the ceiling ripped here and there by the German artillery who we don't hear much of. There is the crisp fire of a machine gun, then nothing. Planes! Boom, boom! Let them flatten everything and let's be done with it all. The thundering goes on, moves away, comes back, disappears and begins again. Nobody is allowed to go out. The camp seems deserted. At last the war is coming closer! There is a deathly silence, indescribable seconds full of anxiety. I feel an immense sadness in thinking of all the dead, our friends, who with us hoped for so long for this liberation, on the sites, in the camps and during the convoys and who will never experience it!

Chapter 37: 30th April, 1945 YOU ARE FREE!

Clack, clack, clack, boom! The staccato sound of machine guns, dull noises from artillery whose distance we cannot estimate and the thudding of planes. How I regret being so weak, so beaten down. I would like to be able to run, to jump when the time comes but it seems as though only my heart has remained young, whilst the rest of my body has become desperately old. Joseph cannot be more than 22 years old either and the Belgian who is weeping because he cannot pass water any more, is only 19! In a few minutes maybe, we will all be engulfed by the bombs! I dream, powerless, on this mattress almost disintegrating by the dampness and our excrement. Those below us are dead and as it often happens that the upper tier caves in, we do not move and so the cursed lice who swarm around like ants, are jealous, it seems to see us still living!

A voice repeats in French: "I've seen a Russian soldier in the wood!" Another madman who is up to no good is coming back from outside when it was forbidden to go out. "Yes chaps, I saw a Russian. He was on horseback,. Among the fir trees". A queer shiver shakes my whole body. Is it possible? Yet the bombing seems to be lessening, moving away even. Only the staccato bursts of fire, there's a great deal of animation in the reviers however. Outside, some are running. What is happening? A Frenchman cries — "We can leave the camp, we have cut the barbed wire. The SS have gone, the watch towers are empty!" The joy which fills my heart knows no limits and yet I remain careful.

- You are free.

- What's the matter? What is it, Mr. French doctor?

- You are free, I say. Do you know what that means? You can leave the camp, the gates are open. The SS have gone. We are all free. The Russians are there though, all around the camp, in the camp, in the blocks. Here, look at them on horseback! The Russians! The Russians! We are free. The SS have gone. The gates are open. These incredible words are spoken by the French doctor. He repeats them in German. Then in all the reviers and other rest blocks, outside in the yards, one hears pitiful voices being raised, but speaking sincerely!

> Arise, damned of the earth
>
> Arise, convicts of hunger.

Crowd of slaves, arise, arise!

French, Greeks, Belgians, Poles, Russians, Czechs, Dutch, Spanish, Latvians, each in his own language but all to the same tune, free our pallets from our boards, from our sad infirmary block, we acclaim our liberators!

We are nothing, let's be everything.......

I can't move. I cannot go out, like some do to kiss the feet of our saviours, while our song takes up again, pathetic. Many are crying with joy. I am myself very moved. Joseph just keeps repeating: "Maurice, we are saved! Maurice, we are going to see France again! Maurice, we are going home!"

It's the final battle...

L'Internationale, everyone knows it (it's a communist song) a little, young, old and despite our weakness, we sing as if we had a conductor.

will be mankind.

One, two, three women, two French women and a Russian approach. We are free. There are no more SS, kapos, whips. "We will give you hot drinks, some bread from the Russian army. You will have something to eat and you will have medicines. Everything will be all right. We are all equal and friends. Point out the SS that you recognise in civilian uniforms. You can go to the village of Furstenberg if you want to, the gates are open. There is no more current in the barbed wire, you can go and pillage the SS village, you will find things to eat and drink there, as much as you like but be careful, don't eat too much and above all don't drink any water." Women! It's a miracle and I can't even drag myself to go and thank them, they who have not hesitated in coming here, to this cesspit of corpses, of putrid things which they have had to step over. Their bodices and skirts of bright colours are like a ray of sun in the night to our grateful eyes but we don't believe what we see yet! Many have therefore, got up and left. I can only sigh as though relieved of a great weight after a long race whose extreme fatigue takes hold of my body and beats my will. I can't go on and the camp is still without water. After one or two hours of acclamations cut off by silence, of cries of all kinds, of shouts, of detonations, of bursts of fire, the crowd of poor men, no longer containing their joy at the thought of living such a day, slowly makes its way between Ravensbruck and Furstenberg, some bent over under a large bag, some dragging a box, some carrying bottles, and buckets. Overloaded, stopping often, they leave nothing behind. Such opulence makes the man a bit mad after having remained for so long in misery. Unfortunately, many collapse, complaining of their weakness, weeping beside a load of jumbled objects, tins of food and packets of American cigarettes which the SS stole from the Red Cross parcels. Some eat a little and take courage again, continuing on their journey. Many remain at Furstenberg but some come back loaded.

What a lot of food, cigarettes and bottles of wine. There are even some who make a distribution but the oddest thing of all is to see old acquaintances come back. Joseph Dauverne and a Frenchman who slept opposite me, almost dead a short time ago, came back not in their rags but in overcoats, bowler hat, stepping in the muck with their patent leather shoes!

Many have done the same thing. It's quite a carnival. Finished are the serial numbers and the striped clothes. You can no longer distinguish the Russians, Latvians, Poles, Belgians – they are all the same, wearing hats or caps. Some Greeks are even dressed as SS with officer's uniforms from which they have torn the insignia. Yet these disguises do not suffice to camouflage the ravages of premature old age and of a still recent suffering. One Russian, a little mad too, has loaded himself with 2 enormous suitcases, crockery basins, a pitcher, a frying pan etc. He begins to make an inventory without worrying about 3 naked and stiffened corpses next to him who seem to be watching him! He examines like a child some scissors as if he had never seen any before, then tired, not knowing why he has brought them, he gives them out. I accept one pair to please him and take advantage of them to cut my claws!

A Belgian, harassed with fatigue, has come back with several corked bottles of wine. I beg him to let me try some. He refuses at first, then I bring him to reason, reminding him that it's the Liberation and that I cannot walk. Already a feast is being organised in the dump. A whole row has been cleared of dead which are now strewn in the quagmire below.

Our first meal as free men is a plentiful one but as sombre as a funeral wake. The Russians, light candles and spread out biscuits, ham, honey, drinking white wine, brandy, St. James Rum by the bottle. To think that all of that has come from here. I no longer watch the preparations. I am so thirsty. I beg the Belgian who says he cannot uncork the bottle. I help him. He has everything he needs which is a corkscrew! It's hard. That's it. What is it in fact? In this cavern as black as an oven, I can see nothing and have to lean out into nothing, (because the great "binge" is happening on the middle tier) in order to read the label in the pale light of the smoking candles. I see "Gevey Chambertin 1934" He pours me out a good measure in the cup from a thermos flask. I try it – it's strong! I sugar it a little, stir it with a spoon and empty the glass. I fall down, fainting!

1st May. The SS did not have a good time with the Mongolians. Some ran away, taking with them all those who could walk but others put on civilian clothes, striped pyjamas like ours, after having shaved their hair. Their subterfuge does not work with the Russians, especially with those, who, like us prisoners, have had to walk and who now dress as soldiers carrying a red armband which differentiates them from the regular army. As soon as they are recognised, the adroit sabre of the Russian horseman cleaves into their neck, splitting their head from top to bottom. It's a rapid retribution, which does not miss its man!

I am not hungry. We have been given coffee but the Russians do not bother about us. The war goes on and there are many bursts of fire and exploding bombs. We are a little apathetic. Happy is the man who can walk and get to Furstenberg! Many are engaged in cooking some poultry, a rabbit, even a pig. Some are plucking chickens, ducks, without knowing how they will be able to cook them! Many are making fires in the open air and warming themselves at them. The heap of bodies has been abandoned too and a frightful odour of hair and cloth burning rises from the pile of discoloured rags which some have taken off. The fire takes hold and an acrid smoke rises and spreads all around. Nobody will agree to share the food stolen from Furstenberg, with friends who cannot move.

Some of the men, through having eaten too much, are violently ill. Me, I mixed some cleo margarine with some biscuits, powdered milk and Russian coffee. I don't think I will ever get over it. After having swallowed three fistfuls of coal dust, I begin to choke. Fortunately, a Belgian gives me another ration of Gevey-Chambertin. All this is of course not recommended for dysentery cases but I don't care! The fleas are attacking with glee all those who remain here. Men have been dragged off by friends, soldiers or civilians towards the kitchen, where they are disinfected in latrine buckets of bleach. Joseph decides with the next man, to go to Furstenberg. What courage! Will they come back? I await them in despair throughout the day and night and they come back half dead with exhaustion, with a load of food and clean linen which we exchange with joy for the filthy rubbish which covers us. Joseph gives me a pullover, white as snow but I have neither the will nor the inclination to put it on. Here is a vest – it is white but smells funny. I at last take off my lousy rags and Joseph rubs my back to get rid of the lice. I am completely grey, completely dirty. I put on the vest and feel as though I have been born again. Dauverne is very ill too but in his brand new civilian clothes, he goes to get some chaps who remained on the bottom tier and who may be dead. "Choux" (nickname of Messaroly from Creusot, dead on his arrival in France) "Choux" he shouts several times but two men have to take him away and when he gets into the passage, his two pointed shoulders indicate under the jacket without colour, the emaciated body which the men want to take out of the rabble. Joseph and myself remain indifferent and I can only feel my fever and the irritating dampness which covers my legs. I dare not look at my hands, whose bones are sticking out and whose nails, too white, make the indelible grime stand out.

Many men have gone. Calm descends again. That should incite me to drag myself to the kitchens so that somebody can take care of me but, unable to move, I remain plunged in a torpor already doubting the well-being so much hoped for. What is happening outside? A Belgian coming back from the old washroom tells me: "There is still no water".

2nd May. Sleep! When you can, you need no will to be patient but I cannot sleep. What time is it? Will they come for us today? The blue tinges of day appear between the wooden posts of the bunks with broken bottoms, from which hang various objects – a jacket sleeve, the bare and stiff arm of a dead man, pieces of straw. What abandonment! Nobody says anything and yet there must be about 50 of us still alive. I have therefore, come to this terrible dilemma! To stay here, satisfied in having this box in which my head makes a hollow and not to feel myself die or to try the impossible, get up, go down these two tiers, walk on the dead, plunge my feet into mud whose depth I know and cross with Joseph the 300 yards to the kitchens! I cannot leave him or the Belgian either. The hours are interminable and I spend my time looking at the ceiling, so as not to see, on the boards of an abandoned bed, a pile of metal and cardboard boxes full of excrement. I would like to throw them down but I can't even do that any more.

I want to dream. I no longer like to think of our freedom. My mind is so full of these visions of horror that it seems that I will never be able to get rid of them and that my plans are just absurd. I feel as though I am really condemned. Joseph thinks so too without a doubt, since he says he is going to die. I moan at him. Moreover, I need only to have an apathetic next to me to stop me from falling into despair. "I don't want to be so weak! Die here? Was it worth the trouble? No! Let's try to share the strength which remains in us. It must be the afternoon. We will get up. We must but we don't move. Joseph, stricken too with dysentery, realises the gravity of his condition and yet I know he will follow me if I can get out of the block.

For more than an hour I call him. Joseph, Joseph! He answers in his hollow voice – Yes, at once, wait for me! I try once, twice, to get down. In descending, I feel yet again my stomach empty itself. Ouch! At long last I'm on the ground! Joseph gets up too. I help him a little to carry his bundle of linen, without knowing if it will be of use to us. On the left is various debris, flip-flops, remains of pyjamas, boxes, empty tins, bowls all heaped up in something black.

There is an alley on the right. I cannot avoid disintegrated mattresses, the remains of some blackened margarine on a box, a blanket shining from use and not even serving to hide a corpse whose paper dressings on its legs give off an abominable stench. On the ground, by the door surrounded by putrid latrine buckets, there is blood, suitcases brought this far and then left once empty, bottles empty too. Some have been broken. Already, on this jumbled heap of broken bottles and various objects reminiscent of a second-hand shop, there is a layer of white excrement, characteristic of the diarrhoea caused by the American dried milk.

At last I am outside, bowled over by the daylight, knocking into obstacles similar to the rubbish tip of a large town. Joseph is following me. The damp sand sticks to my feverish feet, although they cannot feel it. I would like to run, but I am afraid of falling down before I get there. Joseph finds that I walk too fast – exasperated, encumbered with my precious empty box which I don't want to leave, I insult him. My sight is limited to a metre in front of me. I no longer have the will to look far ahead. What's the use?

I go by instinct towards the left, towards the kitchens. My small steps accelerate by themselves, like an exhausted animal who feels that the manger is coming nearer. A coming and going of passers by leaves me indifferent. I bump into things, carry on… it's there! I raise my head, stairs! That increases even more the physical and mental trial to which I am committed. At last I arrive but there are still a few steps up to the big closed door. Me, who went up those of the base at Farge running with 50k on my back, am not even capable of climbing 7 steps! I wait. Joseph comes up slowly behind me. A strong hand seizes my left arm. Another arm covered in a clean green sleeve, a silent face with a large moustache, a cap with a wide red ribbon. I am up and the door opens. There is a lot of movement inside, where it is warm. The Russian soldier takes me to a metal tub. There are some women, other soldiers, some civilians, hot water which steams, a pile of rags on the left, piles of clean linen on the right.

It is our salvation!!

I bath in hot water! The grime which has been accumulating for months is slow to come away under the kindly nurse's brush (Russian or Polish I don't know, for she does not speak!) Joseph washes himself too in my tub, without annoying me however.

No more lice, we have got them! Says a Frenchman who is still strong and who has kept his striped outfit. He is busy by one of the huge red cauldrons in which water has been put to boil.

Out of the bath, I am dried a little. The Polish doctor from Wattenschted gives me a shirt and underpants made of thick rough cloth. Then two enormous blankets, a real burden! In spite of myself, my whole body is caught in a violent nervous shivering. I am standing, and next to me is a 3 legged stool but I cannot sit on it. Joseph is ready too. The door opens. A cart must be there for I can hear the noise of wheels and horses' feet.

"Maurice, come we are going!" says Joseph moving away, bent double and shaking. Muffled up in my heavy blankets I am done in. My will no longer has any command over my weakness which had fixed on the kitchen as a final goal and which now refuses to obey me, just when I must walk some more, advance, carry these legs which don't belong to me, when I can hardly open my eyes to see the ground and Joseph has gone. The noise of wheels, the grating of a horse-drawn cart moving off, the clicking of boots, I must wait for the next one.

Nobody speaks. Some tall strapping women are wearing on their red bodices a Red Cross armband. On the ground, on stretchers, some dying men are also waiting for their turn. In the baths, the procession goes on.

I experience this scene more with my ears than with my eyes. I feel myself once more lifted up by the shoulders. Outside, a carriage is waiting for me. My left leg is dragging pitifully and only my right one is still of some use. The door opens and a portly Russian soldier is there, "Franzouski?" he asks me. "Karacho" I say to him, holding out my hand which he shakes in his own. There are some Frenchmen in civvies there too. They are driving a troika and go to fetch water. They can take me. They put me in with my back to the coachman and close the little door. I am jostled around a bit and my pointed buttocks are bruised in spite of the cushion and the large blankets. My new friends are two Frenchmen, former POW's from Stalag 11A. The sky is clear, the sunset magnificent, the evening air fresh – it's my first day as a free man!!

The kitchen, the WC, the washroom, the Reviers with their piles of dead and the pieces of old rags which are so difficult to get rid of – I am leaving all that behind me. This sad countryside with the abandoned barbed wire is the final scene of a nightmare which has come to the end.

Chapter 38: MY BELOVED FRANCE

A bed with clean sheets and blankets. A bed in which you sleep alone, bowls of rice, of split peas, meat, medicine and injections every day. I have had all this for 6 weeks in our 8 bed room in the former SS block but I have seen about fifteen men die too. Hundreds have been buried all over the camp, the same as in the women's camp. I have been x-rayed twice and I am the only one out of 20 not to have pneumonia. Despite my dysentery, which the Russian treatment has not eradicated, I have gained 4 kilos since the first weighing, for the scales show 42k 500.

The repatriation so long in coming is announced at last! On the 20th June, a Russian lorry takes me away with 22 others to Schwerin. There we take a train, bedecked with branches of fir and red flags, up to the border of the American zone. On our arrival at Lubeck, I am surprised to see Germans going about freely everywhere. Some like policemen are in charge of traffic. Others are driving lorries or are on bikes. I spend one day in a large barracks. I eat a good salad.

On the 23rd we go! An Air France plane has just arrived at the large aerodrome.

We are going to leave! What a magnificent introduction to air travel. The sky is blue and I am not upset. Of the 30 sick men loaded on, 4 are on stretchers. The nurse gives us some rum! I am put behind the radio. We fly over Koblenz. Where ruins stretch for many acres, then we are in France. Here is Soissons – Paris, with the Eiffel Tower in the distance. A large bomber has climbed to our height to say hello. We start to descend. The ground comes up. Another few feet, we are there! I am laid on a stretcher and taken away. I pass between two large lag masts on which tricolours are flying. Tears come to my eyes. In a hall we are given hot chocolate, peaches and beer. A doctor comes over to me and assigns me to the Salpetriere (for those who don't know – a well-known Parisian hospital).

Salvation ! I begin to rediscover France, Paris and tomorrow .... my parents, my friends!

Did I dream it all?

Chapter 39: AFTER THE WAR

After his liberation, Maurice spent 3 weeks in a Parisian hospital. Following his recuperation, he went back to work for the French Railways but this time in Auxerre. Some time later, after passing his exams with flying colours, he was posted to Paris where he was given assignments in the French Alps, Milan and London. He married in France in 1952 and had 2 daughters and 2 sons.

Most of his working life was spent in London where he retired in 1982 and finally he moved back to France to be close to his family. During his retirement, Maurice managed to fulfil his long-life passion for growing plants and trees by helping his landscape-gardening sons. He has achieved his dream.

Gradually and especially since his retirement, Maurice seems more able to relate his story since he feels people are more prepared to listen to it nowadays.

When asked why he never mentioned his story before, he would answer: "I didn't talk about it because people would not have believed me..." Luckily he is able to talk about it now and, on several occasions; he has held lectures in secondary schools. Nevertheless, to this day, he doesn't know how he managed to survive the Extermination Camps when his friends and so many others never came back...

Receiving La Légion d'Honneur in 1968.
La Capelle (Aisne)

Maurice and Colette on their honeymoon.
Milan, February 1952.

Maurice and Gladys, his closest cousin who married a GI at the end of the war.
London, 1960.

Maurice, Colette and Annick, their first born little girl, 1953.

Maurice with his grandmother who died many years later at the age of 95.

Maurice in his parents' garden, 1950.